P9-ECQ-931

"This book is about something we all know intuitively: that money changes everything, from politics to family life to culture—here, there, and everywhere. But Peter Marber brings this important point home in entertaining and enlightening ways with his lively prose and provocative insights into the ever-changing nature of 21st Century politics and economics."

—*Paul Blustein*,
Gerald Loeb Award-winning business journalist, and author of
*The Chastening: Inside the Crisis That Rocked the Global
Financial System and Humbled the IMF*

"With a mass of well-selected data and abundant insight, Peter Marber tackles the essential question of the age: how we are shaped by the way we live. *Money Changes Everything* is an outstanding primer on the awesome social effects of globalization."

—*David Brooks*,
author of *Bobos in Paradise: The New Upper Class and
How They Got There*

"It's not just the start of a new century. It's the beginning of a seminal change in society, culture, and politics, and Peter Marber gives us the blue-print. *Money Changes Everything* should be considered essential reading."

—*Michele Mitchell*,
CNN, and author of *The Latest Bombshell: A Novel*

"*Money Changes Everything* is superb. Evenhanded, fair-minded, loaded with great stuff (especially the graphs), and a coherent and well-developed thesis. At last an honest approach to what is self-evident, at least to the Have-nots. We call them "goods"—as in "goods and services"—not "bads" for a reason. The material world may not be very sophisticated or very deep or even the basis of lasting human happiness. But it is at the center of day-to-day living and the source of much satisfaction as well as much shared meaning. Let's put it this way: Consumption may well be a treadmill going nowhere, but the treadmills are different. This book shows the differences between Biological, Material, and Experiential treadmills, and in so doing, shows how money changes much of the discomfort of living. In so doing, money indeed changes everything.

"I especially like the writing. It's punchy, personal, and to the point. No jargon, no econ mumbo-jumbo, no hiding behind voodoo. *Money Changes Everything* is the ideal antidote to Naomi Klein and the 'I've got what I want, sorry about you' romanticizers of poverty. The book is scholarly without being academic, profound without being polemical."

—*James B. Twitchell,*
Professor of English and Advertising, University of Florida,
and author of *Living It Up: Our Love Affair with Luxury*

Money Changes Everything

How Global Prosperity
Is Reshaping Our Needs,
Values, and Lifestyles

FT Prentice Hall
FINANCIAL TIMES

In an increasingly competitive world, it is quality
of thinking that gives an edge—an idea that opens new
doors, a technique that solves a problem, or an insight
that simply helps make sense of it all.

We work with leading authors in the various arenas
of business and finance to bring cutting-edge thinking
and best learning practice to a global market.

It is our goal to create world-class print publications
and electronic products that give readers
knowledge and understanding which can then be
applied, whether studying or at work.

To find out more about our business
products, you can visit us at www.ft-ph.com

Pearson
Education

Money Changes Everything

How Global Prosperity Is Reshaping Our Needs, Values, and Lifestyles

Peter Marber

FT Prentice Hall
FINANCIAL TIMES

An Imprint of PEARSON EDUCATION
Upper Saddle River, NJ • New York • San Francisco • Toronto • Sydney
Tokyo • Singapore • Hong Kong • Cape Town • Madrid
Paris • Milan • Munich • Amsterdam

www.ft-ph.com

Library of Congress Cataloging-in-Publication Data

Marber, Peter.
Money changes everything: how global prosperity is reshaping our needs, values, and lifestyles / by Peter Marber.
   P. cm.
Includes bibliographical references and index.
ISBN 0-13-065480-9
1. Wealth. 2. Money. 3. Globalization. 1. Title.

HC79.W4M366 2003
306.3--dc21
                    2003040879

Editorial/Production Supervision: Donna Cullen-Dolce
Editor-in-Chief: Tim Moore
Editorial Assistant: Richard Winkler
Development Editor: Russ Hall
Manufacturing Buyer: Maura Zaldivar
Cover Design Director: Jerry Votta
Cover Design: Talar Boorujy
Art Director: Gail Cocker-Bogusz
Composition: Daly Graphics
Cover Author Photograph: A. Marber

 © 2003 by Pearson Education, Inc.
Publishing as Financial Times Prentice Hall
Upper Saddle River, New Jersey 07458

Financial Times Prentice Hall offers excellent discounts on this book when ordered in quantity for bulk purchases or special sales.

For more information please contact U.S. Corporate and Government Sales: 1-800-382-3419, corpsales@pearsontechgroup.com. For sales outside the United States, please contact International Sales: 1-317-581-3793, international@pearsontechgroup.com.

Company and product names mentioned herein are the trademarks or registered trademarks of their respective owners.

Printed in the United States of America
1st printing

ISBN 0-13-065480-9

Pearson Education LTD.
Pearson Education Australia PTY, Limited
Pearson Education Singapore, Pte. Ltd.
Pearson Education North Asia Ltd.
Pearson Education Canada, Ltd.
Pearson Educación de Mexico, S.A. de C.V.
Pearson Education—Japan
Pearson Education Malaysia, Pte. Ltd.

FINANCIAL TIMES PRENTICE HALL BOOKS

For more information, please go to www.ft-ph.com

Business and Technology

Sarv Devaraj and Rajiv Kohli
The IT Payoff: Measuring the Business Value of Information Technology Investments

Nicholas D. Evans
Business Agility: Strategies for Gaining Competitive Advantage through Mobile Business Solutions

Nicholas D. Evans
Business Innovation and Disruptive Technology: Harnessing the Power of Breakthrough Technology…for Competitive Advantage

Nicholas D. Evans
Consumer Gadgets: 50 Ways to Have Fun and Simplify Your Life with Today's Technology…and Tomorrow's

Faisal Hoque
The Alignment Effect: How to Get Real Business Value Out of Technology

Thomas Kern, Mary Cecelia Lacity, and Leslie P. Willcocks
Netsourcing: Renting Business Applications and Services Over a Network

Ecommerce

Dale Neef
E-procurement: From Strategy to Implementation

Economics

David Dranove
What's Your Life Worth? Health Care Rationing…Who Lives? Who Dies? Who Decides?

David R. Henderson
The Joy of Freedom: An Economist's Odyssey

Jonathan Wight
Saving Adam Smith: A Tale of Wealth, Transformation, and Virtue

Entrepreneurship

Oren Fuerst and Uri Geiger
From Concept to Wall Street: A Complete Guide to Entrepreneurship and Venture Capital

David Gladstone and Laura Gladstone
Venture Capital Handbook: An Entrepreneur's Guide to Raising Venture Capital, Revised and Updated

Erica Orloff and Kathy Levinson, Ph.D.
The 60-Second Commute: A Guide to Your 24/7 Home Office Life

Jeff Saperstein and Daniel Rouach
Creating Regional Wealth in the Innovation Economy: Models, Perspectives, and Best Practices

Finance

Aswath Damodaran
The Dark Side of Valuation: Valuing Old Tech, New Tech, and New Economy Companies

Kenneth R. Ferris and Barbara S. Pécherot Petitt
Valuation: Avoiding the Winner's Curse

International Business

Peter Marber
Money Changes Everything: How Global Prosperity Is Reshaping Our Needs, Values, and Lifestyles

Fernando Robles, Françoise Simon, and Jerry Haar
Winning Strategies for the New Latin Markets

Investments

Zvi Bodie and Michael J. Clowes
Worry-Free Investing: A Safe Approach to Achieving Your Lifetime Goals

Harry Domash
Fire Your Stock Analyst! Analyzing Stocks on Your Own

Philip Jenks and Stephen Eckett, Editors
The Global-Investor Book of Investing Rules: Invaluable Advice from 150 Master Investors

Charles P. Jones
Mutual Funds: Your Money, Your Choice. Take Control Now and Build Wealth Wisely

D. Quinn Mills
Buy, Lie, and Sell High: How Investors Lost Out on Enron and the Internet Bubble

D. Quinn Mills
Wheel, Deal, and Steal: Deceptive Accounting, Deceitful CEOs, and Ineffective Reforms

John Nofsinger and Kenneth Kim
Infectious Greed: Restoring Confidence in America's Companies

John R. Nofsinger
Investment Blunders (of the Rich and Famous)…And What You Can Learn from Them

John R. Nofsinger
Investment Madness: How Psychology Affects Your Investing…And What to Do About It

Leadership

Jim Despain and Jane Bodman Converse
And Dignity for All: Unlocking Greatness through Values-Based Leadership

Marshall Goldsmith, Vijay Govindarajan, Beverly Kaye, and Albert A. Vicere
The Many Facets of Leadership

Marshall Goldsmith, Cathy Greenberg, Alastair Robertson, and Maya Hu-Chan
Global Leadership: The Next Generation

Contents

Preface

It may seem a bit audacious to include the phrase "global prosperity" in a mid-2003 book title. In fact, many friends have suggested that I substitute the word "anxiety" for "prosperity" to sell more books. Titles with pessimistic or alarmist expressions like "The End of," "The Decline of," or "The Crash of " invariably catch more attention and register more sales, and unfortunately too many of them fill our bookstores.

However, it's exactly at such a time that readers need a reality check. Not a reality based upon what's covered on CNN or printed in the newspapers; these are often simplified sound bites pandering to our collective economic and social insecurities. Rather, a factual reality based on successful trends in so many areas of human existence. Believe it or not, the world is growing measurably more prosperous everyday. Not understanding how these wealth trends filter into the world, or America's unique position amid this abundance, merely contributes to our anxiety and obfuscates the actual issues of globalization.

I have three intentions expressed through this book. First, I want to document the tremendous progress—or "wealth"—made in the last 200 years, particularly since 1950. Human history has been a long, sad tale of struggling with scarcity. Up until 200 years ago, most of our species lived very similar agricultural lives. Since then, the scarcity conundrum has been slowly and miraculously unraveled, with human capital unleashing an astounding ability to produce more of the things we need and desire. In the last two or three generations, these trends have accelerated. As I explore in the book, wealth and prosperity mean more than money; they are larger concepts that encompass everything from better education, improved health, greater democracy, and greater choice. Much of this advancement is the result of increased knowledge and human capital, burgeoning technology, economic growth, and excess financial capital that mutually reinforce each in other in a virtuous cycle.

Second, I attempt to describe how this wealth creation process has profoundly altered—and should continue to alter—the human experience. While factories may be closing down in the U.S. and other wealthy countries, many more are opening in boomtowns scattered among developing nations, from Latin America to Asia. New forms of democracy and wider-ranging political demands are reshaping governments everywhere. Mobile non-nuclear families are replacing traditional households; middle-class enclaves are sprouting up everywhere; women are more participatory in social life than ever before; new and old religions are fading, rising, and morphing everyday. What humans need and value in this century is very different than 200 years ago, or even three or four generations ago; and the stratification of needs, values, and lifestyles in the world is greater today than it has ever been.

Third, I wish to suggest that by analyzing these life-altering processes and changes, we'll all be better equipped to cooperate and continue prospering globally, hopefully with less anxiety. The new economic order of the 21st Century relies almost entirely on well-intentioned cooperation and coordination—for international trade, intellectual and cultural exchange, and collective security. No country, even a hyper-power like the U.S., can achieve greater, long-lasting prosperity on its own. Moreover, no nation can afford to shut itself off from globalizing forces no matter how frightening, foreign, and incomprehensible they may seem.

The U.S. has been thrust into the epicenter of these seminal changes, not merely as an economic and military superpower, but a social, cultural and political—or civilizational—vanguard as well. Through technology beamed into living rooms around the world, our American society is a lightning rod—perhaps *the* lightning rod—for both the enthusiastic embrace and the violent rejection of this 21st Century world. Frequently, strong opposing views occur within the same countries or societies, and even within the same individuals. We Americans love our wealthy, free capitalist system, but we may feel guilty and apologetic about our materialistic existence. We love our SUVs but hate our dependence on foreign oil and the entanglements it brings. We love abundance and choice, but we worry over environmental degradation.

There are similar mixed emotions in the developing world: Yes, many idolize and dream about the cushy American way of life and hope for a prosperous future of greater ease and material comfort. At the same time, they cling fiercely to their own traditions, even sympathizing with Al-Qaeda terrorists seeking to destroy the U.S., a country often perceived as a modern imperialist driven its own self-interests. Americans should remember that our country endured 200 tumultuous years of unjust and often violent history to reach its current state of freedom, tolerance, diversity, and wealth—and we still have much progress to make. We cannot expect traditional values and perceptions to be dropped so quickly elsewhere, particularly in ancient cultures that can be measured in millennia, not centuries.

This civilizational unmooring underpins much of the current anti-globalization and anti-American sentiments (indeed, they are often intertwined). It certainly is convenient to have some clear target for rage. It is far easier for foreign nations and individuals to lash out at the U.S. government, an American hedge fund, or multinational operators than to address difficult domestic issues of economy and taxation, budget deficits, social repression, or trade competitiveness. Poorer countries are in the awkward position of wanting to attract investment from wealthier ones and export goods to those markets. Therefore, they start from a disadvantaged position that may lead to a variety of fears and resentments. Likewise, it is easy for Americans to lash out at big business (companies whose stock many of us own in retirement accounts, directly or indirectly), protectionist foreign governments, and "backward" policies overseas. We want access to inexpensive imported goods and cheap gasoline, but we don't want to deal with the social and political responsibilities that may come with such commercial entanglements. Often we are insensitive to—or even blithely unaware of—the needs, values, and lifestyles of less fortunate countries, and our actions may be seen as arrogant, boorish, antagonistic, and self-righteous.

This individual and national confusion unfortunately taints the globalization debate here and abroad, where the focus is often on anecdotal successes or failures. However difficult it may be, we must remember that the long-term, universal benefits of globalization—the raising of human living standards on all fronts—are indisputable. Anxieties and economies may ebb and flow in the short run, but the responsibility to manage these progressive evolutions and revolutions—with worldwide human prosperity as the goal—should be our consistent aim in both government and the marketplace.

Since so many people have become interested in the globalization debate in recent years, I've attempted to keep the material fairly broad, fluid, and useful for the general reader. The chapter endnotes serve not only to identify my research sources, but also as starting places for further exploration by readers. There are so many perspectives and facets of this wealth and globalization debate; I hope that these references will spur additional research and discussion into the pressing questions of our time.

Acknowledgments

Books like this always require an immense amount of support, and I can only attempt to acknowledge the gracious assistance and guidance received during this project. Several writers, scholars, and market practitioners have spent time chatting with me about specific ideas and issues that populate the book including Sam Ahmad, Gerard Baker, Federico Bauer, David Brooks, Charlie Calomiris, Joyce Chang, John Edmunds, Albert Fishlow, Frank Fukuyama, Derik Gelderblom, Steve Hanke, Craig Karmin, Naomi Klein, Enrique Krauze, Albert Laverge, Michael Lewitt, Price Lowenstein, Ted Merz, Pedro Molina, Paul Zane Pilzer, Lynn Patterson, Virginia Postrel, Jeff Sachs, Amity Shlaes, and Jim Twitchell. Dr. William Robert Fogel of the University of Chicago deserves special mention. He is one of the more human-oriented economists, who proved to me that, occasionally in life, one can get a free lunch. Lisa Anderson and Steven David provided excellent feedback on early drafts and many of their suggestions have been incorporated into this final version. There are also many debts owed to scholars I've never met except through their writing. Among these, I must thank Lynn White, Jr., the great historian at UCLA, whose work on medieval technology and social change has inspired so much of my multidisciplinary interests.

On the publishing front, the Financial Times Prentice Hall team has been exceptionally encouraging and accommodating. My publisher Tim Moore and his team—Russ Hall, Jerry Votta, Talar Boorujy, Donna Cullen-Dolce, and Rick Winkler—have worked closely with me from day one of the project. My agent, Henning Gutmann, also deserves thanks for shaping my original proposal and approaching the FT team with my ambitious topic. Jon Beckmann, who helped organize and edit my first book, fortunately did not tire of my shortcomings and provided similar support for this book as well.

I owe much to my Columbia University students, and it is to them that I dedicate this book. Many of the themes have been debated with them over the last decade. A few students have assisted me with specific research including Lisa Bryant and Stephanie Meade. Gretchen Heefner, in particular, supplied heavy lifting in early drafts and Arif Joshi dutifully mined for difficult data in many chapters.

A certain amount of psychic support is always necessary for projects like this. My day-job colleagues—Mike Gagliardi, Lisa Sherk, Denise Simon, Ken Glynn, and Rich Crochet—deserve much praise for helping my research while keeping our business bliplessly on track. They, along with other colleagues such as Hernando Perez and Christina Almeida, have also contributed many economic, financial, and political, and cultural insights over the last decade. Kat Arturi, my assistant, assembled and packaged multiple versions of the manuscript, and kept the project organized when things were almost spiraling into chaos. Deb Killmon kept my energy levels high through the last year and a half, and David Rapkin has been an excellent early-morning sounding board for dozens of factoids strewn throughout the book.

There's probably not a big idea in the book that hasn't been bantered about with some members of my family at one time or another, and my brother-in-law Matt Hill has been part of many of those discussions for nearly two decades. Finally, a special thanks to my wife, Andrea, who never reminds me that book editing wasn't part of our wedding vows. Her valuable comments have helped smooth many arguments that you'll read, and there's probably not a page in the book untouched by her hands.

1
Living Large in the New Millennium

We are the first stage since the dawn of civilization in which people dared to think it is practicable to make the benefits of civilization available to the whole human race.

Arnold Toynbee (1889–1975)

At first glance, the new millennium has brought us more of the strife and uncertainty that haunted the 20th Century. This perspective, unfortunately, has been shaped largely by gut-wrenching headlines: roller-coaster financial markets, corporate bankruptcies and malfeasance, international political and economic crises, sporadic terrorism, and environmental degradation, to name a few. For many, our liberal free-market system *feels* seriously broken. Yet behind the daily media assaults, monumental, positive forces are transforming the world—largely for the better.

This book explores the ways in which life is changing and improving, providing greater wealth and opportunity for more people than ever before. Such prosperity is altering not only the material world, but also human needs, values, and virtually every aspect of life. Many social upheavals in rich, middle-income, and even poor countries reported in the media reflect the current warp-speed changes in global lifestyles. While such historic changes do indeed create painful adjustments, make no mistake: The world is wealthier today than it has ever been.

Measured by virtually any yardstick, you are—whether or not you know it—*wealthy*.

This is particularly true for any college-educated American. Yes, we Americans must work, but not as our grandparents or great-grandparents did to eke out survival minimums of food, clothing, and shelter. We still work to eat, but today, it's for food we *desire*, not the minimum calories needed to survive. Our choices are vast, from fresh organic vegetables and exotic fruits from around the world to prepared microwavable meals. We also work to eat out, whether it's at a diner, an Outback Steakhouse, or a trendy Zagat-rated restaurant. Americans now spend almost as much money dining out as we spend eating at home.

We still work for clothes, but not simply to cover our naked bodies. We want to wear the *right* clothes, whether they're from Old Navy, Eddie Bauer, the J Crew catalog, or a chic boutique. We don't buy basic shoes; we buy Nike Air Jordans, Timberland boots, or Gucci loafers. We want new, stylish wardrobes every year, and most of us discard clothes well before they're worn out.

We still work for shelter, but more for nesting in houses or apartments that we own, or will own when our mortgages are paid. We work to live in taller high-rises with views, prettier suburbs with better schools, or luxury condominiums with health clubs. We work to live in gated communities, to have vacation homes and time-shares, to renovate or add on, to decorate and redecorate from IKEA, Pottery Barn, Crate & Barrel, or Horchow.

Perhaps most importantly, we work to entertain ourselves when we're not working. We work to buy Sony's largest and flattest television, theater tickets, the best sports or movie packages on satellite TV, Dell's newest Pentium computer, Madonna's latest compact disc (CD) or download, and Barbie dolls, BMX bikes, and X-Boxes for our kids. We work to relax and read *Forbes* or *Entertainment Weekly* and watch rented videos from Blockbuster. We work to sun at the beach, fish at the lake, gamble in Las Vegas, fly to Hawaii or Disney World, take a cruise, or maybe sightsee in Europe. Many work not to own just any car, but to buy a second or even third car, or to upgrade to the latest Lexus or Jeep.

These trends underpin my definition of wealth in the new millennium: freedom. Freedom from hunger, from disease, from short lives, from illiteracy, from debilitating physical labor, from poor housing, from shabby clothing, and not unimportantly, from boredom. It is this physical and psychological wealth—or freedom—for which all humans strive. While this wealth has largely been concentrated in a handful of Western economies, wealth has grown around the globe: There are 1–2 billion people alive today whose lifestyle exceeds anything kings and queens dreamed of 150 years ago, and another 2–3 billion only a generation or two behind.

A key driver of wealth has been the historic migration in labor from back-breaking agriculture toward industry and services.

Having spent more than 15 years working with developing countries, I can say that these trends are altering life in Asia, Africa, Latin America, and the former Soviet Union, in some ways, more than in the West. For example, India's middle class is more than twice as large as the entire Canadian population. China, the world's most populous country with more than 1.3 billion people, now doubles its economic output every 10 or 12 years, or 3 times faster than the U.S. By 2030, China could easily have a consuming middle class the size of the entire U.S. population.

Current living standards in most of the world—including much of Asia, Latin America, and the former Soviet Union—have risen dramatically beyond those of the 19th Century, and a formula for meeting humans' basic needs has been found. Yes, much of the world lives on less than $5 a day. And tragically, there are still over 1 billion people who live in abject poverty—on less than $1 a day. But striking progress has been made over the last 50 years, and recent World Bank studies project true abject poverty will halve by the year 2020.[1]

One of the key drivers of wealth has been the shift in labor away from back-breaking agriculture. Two hundred years ago, almost all of humanity toiled 16-hour days, 6 or 7 days a week, just to feed, clothe, and shelter themselves. Few people lived past 60, and many died at birth or early in childhood. But improved pre-natal and maternal healthcare and education have boosted life expectancies, and better nourishment has bolstered the underlying health of all people. In fact, there has been a larger leap in worldwide life expectancy over the past century than at all other times in history, combined.[2]

As economies move away from agriculture toward industry and services—as first seen in the West—economic output, or Gross National Product (GNP), expands dramatically, triggering profound lifestyle changes (refer to Table 1–1).[3] For example, in Kenya, where 80% of the labor force is in agriculture, GNP per capita is a mere

Table 1-1   The Nature of Labor and Wealth in the New Millennium

Country	Kenya	India	China	Egypt	Mexico	Poland	Hungary	Taiwan	Spain	Canada	Australia	U.S.
GNP Per Capita ($000, p.a.)	0.35	0.44	0.75	1.3	3.8	3.9	4.5	12.0	14.1	19.2	20.0	29.2
% of Labor Force in:												
Agriculture	80	60	50	34	17	19	8	8	7	4	5	3
Industry	7	18	23	22	27	32	35	37	31	22	21	23
Services	13	22	27	44	56	49	57	55	62	74	74	74

Sources: *The Economist, CIA Factbook 2002.*

$350 per year. In Spain, where less than 10% of the population farms, GNP per capita is 40 times higher. Keep in mind that only 5 generations ago in America, it took 19 farmers to feed themselves and just 1 non-farmer. Today, one American farmer harvests for 200 non-farmers, not only in the U.S. but also for export markets.

As wealth is created and the ability to satisfy basic needs increases, individual and community values shift. These values underpin how societies are organized, from economic philosophies to politics, religion, family, culture, education, and the environment. Money does change everything.

Shedding light on these complicated economic, political, and social trends requires a holistic approach, combining seemingly unrelated fields of basic science, demography, sociology, psychology, economics, history, popular culture, and mass media. At the core of my wide-ranging, multidisciplinary exploration of how wealth changes the human condition is the concept of a hierarchical values system. Societies with different needs will, ultimately, promote different values. A married couple in Peru that needs to feed their family on $3,000 per year will not be interested in the latest Maytag dishwasher that captures the attention of a couple making $50,000 per year in Peoria. Simply stated, what a particular group of people needs to physically, emotionally, and psychologically sustain itself ultimately shapes its value system and way of life.

With this focus on human motivation, I am proposing three broad classifications of modern existence: Biological, Material, and Experiential. These categories correlate generally to annual per-capita GNP levels: perhaps up to $2,000 per annum for Biological societies, $2,000–50,000 in the wide Material range, and $50,000 and above in Experiential-trending populations. However, these terms are meant to encompass broader measures of socio-economic progress than pure output and income, such as education and health levels, gender and minority participation, and leisure time. Where a particular society falls in my framework is an important indicator and driver of the lifestyle and value transformations we'll discuss.

This division of life into three catagories is, of course, a conceptual device. There are no simple or absolute categories for complex social, political, and economic development. There are few countries that fit neatly into just one of these classifications; all three exist in every society to some degree, although the number of Experientials in Ghana or Biologicals in the U.S. is relatively small. In fact, the uneven mix of these three groups *within* and *between* countries may lead to some of the most significant conflicts for the world in the coming decades.

During my career on Wall Street, I have seen the limits of studying development in traditional financial terms. What drives progress is far more complicated than cold economic theory; this is why my framework draws heavily from motivational psychologists and social scientists. In the 1960s and 1970s, personality theorist Abraham Maslow popularized the notion of a hierarchy of human needs: All people have a rough pecking order of wants. Such needs are arranged in a motivational ladder (see Figure 1–1), requiring satisfaction of needs on the lower rungs before those on the top rungs.[4] This provides an interesting starting point to discuss my three classifications of societal development.

Figure 1–1   Maslow's pyramid of human needs.

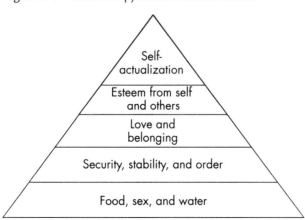

THE BIOLOGICAL PHASE

First, all humans must satisfy their physiological and safety needs, which correspond roughly with Maslow's bottom rungs. Such needs are unbelievably powerful. Imagine not eating or sleeping for a couple of days, or being stranded in a snowstorm; all other non-survival needs would be blocked out. For the average American, meeting such basic "Biological" needs is not an everyday challenge. But for some 2–3 billion people around the developing world, the next batch of calories is still a prime motivator to work.

Once the subsistent needs are met, humans crave security and order. Without such stability, planning for the future and creating widespread wealth are virtually impossible. One only needs to look at war-torn parts of Asia, the Middle East, and Africa to see how economic growth is stunted by a variety of physical and political instabilities. While everyone has higher needs and aspirations, physiological imperatives tend to shape behavior, values, and social institutions in Biological societies.

In places where people now live on $1–5 a day, life is not much different from how it might have been in the U.S. or Europe some 150–200 years ago, before the Industrial Revolution. These Biological economies tend to be agrarian, with long days spent toiling in fields. Life expectancy in these countries is among the world's lowest, ranging from 40–65 years, versus nearly 80 years in the richest countries. Short life expectancy is also linked to infant mortality rates, which are typically between 30–90 per 1,000 births, versus 5 in the U.S. As a result of high infant mortality, birth rates tend to be greatest, along with family size. The average Biological household is roughly twice as large as the average in wealthy North American or European countries, with maybe 3–4 children versus 1 or 2, and with grandparents sometimes living under the same roof. Literacy rates, too, are low in Biological societies—often less than 50%, and large segments of the population are never formally educated. Women are often second-class citizens, legally and culturally, and minority rights rarely exist.

Biological economies tend to be statist, or centrally managed, with frequent government intervention, and geared toward meeting only basic human needs. Often, these impoverished societies can be dominated by religious beliefs that reinforce the value of order, structure, and predictability. Sometimes religious groups control government, like the Taliban did in Afghanistan. Biological populations tend to be organized in small communal units that stress conformity and tradition, with social and economic mobility virtually nonexistent. In the societies, democracy often takes a backseat to autocracy.

In short, how a society's needs are met determines the values of that society, and Biological governmental and community networks are organized primarily around survival principles. Countries characterized as largely Biological might include Haiti, Kenya, and Bangladesh. However, some more populous, stratified countries like India and China also have large Biological-oriented segments.

THE DAYS OF OUR LIVES

While a woman in the U.S. is waking up to go to Starbuck's before work, her counterpart in Ghana may be collecting firewood to make the morning's breakfast. A South Korean woman may be heating breakfast over the stovetop when her cell phone rings.

So begins the day of different women in Biological, Material, and Experiential societies. While there are no countries that fall completely within one category, certain parts of the world are more representative of each phase than others. Ghana, with an annual GNP per capita under $400, is almost entirely Biological; South Korea has elements of all phases, but generally falls into the Material; and the U.S.—though largely Material—has large segments that have entered the Experiential phase.

Ghana: The Biological Day[5]

For a woman in Ghana, the day consists largely of work: Each day she will spend 25 minutes collecting water and 43 minutes collecting the firewood needed to heat the water and prepare meals. She will walk 48 minutes to work because the country lacks the basic infrastructure to provide for buses and bicycles. Like most of the population of her sub-Saharan African country, she farms for a living. Indeed, the nation's domestic economy continues to revolve around subsistence agriculture, which accounts for 36% of GNP and employs 60% of the workforce, mainly small landholders. She makes just over $1 a day.

Each morning, she wakes before sunrise and prepares breakfast by the light of a kerosene lamp. The house lacks electricity, a telephone, or a TV. During the day, this woman and her husband will work in their cassava field a few kilometers from their hut of mud walls and thatched roof. She will carry her baby on her back all day. After a lunch of yams, she will walk 28 minutes to the nearest mill to have the cassava ground. If it is market day, she will spend 2 hours and 8 minutes regardless of weather to walk to the market to buy the things the family cannot produce and to trade their surplus. If someone in the family falls seriously ill, it is unlikely that they will see a trained doctor; only one-quarter of the population has access to such healthcare. Long-term malnutrition stunts the growth of 31% of Ghanaian children. This woman has five young children. The two eldest attend primary school, but are unlikely to go on to secondary school. Only 1 in 3 children are in school for any given age group—this number has declined from the 1980s when enrollment rates were higher. Female children have even less opportunity than males; adult female literacy is about 75% of the male rate.

GHANA at a Glance:

Output per capita:	$340
Life expectancy:	61
Calories per day:	2,237
Adult literacy (male/female)	80/62%
Fertility rate:	4.2
Phones, fixed and mobile (per 1,000):	18
Computers (per 1,000):	3

Like most of its neighbors, Ghana suffered from serious post-colonial political instability and experienced nine changes in government and four military coups between 1957 and 1983. Today, Ghana is a constitutional democracy with an elected president. While there have been charges of corruption and dubious political practices, the country is moving toward greater openness and political participation. In fact, compared to its sub-Saharan neighbors, Ghanaians enjoy relatively high levels of political freedom, though most do not vote. A large portion of the population is Christian, but traditional religions and rituals are still important and Islam is practiced by 13% of the population.

While social progress is being made in Ghana, at the present rate of growth, it will be two decades before a significant Material middle class develops. Even then, a majority of the population will still live in the Biological phase.

THE MATERIAL PHASE

This stage begins to evolve when large segments of a population move from subsistence agriculture to factory and service jobs. The Industrial Revolution ushered in this phase in the West, raising productivity, and promoting the mass production of goods, new economic efficiencies, and the advent of true markets. This migration from farming has a profound impact on people's lives, as the amount of time and income spent on necessities falls precipitously, providing people the new opportunity to enjoy *leisure*. This is the great legacy of technology and industrialization: People produce more in less time and come away from work with more disposable income and time to spend it.[6]

As personal income grows beyond what's necessary to cover basic food, clothing, and shelter, work becomes intertwined with social and status-linked needs. Figure 1-2 shows that as societies move from agriculture to manufacturing and services, income grows and people net more leisure time and money to consume nonessential items. In 1875, when more than 95% of Americans farmed, only 18% of income was spent on leisure. By 1995, leisure spending ballooned to 67.5%, with less than 3% of Americans engaged in farming. Over the same period, the percentages of income spent on food, clothing, and shelter fell dramatically.[7]

Economist and author Paul Zane Pilzer argues that once basic biological and security imperatives are met, people are thrown into the realm of *alchemic demand*, a phase that neatly describes how economics and human needs are joined at the hip. Pilzer believes that 90% of what is consumed today in wealthy countries like the U.S. is unnecessary for Biological existence, but satisfies alchemic "quantity" and "quality" demands. A "quantity" demand is the want for more of what one already has: more food, another pair of jeans, an extra CD player. Indeed, the demand for a second or third item—like a telephone or car—is often greater than the demand for a first one in wealthy countries.[8]

Figure 1-2   The changing pattern of the consumption composition of American household spending, 1875 and 1995.

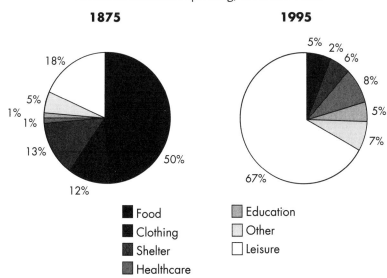

However, demand for increased quantity is often capped by *Engel's Law*: One can only eat so much regardless of income.[9] Once well-fed and clothed in a moderately wealthy society, people want *better* food and clothing versus more. This creates what Pilzer calls "quality" demand. There are entire industries and movements built on quality demands, segmenting products and services beyond imagination. As Pilzer observes:

> A typical middle-class American couple would have little interest in buying a third Chevrolet to add to the two they already own. But they might jump at the chance to get rid of one of the Chevrolets and upgrade to a BMW. A young executive whose closet is filled with eight $400 suits would probably have little interest in purchasing a ninth one. But he might jump at the chance to purchase a new $800 designer suit.[10]

In Material societies, people tend to focus on status and esteem needs, since they are no longer struggling to meet the physiological needs described earlier. In countries where large middle classes are developing, communal values tend to weaken while individualism grows stronger. Simultaneously, secularization of economic and political institutions occurs. With greater freedom from concern over survival necessities, Material populations begin to consider the possibility of controlling their own destiny, which may translate into greater democratic tendencies. Material life in the new millennium is dominated by the desires for status, recognition, and the freedom to live a life of choice.

Don't underestimate the far-reaching importance of these social needs. In his seminal book, *The End of History and the Last Man*, Francis Fukuyama calls the universal need for esteem, or "recognition," the greatest and most misunderstood motivator in history. Indeed, while such social needs manifest themselves economically in where people decide to work and what they buy, Fukuyama wisely notes that these needs ultimately create demands for democracy and liberal economics—for a strong popular voice as to how government will operate. While democratic yearnings are not limited to rich populations, they are suppressed, often severely, in countries where subsistent needs are not readily met. As a result, greater popular political participation and a tendency toward democratic governance characterize the Material phase.

Material governments and institutions are built to foster economic growth and wealth creation. They become more bureaucratic and centralized than those in Biological societies, and are focused less on supporting traditional community units. A significant feature of Material societies is the separation of traditional religious structures from everyday functions and institutions.

Material segments come away from work with more disposable income and free time to spend it.

This evolves when secular conventions—versus holy scriptures—become life's rulebook, ultimately creating "civil" society with personal and property rights codified by laws and regulations, and enforced by an impartial justice system.

Depending on the country, life expectancy in Material societies is averaging 70–80 years. Minimum daily caloric intake is not a problem for most; in fact, obesity might even become more prevalent, as in the U.S. Literacy rates often range between 60–99%. Family size tends to be smaller than in Biological countries, and there are better medical and health practices. Urbanization trends are well-established, and suburbanization is increasing in higher income Material countries.

Some countries newly entering the Material phase still have large segments of Biological populations, like Mexico, Brazil, Russia, Poland, South Korea, and Malaysia. Middle-stage Material countries include Spain, Israel, Taiwan, and others countries with $10,000–20,000 per-capita average incomes. Material populations dominate wealthier countries like the U.S., Great Britain, Japan, and Germany. Indeed, most of these nations are more than two-thirds Material.

SOUTH KOREA: LIVING IN THE MATERIAL WORLD[11]

Halfway around the world from Ghana, a woman in South Korea has awakened to an alarm clock and a quick shower. She may prepare breakfast for her family (two children and her husband)—possibly rice, fruit, and vegetables or kimchi (Korea's staple spicy cabbage dish)—over her stovetop and wash the dishes under warm tap water, or perhaps in a small dishwasher. She will take public transportation to work. While more and more Koreans are buying cars, most do not have one. Like most Koreans, this family lives in a high-rise apartment building in a major urban area.

This woman works in a bank. Just over half of South Korea's economy is in services. She makes over 40 times what the woman in Ghana makes each year, and uses her disposable income on a variety of goodies. A movie ticket in South Korea costs over $6, dinner for two at an average restaurant will be $25, and a pair of designer jeans will cost $40.

While this woman's grandmother probably could not read and write, a rapid program of industrialization and economic advancement implemented in the mid-20th Century has boosted Korea's primary and secondary enrollment rates to almost 99%. The woman holds a bachelor's degree from a local university, and she has studied English since grade school. Her husband, an engineer for a large electronics company, works long hours and makes more than twice what she does. Her two children—a boy and a girl—will most likely attend college and find jobs in the service sector.

The daughter loves to chat with friends on the Internet. She recently upgraded her cell phone for a newer, flashier model with changeable color cases. She seems to constantly be typing messages and will run off during dinner when her phone beeps, indicating an incoming message. Korean women are reported to be Asia's most active and sophisticated Internet chat users. They have affordable and fast Internet access through computers and through their mobile phones.

SOUTH KOREA at a Glance:

Output per capita:	$8,600
Life expectancy:	73.2
Calories per day:	2,717
Adult literacy (male/female):	99/96%
Fertility rate:	1.7
Phones (per 1,000):	433
Computers (per 1,000):	153

Along with the rapid rise in education and economic opportunity, South Korea has undertaken a concerted effort at government reform. The president and National Assembly are elected by popular vote. Koreans enjoy relative political freedom. The state is highly secular and religious authority plays little, if any, role in public life.

THE EXPERIENTIAL PHASE

Generally freed from economic and social hardship, some wealthier societies have large populations that are increasingly focused on psychologically rooted needs: the Experiential phase of greater personal fulfillment.[12] At this level, the desired quantity and quality of material accumulation have been achieved and individuals look outside of the traditional social structure to find purpose and meaning in their efforts.

No country has a majority Experiential population yet, but there are growing numbers in the U.S., Canada, Western Europe (particularly Scandinavia), Japan, and Australia. And as mentioned above, there are small segments of Experientials in virtually all countries, particularly in highly populated Biological societies such as India and China, as well as in dozens of Material-dominated countries. It should go without saying that everyone yearns for individualized, personal fulfillment, but economic circumstances often determine whether Experiential needs are pursued or lay dormant.

The University of Michigan's *Human Values Survey* highlights the connection between wealth, personal well-being, and the search for greater self-expression. There is a direct relationship between output per capita and the Michigan's Subjective Well-Being Index. Simply stated, higher output countries almost universally have more "satisfied" populations, although of course that does not mean wealthy individuals have problem-free lives.

Experiential people put less faith in traditional political and religious institutions and concentrate more on their own physical, mental, and spiritual fulfillment. In countries with growing Experiential populations, traditional government recedes into the background as people choose to participate in activities that fit their individual values and needs. The rise of tourism, the booming "wellness" industry (including everything from nutritional concerns, fitness, and cosmetic surgery to advanced medicines), and a growing interest in non-traditional spiritual practices (which may include new religious movements, or NRMs) are examples of this. Ironically, another Experiential trend is the "simplicity" movement, in which people drop out of the Material phase, believing that "less is more" in terms of achieving happiness. Having reached a level of economic security unprecedented in the world, these people are rejecting the purely material world in their search for greater holistic fulfillment. Echoing Maslow's "self-actualization" stage, Ronald Inglehart notes that once all physical and material needs are sated, people often place higher priority on self-expression than on pure economic effectiveness.[13]

AN EXPERIENTIAL SLICE OF AMERICA[14]

A woman in an Atlanta suburb wakes to National Public Radio on her clock radio. On her way to work (she drives a new Toyota hybrid, gas/electric car), she stops by the local Starbucks to get a skim milk latte and low-fat muffin. She works in marketing for a multinational corporation and earns almost $70,000 each year in salary and bonus. She has both a bachelor's and master's degree from major American universities. Her husband is a corporate lawyer and makes more than $100,000.

At noon, this American woman attends a yoga class at the company gym. She grabs a made-to-order sandwich from a nearby shop and often eats at her desk. She leaves work a few minutes early to make it to her son's T-ball game. The family's nanny (from Mexico; she is teaching the kids Spanish) will pick up the little girl from her private Montessori kindergarten. After the game, the family will eat at a nearby Japanese restaurant.

When the family needs groceries, they no longer shop exclusively at a supermarket or Wal-Mart. Instead, they frequently opt for a small, local shop where produce is organic and meats are hormone-free. The family recycles all bottles, cans, and plastics each week, as mandated by town ordinance.

Once home, the boy will log online to research a school project. The father will watch his favorite TV show from the night before—saved on Tivo. The mother will relax with a glass of California Merlot and will read a book on Costa Rica. The family is planning a vacation there next month. They will spend one week learning about sustainable rainforest tourism, including a camping trip into the jungle.

U.S. at a Glance:

Output per capita:	$29,240
Life expectancy:	80
Calories per day:	3,157
Adult literacy (male/female):	100/100%
Fertility rate:	2.0
Phones (per 1,000):	661
Computers (per 1,000):	459

Both parents are active in causes that are important to them: environmentalism and education. They serve on the board of a large environmental group and make large campaign contributions to local candidates promising to make changes. As wealthy Americans, their political and social freedoms are unrivaled in the world.

The two children will almost certainly go to college, and maybe even spend a semester abroad. Both are encouraged to excel in school, sports, and extracurricular volunteer activities. The family does not participate in any organized religious activities though the mother is from a Christian background and the father is Jewish. The children are educated about these beliefs, but are not encouraged to subscribe to either. It will be their choice when they are older.

GOING FORWARD

Money Changes Everything begins with a historical overview of the world's shifting economies, followed by an investigation of how wealth is being created today. The remaining chapters will examine how specific aspects of the human experience—government, family, religion, education, leisure, and the environment—are being transformed by prosperity. Most chapters will include a chart like Figure 1–3, showing the economic growth and historic changes that have occurred within each chapter's area of focus.[15]

From my lucky perspective as a 21st Century American, wealth creates freedom: freedom to choose how one spends one's time on earth. And because I see wealth increasing around the globe, I am unabashedly optimistic. But I am also realistic; I understand that wealth creation is not always fair or equal. Comparative advantage and free trade—the main engines of prosperity—are philosophies that inherently divide and segment people; not everyone gains evenly under them. The fact that some countries are split into my three phases within their own borders highlights this inequality. Moreover, it should not be overlooked that some 2000 privileged families in the world control more assets than the 2 billion poorest. Wealth creation is a tide that lifts most boats, but it certainly raises some higher and faster.

Figure 1-3   Wealth and human progression, 2000BCE–2000CE.

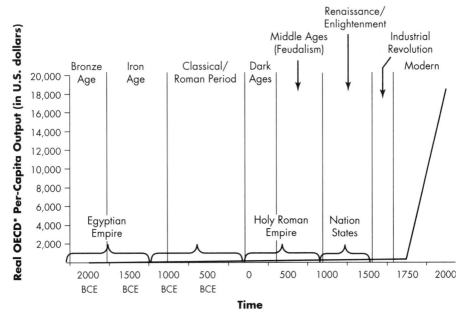

*Organization for Economic and Cultural Development

Table 1-2 Framework for Understanding Societal Development

	Biological	Material	Experiential
Economics	Steady-state, less-diversified agrarian or mineral-oriented; poor efficiency; some oligopols; limited capital formation; largely essential goods; small middle class; vulnerable to external shocks	Market-oriented, more diversified mix of agrarian, industrial, and services; greater efficiency; some capital market formation; mix of essential and non-essential goods; less vulnerable to external shocks	*Laissez-faire* markets; highly industrial and service-oriented; little agriculture; great efficiency; high capital market formation; non-essentials very important; large domestic market, less vulnerable to external shocks
Government	Autocratic, possibly totalitarian; questionable voting and democracy; poor tax collections; limited legal system	Greater democracy, parliamentarian; greater tax collection; improving legal system	Fully tested democracies; functioning accountable parliaments; reliable tax collection; fully enforceable, tested legal systems
Religion	Traditional and prevalent; possibly fundamentalist; still important sphere in government and culture	Becoming more secular; traditions fading; church less important in society; formal attendance and belief down; traditional values questioned	Very secular; formal religion less prevalent; formal churches less visible; rising spiritual and/or "self-actualizing" needs
Family	Larger, with high birth rates; multigenerational homes; largely heterosexual households; some female and child labor	Medium-sized, with modest fertility rates; single-generational homes; largely heterosexual, married households; growing female labor, and declining child labor (if any)	Small-sized, with low or negative birth rates; dispersed generational households; mix of single and marrieds, heterosexual and homosexual households; full female workforce; protective child labor laws
Leisure/ Culture	Traditional, religious, fundamental; little money spent on culture consumption; rural, but urbanizing; indigenous versus cosmopolitan	Traditions fading; secular cosmopolitanism growing; expanding income spent on leisure, entertainment, and sports; widespread urbanization, declining rural life	Secular, cosmopolitan; focus on work objective; high amounts spent on leisure, entertainment, and sports; urban and suburban, with little rural population

Constituencies not yet engaged in the wealth process, often illiterate and living under despot regimes, maintain traditional values at odds with those treasured in wealthy nations. The intellectually dynamic, free-market, democratic, secular lifestyle that usually accompanies greater affluence often can be despised and thought of as wanton, sacrilegious, and shameful by non-participants. Ironically, many technologies that have helped create wealth can be used to disseminate hateful propaganda or can even be fashioned into weapons to attack richer democratic societies, a risk that has greatly increased in the last three decades. The tragic terrorist attacks of September 11th are a stark example of this.

This is why everyone, everywhere should be concerned about wealth creation and globalization. It should be clear that a sagging Japanese economy, or a surging one in China, or a politically unstable African continent, or rising Islamic fundamentalism, or global warming trends resonate across all borders and affect all lives. The needs, values, and lifestyles of every society affect many abroad, and not always positively.

My objectives in *Money Changes Everything* are to demonstrate that wealth is a multi-dimensional concept, and that prosperity is altering human needs, values, and lifestyles around the globe—first in the West, and now for billions elsewhere. Not every person or every society will welcome these changes, and some may reject them completely. There will be many who adopt them, but might not benefit much from them in their own lifetimes. This book will show why these monumental forces should be understood, humanely and intelligently managed, and universally embraced.

Table 1–2 outlines a framework for understanding societal development.

2
Wealth and History:

How the World is Growing Richer

Gross National Product is our Holy Grail.

Stuart L. Udall (b. 1920)
Former U.S. Interior Secretary[1]

During the last century, the world has grown dramatically wealthier, and most of us have experienced it personally. But the dimensions and background of this historic progression are not so readily understood. How rich are we? How much better off are we than a few generations ago? Examining this pivotal period of human history dramatically reveals that not only has wealth creation accelerated sharply, but also that its consequences go far beyond the usual economic definitions.

Wealth needs to be measured not only by economic concepts like net disposable income, GNP, and global stock market capitalization, but also by living standards such as life expectancy, daily caloric intake, morbidity and mortality rates, and education levels. By all these measures, wealth has climbed beyond any expectation of the late 19th Century. On average, people are living twice as long as they did a century ago, and the quality of health during those extra years has also improved. The visible, material infrastructure of modern societies—houses, roads, schools, bridges, tunnels, cars and trucks, factories, hospitals, stores, mines, farms, shopping malls, rail lines, airplanes, power

Figure 2–1   Wealth and human progression, 2000BCE–2000CE.

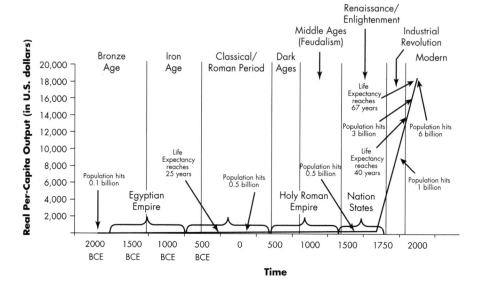

plants and grids, and phone networks—all demonstrate that the world has capacities undreamed of a century and a half ago. Based on estimates by economic historian Angus Maddison, this aggregate material infrastructure is hundreds of times greater than what it was in the early 19th century.[2]

The lifestyles of 1–2 billion people living in the U.S. and the other 25 industrialized countries surpass that of any royalty living in the 18th and 19th Centuries. For 4–5 billion citizens in developing countries, the process of wealth creation has begun to take root in the last two generations, with large segments of these populations making major progress. According to the United Nations (UN), in the year 2000, more than 3.5 billion people lived in what it classifies as "medium development" versus only 1.6 billion in 1975.[3]

As Figure 2–1 notes, life expectancy was low and world population small up until 100 years ago. Technological improvements in medicine, chemistry, and mechanical science have brought about a true golden age for many, correlated with a spike in real per-capita income in the 20th Century.

Note that the ability to increase human living standards at all, let alone within one's own lifetime, is a relatively new phenomenon. For much of homo sapiens' 100,000 years of recorded existence, life was indeed nasty, brutish, and short, as Hobbes remarked in *The Leviathan*. Even in the last millennium, economic output expanded at less than .2% per year up until a century or so ago. That means it took some 500 years for output to double. However, this changed during the 20th Century, when output doubled in less than 30 years in the U.S. and other Western European countries, and Japan's economy doubled in less than 16 years. In recent decades, developing country economies have surged so quickly that some—like South Korea in the 1960s and 1970s, and China in the 1990s—have often doubled productive output in just 7–10 years.

The ability to increase human living standards at all, let alone within one's own lifetime, is a relatively new phenomenon.

Around 500 years ago, ideas from the Renaissance and then the Enlightenment revved up the ability to harness the earth's resources. Building on this foundation, scientific knowledge and its technological applications changed political and economic thinking, which—combined with modern finance in the last century—produced unprecedented, measurable gains in human wealth. This has intensified in the last 50 years, arguably with what one author calls "turbo-capitalism,"[4] that is, the hyper-pursuit of efficiency and innovation through technology, trade, and mobile capital.

The miracle of modern prosperity and the underlying philosophies that support it have helped to conquer hunger for most, stretch life expectancy and eliminate diseases of the past, and is providing the keys to unlock a continually progressive future. The clearest evidence of such success is in sheer population; there are now more than 6 billion humans living on earth. Twelve thousand years ago, perhaps there were only 6 million, and even 2,000 years ago, world population reached only 252 million.[5] After the Earth's population passed 1 billion around 1800, Thomas Malthus and others predicted that overpopulation would lead to global famine. Happily, they were wrong. Today, billions have triumphed over bare necessity, and are, by historical standards, rich.

HOW WE'RE ALL DOING BETTER

Is the world better off in this new millennium than it was 50 or 100 years ago? No matter how one measures wealth—by economic, social, or physical indicators—the answer is unequivocally "yes." As

Table 2-1   Measured Wealth Creation, 1950-2050

	1950	2000	2050E
Global Output, Per Capita ($)	$586	$6,666	$15,155
Global Financial Market			
Capitalization, Per Capita ($)	$158	$13,333	$75,000
% of Global GDP,			
Emerging Markets	5	73	55
Industrial Countries	95	77	45
Life Expectancy (years),			
Emerging Markets	41	64	78
Industrialized Countries	65	77	84
Daily Caloric Intake,			
Emerging Markets	1,200	2,600	3,000
Industrial Countries	2,200	3,100	3,200
Infant Mortality (per 1000),			
Emerging Markets	140	65	10
Industrial Countries,	30	8	4
Literacy Rate (per 100),			
Emerging Markets	33	64	88
Industrialized Countries	95	98	99

Sources: Bloomberg, World Bank, United Nations, and author's estimates. Output and financial market capitalization figures are adjusted for inflation.

Table 2–1 illustrates, progress has been made in virtually every meaningful aspect of life, and this trend should continue for the foreseeable future.

While it is clear that the world as a whole is earning more money and buying more things, what is probably more important is that people are living longer, healthier, fuller lives. For much of the developing world, life has improved rapidly since 1950. Life expectancy for emerging market countries, for example, has been stretched by more than 50% from 41 years to 64, reaching levels the West enjoyed back in 1950. Many Biological societies are merely two generations behind the wealthiest nations (keep in mind that in 1820, life expectancy in Sweden was just 35). Life expectancy gains are linked to better pre-natal care and lower infant mortality, the results of better nutrition (including a doubling in daily caloric intake), improved sanitation, immunizations, and other public health advances. Because fertility rates have not declined as fast as mortality rates, population growth surged in the 20th Century. It is interesting to note that after similar improvements in the 19th Century, European and North American populations swelled, though they are now static (or even declining in some parts of Europe) as a result of conscious choices regarding family size.

The essence of wealth in the modern world is strong price deflation and greater purchasing power.

The fact that the world is producing enough food to keep pace with the growing population (Table 2–2) means that freedom from hunger—the most basic Biological need—will allow billions of people to possess the physical health to begin tackling their next set of needs. There is already evidence that this is happening.

Literacy rates in developing countries, for example, have risen dramatically in the last 50 years. In 1950, only one-third of their populations (roughly 800 million people) could read or write; today two-thirds can—for a total of more than 3.2 billion. This literacy trend continues as attendance in primary and secondary school grows, and as more men and women continue at the tertiary level. The world now has a far more educated population with greater intellectual capacity than at any other time in history.

Table 2–2   How Food Production Has Outpaced Population Growth

Per Capita	1961	2001
Wheat Production (Metric tons (Mt)/per 1000 capita)	72.22	94.99
Total Wheat Yield (hectogram per hectare [Hg/Ha])	10,889	27,252
Soybean Production (Mt/per 1000 capita)	8.73	28.80
Fertilizer Use (Mt/per 1000 capita)	5.1	22.2
Rice Production (Mt/per 1000 capita)	70.04	96.64
Meat Production (Mt/per 1000 capita)	23.12	38.56
Marine Fish Production (Mt/per 1000 capita)	9.86	11.89
Marine Fish Catch Production (Mt/per 1000 capita)	12.73	21.10
World Population (in 1000s)	3,078,867	6,134,138

Source: Food and Agriculture Organization, FAOSTAT Agricultural Data, online at: *http://apps.fao.org/cgi-bin/nph-db.pl?subset=agriculture.*

The combination of lower infant mortality, longer life expectancy, greater literacy, and education has resulted in tremendous gains in human economic productivity. The world has increased its human "capital" more than ever before, and is producing more goods and services than ever before, as demonstrated by sharp increases in economic output such as the GNP, disposable income, and global financial aggregates.

Some who may remember the 1970s and 1980s, regardless of a background in economics, may note that rising GNP and stock market capitalization numbers don't immediately mean "wealthier"; these numbers may also reflect inflation. According to sticker prices, almost everything we buy today costs more than it did in the past. However, inflation and higher absolute prices obfuscate the real economic trend: At its center, wealth creation in the modern world is strong price **deflation**.

The most dramatic illustration of greater prosperity, by far, is *purchasing power*. Ultimately, what determines wealth is the ability to work less, yet produce more. The time needed for an average U.S. worker to earn the purchase price of various commodities, goods, and services drastically *decreased* during the 20th Century. Anyone born in the U.S. since 1950—and even in the last three decades in many countries around the world—has had access to things and experiences previously reserved for only the ultra-wealthy, and many never available to anyone in history. As economist Brad DeLong points out:

> Today the average American possesses a degree of material comfort that in many ways outstrips the reach of even the richest humans of previous centuries. Perhaps a billion people living today are within striking distance of middle-class American productivity levels and living standards. Moreover, even lower middle-class households in relatively poor countries have material standards of living that in many dimensions—access to entertainment and news, public health, variety and extent of diet, potential literacy, materials with which to build shelter—would make them the envy of many of the prosperous of past centuries.[6]

To illustrate this point, examine how much work time it has taken an average American to earn enough for certain household items throughout history, constructing a rough index of American productivity. In 1919, it took 30 minutes of labor to earn enough to buy a pound of ground beef. That time decreased to 23 minutes by 1950, 11 minutes by 1975, and just 6 minutes by 1997.[7] As Figure

Figure 2-2 Growing richer by working less, labor and consumer costs, 1919-1997.

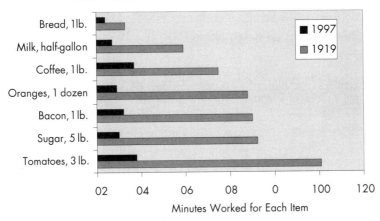

Source: U.S. Federal Reserve Bank (1997).

2-2 notes, the *time* spent to produce food has decreased in the last century, freeing workers to consume and do more.

But this deflation goes well beyond groceries, and has had even greater impact on manufactured goods and services. DeLong constructs a similar productivity index with comparisons from the 1895 *Montgomery Ward* catalog, the largest mail-order retailer in the U.S. at that time. Take a bicycle that, in 1895, cost $65. Measured in actual dollars, the bike now costs roughly twice as much largely due to inflation of nominal prices.[8] But the nominal amount of money is merely a shorthand calculation; what actually matters is the "real" price, that is, the number of hours of labor needed to buy the bike. Based on DeLong's calculations, an average American needed to work some 260 hours in 1895 to purchase the bike; *but it costs less than 8 hours, or 1/36 as much, in labor time today.*[9] Using DeLong's bicycle example, the average American worker today is 36 times richer than his or her counterpart was back in 1895.[10]

A trip back to the late 19th Century isn't necessary to understand this point; clearly, this price deflation phenomenon is evident in our own lifetimes as well. The costs of goods and services—everything from TVs, to household appliances, to telephone calls, computers, and airplane travel—have plummeted relative to growing incomes. In 1975, a 19-inch color TV cost $300. By 2003, it cost less than $150, and keep in mind that $300 in 1975 was equal to about $1,000 in 2003. In the last quarter century, TV prices have effectively dropped 85% in terms of labor needed to buy one.

Similarly, look at commercial air travel, once only reserved for corporate titans and Hollywood legends. In 1975, a round-trip coach seat from New York to Los Angeles cost approximately $700.

The costs of most goods have plummeted relative to our growing incomes.

At times during 2003, some airlines were offering such tickets for roughly $200. In 1975 dollars, that would deflate to approximately $60—making air travel less than one-tenth the cost of just a quarter of a century ago.

More remarkable are the deflationary trends in high-technology goods. Take the price of personal computers (PCs), one of our most recent revolutionary inventions. Just compare Dell Computer's desktop model offered in mid-1991 versus early-2003:[11]

	1991	2003
Price:	$2,699	$599
Memory:	2MB	256 MB
Internal Storage:	80 MBs	20 GB
Processor:	25 MHz	2 GHz

First, keep in mind that $2,699 in 1991 is the equivalent of approximately $3,400 in 2003. So the 2003 price is already *less than 20% of what it was in 1991.* Second, the 2003 model has capacities that are anywhere from 100–250 times *greater* than that of the 1991 model. That means to get the same computing capacity from one single Dell desktop computer in 2003, one would have had to buy 100–250 desktop PCs in 1991. Simply stated, in 2003, for $599, one could buy the computing power equivalent of more than $500,000 Dell desktops in 1991. *That* is price deflation.[12] And this doesn't take into account that the 2003 model has a variety of features like DVD, stereo, and Internet connectivity that were not even available in 1991.

WEALTH, EQUALITY, AND GROWTH

The discussion of economic equality, particularly in globalization circles, is extremely heated with both sides pointing to a variety of statistics to show growing or narrowing gaps. While some may argue that the world is wealthier overall, many critics of liberal economics cite growing income inequality around the globe. The science of analyzing such long-term trends is far from perfect, but there are sufficient indicators that point absolutely to measurable progress.[13]

One of the biggest problems in this discussion is an unfortunate preoccupation with "income" or "GNP" as a measure of welfare. Income is just one measure of wealth, but not the only one. And income comparisons don't always capture full household money from informal or unreported economic activity, which tends to be more prevalent in poorer countries.

Many social scientists apply GINI coefficients for income (a measure of income dispersion between and within countries) to such equality analysis. The lower the GINI figure, the more equal income tends to be. Unfortunately, GINI doesn't take into account purchasing power parity (PPP), the age dispersion of a population, and other variables that could breathe a little wisdom into the dry GINI income statistic. GINI might be better applied to life expectancy, education, or daily caloric intake to see if gaps are closing in these measures (which they are). Even with this income limitation, when adjusted for PPP, GINI for world income distribution from 1965–1997 decreased from .59 to .52, an improvement of nearly 12%.[14]

Others like to cite "poverty" rates, an approach that is also problematic. Poverty is often defined as the percentage of a population that earns 50% less than the median income in a country. But because 50% of median American income is very different from 50% of median income in Bangladesh, poverty rates often don't reveal much.[15]

Perhaps broader trends in human development are better progress gauges than simple income analyses. A yardstick like the UNDP's Human Development Index (HDI), for example, which looks at not only income but also life expectancy and education (including literacy and school enrollment), may provide a clearer picture of well-being. In this respect, there has been progress for wealthy, developing, *and* the least developed countries between 1960 and 2000:

HDI	1960	1993	2000
OECD	.798	.909	.905
Developing	.260	.563	.654
Least Developed	.161	.331	.445

This index underscores that well-being gaps are closing. While wealthy OECD countries have advanced 13.9% in the period, developing countries rose 116+%, and the least developed countries also more than doubled. Looking at the ratios of HDI between segments, the poorest countries climbed from 20.2% of the wealthiest to 49.1%, and developing countries from 32.6% to 72.1%. More importantly, the greatest gains are from the recent 1993–2000 period, a time of accelerated international trade that helped developing countries ratchet up an additional 20–30% on the HDI, at a time while OECD HDI actually *declined* (even though incomes grew). Critics of globalization tend to gloss over these facts.

To most, the HDI findings make intuitive sense. Of course poorer countries are making much greater advances in life expectancy, education, and daily caloric intake than wealthier countries. They're catching up from a low base. And those gaps are narrowing. Nobel-winning economists Simon Kuznets and Robert E. Lucas have noted that such inequality and catch-ups are to be expected,[16] and that we should expect the gaps to close further in the next 50 years. Several studies note that on average, growth in the income of the poor rise about one-for-one with the growth rate of overall per capita income in a given country.[17] And developing countries now contribute nearly 25% of global economic output, three times their contribution in 1950.

This by no means negates the reality of global poverty. There is still substantial work to be done. While the UN notes the world's percentage of poor people has declined from 28% to 24%, 24% is still too large a number. There are an estimated one billion people in "abject" poverty—defined as living on $1 a day. But the World Bank estimates that this number should halve by 20 at current growth trends.

This rise of productivity, price deflation, and resulting wealth has not been confined to the world's elite economies. The greatest leaps forward have happened in some of the world's poorest Biological-oriented economies. Certain consumer goods, like TVs, have become universal commodities owned by most households on the planet (see Table 2–3). Indeed, the 50 most populous countries in the world average more than 95 TVs per 100 households. That includes some of the world's largest and poorest countries, such as China, with 95.6 TVs per 100 households. Keep in mind that China's output per capita, while growing at a blistering rate, is still not among the world's top 100 at only $750 per annum as of 1998.[18] Even for high-priced items like automobiles, there is a growing universal usage. For the 25 wealthiest countries in the world, there are approximately 425 automobiles per 1,000 people.

Table 2-3 Global Consumption Patterns (People All Over the World Have Access to More and More Goods)[19]

	China	Brazil	Hungary	Japan	U.S.
Energy Consumption per Head (Kilowatt-hours), 1997	714	1,743	2,840	7,241	11,822
Cars (per 1,000 people), 1998	12	70	229	394	486
Telephone Main Lines (per 1,000), 1998	70	121	336	503	661
Daily Newspapers (per 1,000), 1996	29	40	186	578	215
Radios (per 1,000), 1997	333	444	689	955	2,146
TVs (per 1,000), 1998	272	316	437	707	847
Coca-Cola (units per capita per year), 2001	9	144	39	168	419

While some may decry industrialization as a spirit-numbing process, more people in more places have access not only to goods, but also to art, ideas, and innovation. One of DeLong's best examples is music: Think about what it took to hear a classical orchestral piece in 1900 compared to today. To listen to music on-demand then, one would have had to be either a real baron or a robber baron. DeLong estimates that it would have cost the average U.S. worker 2400 hours, roughly a year at a 50-hour workweek, to earn enough money to buy a high-quality piano, let alone have a concert pianist on hand to play it.[20] Today, to listen to music on-demand, one could buy a boom box or mini-stereo for a mere 10 hours of work, or a simple $5 transistor radio for 1 hour of work at current U.S. minimum wages—an utter impossibility 100 years ago.

What about wealth derived from new products and services not even invented 100 years ago? There are thousands of medical techniques, diagnostics, procedures, and pharmacological remedies that have dramatically improved our physical quality of life. Inexpensive vaccines and medications, for example, are accessible to billions today for very little labor. These wealth gains are almost impossible to quantify, but it is indisputable that they have enriched the human condition.

Perhaps one of the biggest stories of the 21ˢᵗ Century will be the growth of what we call the "middle class"; hundreds of millions of people are joining the ranks of the Material layer all over the globe. Indeed, the American middle-class family has gone global. What's surprising is that the *Father Knows Best* family, house, car, and pet are as alluring today in China as they were in the U.S. some 50 years ago: There are new suburbs in China where some homes have American-style white picket fences and manicured green lawns. In newly industrializing countries like Mexico and Poland, a large swath of the population now shops in malls, uses cellular phones, and eats at the local McDonald's.

Of course, this is not to suggest that all middle classes are alike. There are clearly significant differences between the Malaysian middle class, for example, and that in Brazil. However, there is a remarkable consistency in the underlying *values* exhibited by the world's growing middle class, probably since most basic needs have been met for these groups. They value Material comforts and pleasures—they like cars, TVs, and the latest computer games. They like to borrow from other middle-class cultures, sharing products and ideas. And, they appreciate political and economic stability—the world's middle class is unlikely to rock the boat much.

A recent poll of middle-class Indians in *India Today* found striking similarities with middle-class attitudes across the world. These Indians ranked travel and outdoor enjoyment as their top interests. They were concerned about crime, inflation, unemployment, and especially education, which they saw as the key to upward mobility. This is in a country with a very different culture than America's, with thousands of years of Hindu traditions and culture that contrast sharply to those in the West. Nevertheless, two-thirds of the "consuming class"[21] owns a scooter, iron, blender, and sewing machine. Sixty percent of all urban homes have TV sets, and 68 million of all Indian homes have TV sets. More than 32 million of those have cable, growing 8% a year.

In China, urban family spending on durables nearly doubled between 1980 and 1994 according to the UN *Health Development Report* in 1998 (Chapter 3), while spending on traditional consumables like food and clothing declined by nearly 10% (partially the result of price deflation). With per-capita incomes in urban areas rising 50% in less than a decade, purchases of durables (washing machines, refrigerators, and TVs) rose between 8–40 times. It is estimated that China will have a broad Material population of 40–600 million in the next three decades.

A thriving middle class is an important component of economic, political, and social stability. According to the World Bank, a higher share of income for the middle class is associated with higher national income, higher growth, more education, better health, better infrastructure, better economic policies, less instability, less civil war, more social modernization, and more democracy. We're even seeing some developing regions' middle classes penetrate the world's millionaire club. According to the *World Wealth Report 2001* published by Merrill Lynch and Cap Gemini Ernst & Young, the number of Asia's millionaires grew 600% from 1985–2000, and Asia now comprises more than 18.2% of the world market share of millionaires.

PROGRESS BEGETS PROGRESS

At the beginning of the 21st Century, 66% of the world still lives on less than $5,000 per capita per year, the approximate income of many Americans in the early 20th Century. But even in poor Biological countries today, most inhabitants are living much better than their predecessors as the costs of food, clothing, low-tech electronics like TVs and radios, and basic medicines have been deflated in terms of work required. In short, the average life on earth today is far "richer" than 100 years ago.

It should come as no surprise that the rapid rise in global living standards has coincided with a phenomenal rise in technological innovations during the last 200 years. From 1000–1500CE, economic output perhaps doubled, and then doubled again by 1800. Rough estimates show that output since 1800 has risen after that more than 20-fold when adjusted for inflation, and this spike is largely the result of the introduction of thousands of technologies, applications, and consumer products. The methods by which technology was refined, financed, and brought to market were just as important as the innovative ideas themselves.

This sudden shift in humankind's fortunes—occurring in a relative nanosecond of human history—is genuine and profound. The wealthy world of today was made possible by a convergence of powerful forces not limited to economics. Human value systems propel the wealth creation process, and in turn, are changed by it. Indeed, making prosperity function for the benefit of billions of people imposes fundamental changes in how societies organize and govern themselves, manage workplaces, handle religious beliefs, cultivate family life, forge educational opportunities, use leisure time—in essence, all aspects of human culture. That's what we'll explore in the rest of this book.

3
Wealth and
Economics:

The Proven Formula for Progress

*Communication, creativity, and growth occur together
or they do not occur at all.*[1]

Marshall McLuhan (1911–1980)

How did our recent prosperity arise, and, more importantly, how do we continue the process? Economics and its core concepts reveal some answers, but a thorough discussion requires an examination of culture and how human capital can shape economic outcomes. In this chapter, we'll analyze the broad formula for wealth creation and explore its relationships to the Biological, Material, and Experiential phases.

Many economists, historians, political scientists, and demographers writing about the Industrial Revolution, economic growth, and development provide clues to the mystery of wealth creation.[2] John Maynard Keynes' great observation in his 1930 *Essays in Persuasion* provides simple, powerful insight:

From the earliest times of which we have record—back, say, to two thousand years before Christ—down to the beginning of the 18th Century, there was no very great change in the standard life of the average man living in civilised centers of the earth. Ups and downs certainly. Visitation of plague, famine, and war. Golden intervals. But no progressive violent change. This slow rate of progress was due to two reasons—to the remarkable absence of technical improvements and the failure of capital to accumulate.

What Keynes wrote more than 70 years ago has great relevance in discussing wealth today. The application of mass production technology and its foundation—excess capital and a free market to exploit such technologies—gets at the roots of modern prosperity. This complex process can be reduced to the miraculous confluence of three equally important catalysts: (1) greater human capital; (2) more efficient free-market economics; and (3) sophisticated finance. These three, like well-oiled, synchronized cogs, have interacted harmoniously to produce the wealthy world of the 21st Century.

GROWING HUMAN CAPITAL AND TECHNOLOGY

The previous chapter discussed how technological innovation was a prerequisite for growth based on greater human capital—our collective ability to apply knowledge to manipulate our environment, to think abstractly, to measure possibilities, and gauge outcomes empirically. In the economic sphere, this equals efficiency, producing a desired good or service with as little waste of effort and resources as possible. But there's more to this story. Greater human capital during the Industrial Revolution not only increased production and therefore wealth; it changed social organization. Most importantly, it altered the ways people thought of their livelihoods, their tools, and the expectations for their lives. Without greater human capital, the changes in life we have seen in the last two centuries would not have been possible.

Increased human capital and the ability of people to generate new ideas are directly related to literacy and formal education. Prior to the Renaissance, the world was, in essence, walking in the dark; it had few technological advances beyond those existing for perhaps 10,000 years. After paper was introduced in the 2nd Century CE, there was at least a 1,000-year gap before any lasting innovation was introduced to improve the human condition. Eventually, educational opportunity expanded, resulting in rapid technological and intellectual progress (see Figure 3–1).

As Figure 3–1 illustrates, the historic spike in per-capita output in the past 150 years is largely intertwined with the introduction of thousands of techniques, applications, and consumer products. Technological development was limited until the 19th Century, and so was global and individual wealth. As you'll see in later chapters, in addition to the massive technological changes that are concurrent with wealth, social, political, and culture changes will also occur.

Figure 3-1   Wealth and technology, 2000BCE–2000CE.

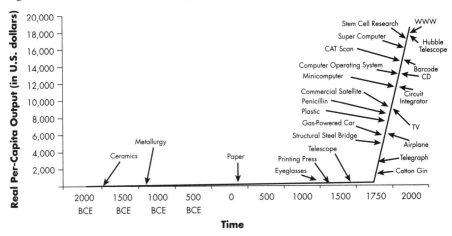

Some of the first universities sprang up in mercantile Italy, including Salerno (9th Century) and Bologna (1088CE), but it would take a couple hundred years of Renaissance thought before knowledge began to result in useful inventions during the 15th, 16th, and 17th Centuries. The watch, the printing press, and the telescope would help further the notion that human knowledge could be expanded with effort through scientific method, a concept that would unleash the seminal changes in technology of the next three centuries.

The Enlightenment was an important precursor to industrialization because it convinced people that human reason could be used to combat ignorance, superstition, and tyranny. Human potential no longer needed to be constricted by the rules of religion and hereditary aristocracy; instead, individuals could take charge and make choices for their own well-being. This philosophical premise was essential for the growth of human capability and capital.

The link between education and growth reveals an important process. Education leads to ingenuity, invention, and greater productivity, which in turn leads to greater wealth. At the same time, wealth generates more resources (time and money) for even better education and innovation. It is a virtuous cycle that has been at play in the U.S. and Western Europe since the 1800s (and now in other parts of the world as well). As Maddison has shown, the number of years of education for people aged 15–64 in the U.S. and Western Europe grew dramatically between 1820 and 1993. In the U.S., it jumped from 1.75 to 18 years, and in the UK, years of schooling increased from 2 to 14.[3]

The cycle of greater human capital during the Industrial era freed workers to produce goods beyond those needed for survival and to engage in nonessential pursuits. Inventions like the spinning jenny, the steam engine, and a variety of farm implements helped dramatically improve output while simultaneously reducing human labor required. Wool production, for example, increased 40-fold in less than 40 years after motorized looms were introduced in England, and prices dropped 10-fold.[4] The steam engine—applied to many industries—dramatically cut the need for human and animal power.

As the application of technology accelerated production in the industrializing West, human capital became increasingly central to the wealth creation process. Labor moved from farms to factories, and then to shops and offices (see Figure 3–2). This transition was often tied to trends in fertility and population growth. Greater education fostered longer life expectancy, which in turn reduced fertility and population growth. Lower birthrates allowed parents to invest more in the well-being of fewer children. This cycle is one factor that allows countries to accelerate what's called the "demographic transition" from an agrarian to industrial lifestyle in terms of family size, and boosts per-capita living standards in the process.

By developing a more efficient paradigm for satisfying basic Biological human needs, industrialization in the West produced a

Figure 3-2   From factories to offices, labor in the U.S. 1800-2020.

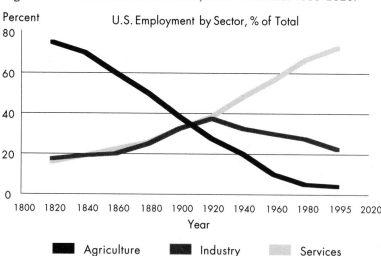

Sources: U.S. Department of Commerce, OECD, *The Economist*.

two-century-long blend of economic, social, political, and cultural changes that influenced the rate and course of technological development[5] that still reverberates today. The processes by which new technologies would be invented, developed, manufactured, and distributed during the Industrial era would ultimately be used by virtually every society in the race for greater living standards.

IMMIGRATION, SOCIAL MOBILITY, AND WEALTH

Just as free trade optimizes resources, a flexible workforce optimizes a country's human capital. Think of how rapidly the U.S. workforce has changed over the past 100 years—moving en masse from farms to factories to offices. Accompanying this movement has been the most impressive economic expansion ever witnessed. Computing and higher tech sectors, for example, have pulled many Americans into higher skilled jobs since the late 1970s. The positions they vacated in manufacturing have since been filled by people who once worked in agriculture, and so on. Just as mass electronics are no longer produced in the U.S., America has reduced agricultural and low-skill jobs: Our comparative advantage lies in higher skilled areas like computer software, finance, and healthcare services.

To fill these lower skilled employment vacancies, economies can depend on immigrants and foster a flexible labor pool that allows more skilled workers to "move up the food chain." It is another virtuous cycle of growth as workers enter the positions that have been vacated by those who are able to advance.

Of course, immigration is not limited to low skilled areas. There are many advanced economies that have had to recruit well-trained foreign workers to maintain a domestic edge. This has been particularly true in the high-tech arena. In 1992, the U.S. reformed its visa laws to provide for more high-skilled workers. Germany, too, in recent years has altered immigration laws to acquire foreign engineers needed for economic progress.

Immigration is not only good for the economy that imports labor, but also for the laborers themselves who often leave impoverished areas with few opportunities. Latin American migrant workers, for example, are essential to the giant American agricultural industry: They provide the day labor for which college-educated workers would be too expensive. At the same time, they are important sources of income for families back at home. The Inter-American Development Bank estimates that at least $300 billion will be sent back to Latin America over the next 10 years. All told, global immigrant remittances now total $60+ billion per annum, more than the $50 billion spent on foreign aid.[6]

Aging populations, where workforces are shrinking, such as West Europe and Japan, are natural targets for select immigration. However, older populations are often less receptive to change. While America has spent more than a century managing the cultural integration of immigrants, Europe and Japan are relatively new to the game and need to develop such policies quickly amid much cultural resistance. To maintain its current working age population, UNDP reports that Germany must add 600,000 immigrants per annum, and Japan 500,000. In comparison, the U.S. needs only 150,000 (while the U.S. is three times bigger than Germany and two times Japan's size). Immigration is a piece of the wealth puzzle that governments need to consider.

COMPARATIVE ADVANTAGE AND FREE TRADE

What was the greatest single technological development to emanate from the Industrial Revolution? One could argue that it was not any specific invention as much as a new philosophy of how to conduct commerce.[7] Indeed, the great legacy of the Industrial Revolution was the shift of economic production away from personal consumption to the marketplace. Humans had spent centuries toiling in fields for subsistence food and clothing. Suddenly, the standardization of products and specialization of labor set the stage for the wealth creation paradigm to follow. It is mass production and a functioning marketplace that ultimately drive down the price of goods and services—whatever they may be—thereby, creating "wealth" in the process.

With technological development, standardization, and industrialization taking root, the world needed ways to make these monumental changes efficient. As people in the West began working to produce for the marketplace (versus personal consumption) in the late 18th and early 19th Centuries, it became clear that there would be benefits for countries to specialize in producing certain goods. How should people spend their time now? Which countries, or segments thereof, should continue to be farmers, and which industrialized? Would it pay to build redundant factories all around the world to produce the same goods, or was there a more efficient answer?

Economic theorist David Ricardo (1772–1823), influenced by Adam Smith's late 18th Century theories on international trade, began to lay out some simple concepts that would help answer these questions.[8] Let's look at two countries, England and Spain, and their abilities to produce two goods, wine and wheat. Spain can produce both wheat and wine more cheaply in terms of hours than England (what economists call an *absolute advantage* in both products). However, Ricardo believed that it could still be mutually beneficial for both countries to specialize and trade.[9]

Table 3-1   Country Production before Trade

Country	Wheat	Wine
	Cost Per Unit Hours	*Cost Per Unit Hours*
England	15	30
Spain	10	15

In Table 3–1, a unit of wine in England costs the same amount of labor to produce two units of wheat. This means that for England to produce an extra unit of wine, it must give up producing two units of wheat. However, the cost in Spain for a unit of wine is only 1.5 units of wheat. This example notes that Spain is *relatively* better at producing wine than wheat; therefore, Spain is said to have a *comparative advantage* in wine production. England is relatively better at producing wheat than wine; it has a *comparative advantage* in wheat.

However, Table 3–2 shows how trade might prove mutually rewarding. Let's assume that England has 270 hours of labor available for production. Before trading with Spain, it produces and consumes eight units of wheat and five units of wine. Spain has a smaller population and has only 180 hours of labor available for production. Before trade with England, it produces and consumes nine units of wheat and six units of wine. Before trading with each other, total production by the two countries combined is 17 units of wheat and 11 units of wine.

If both countries focus their efforts, Spain would produce only wine and England would produce only wheat. Net total production under this specialist scenario would be 18 units of wheat and 12 units of wine. By specializing, England can exchange its extra 10 units of wheat and take in 6 of wine, a net increase of 1 unit of wine. Spain, in turn, can net an extra unit of wheat—all with the *same* amount of labor.[10]

Table 3-2   The Wealth Benefits of Trade

Country	Production Before Trade		Production After Trade	
	Wheat	Wine	Wheat	Wine
England	8	5	18	0
Spain	9	6	0	12
Total	17	11	18	12

This simple model of comparative advantage proved to have a great impact on rising living standards around the globe in the 19th and 20th Centuries, and still offers us a glimpse into today and the future. The Ricardo paradigm has relevance today regarding who makes CAT scans, cantaloupes, and Caterpillar tractors. It also provides an uncluttered introduction to the economically integrative nature of technology and global production.

When a developing country first enters the global economy, it exports simple products—typically something like commodities and other goods requiring low-skilled labor—to more advanced places, a process that reflects the differentiated cost structures of wealthier and less wealthy nations. Trade develops in the Ricardo model, and profits from exports are accumulated by the developing country. These profits—excess capital that the developing country didn't have before trade—increase local demand for consumer goods such as foodstuffs, beverages, clothes, health products, etc. The consumer goods are then imported from the more advanced countries that have already set up efficient production of those goods.

Eventually, *domestic production* of consumer goods previously imported begins in the developing country, using the new trade-related, wealthier local consumer market as the outlet. The developing country no longer imports consumer goods since it now produces them domestically, but it does import "higher tech," or capital goods that it does not produce, such as power looms for sewing. Those power looms allow local labor to create a small clothing industry, which helps employ people and expand the local developing economy. The developing country now no longer needs to import certain types of clothes. In turn, it begins to *export* the clothes it used to import, but to even *lesser* developed countries (and maybe even to more advanced countries if it produces them cheaply enough). As wealthier countries continue to innovate and bring new products and services to the world, this process should, theoretically, continue and raise living standards. Indeed, this is what has made cars from Japan, cocoa from West Africa, clothes from the Caribbean, and laptops from Taiwan commonplace in America. It is also a process that forces countries to continually improve their efficiencies, particularly in low-skill sectors, where there are always aspiring poorer countries hoping to compete in the global economy.

COMPARATIVE ADVANTAGE IN ACTION

How Labor Shifts from Country to Country in
Blue Jean Production

	Hourly Wages	Hourly Output	Unit Cost
U.S. Worker	$16.	8 pairs	$2.
Developing Country Worker	$2.	3 pairs	$.67

As the above chart illustrates, comparative advantage tries to take into consideration the productivity of labor between countries. For example, a U.S. worker may be more than twice as productive in making blue jeans than a developing country worker, but if the U.S. worker makes eight times the wages, the net labor cost per pair of jeans dictates that the labor shift to another country, freeing the U.S. worker to pursue something else. Note that this game also works two ways. The South Koreans, for example, used their comparatively cheap labor and good productivity to make huge inroads into a variety of cut-and-sew and lower skilled sectors in the 1970s and 1980s. But with economic success comes higher wages. However, by the mid-1990s, which saw competition from a variety of other countries such as China and India, South Korea found itself less competitive in many lower end manufacturing sectors such as sneakers and metal fabrication (along with middle-skill sectors as well). They were eventually forced to exit the lower skilled sectors and focus more on higher skilled industries. Such is the nature of comparative advantage and free trade, a neverending race for greater productivity and efficiency that helps create wealth in the process. While transition periods are often painful, they are necessary for continued wealth gains.

Richard Rosecrance has theorized about trade's interconnected nature by classifying some countries as "head" states focusing on high-value planning and design, and others as "body" states concentrating more on efficient

Trade forces an economy to optimize its resources, by allowing imports of goods and services at lower costs than for which they could be domestically produced.

production and manufacturing. Over time, "body" states can evolve into "heads," reshaping their trade patterns to reflect their relative human capital capacities.[11]

Free trade has reshaped the global economy and wealth creation. It is a philosophy that forces an economy to optimize its resources, by allowing imports of goods and services at lower costs than they could be domestically produced. Trade enables developing countries to import capital equipment and intermediate inputs that are critical to long-run economic growth, but which would be expensive or impossible to produce domestically. For much of the 20th Century, authoritarian states such as the former Soviet Union and Communist China decided that central planning and domestic protectionist policies—and not free trade—were the ways to raise living standards. However, those countries' abandonment of such economic philosophies—along with much of Latin America and other developing regions—demonstrated the limits of protectionism. Exports are the price a country pays to get access to desirable imports. Other potential benefits of free trade include more intense competition, which obliges local firms to operate more efficiently than if they were protected, and a greater awareness of new ideas and technologies.[12]

It is often argued that free trade harms economic growth and the poor by causing a loss in jobs, particularly in wealthier countries. But, trade liberalization works by encouraging a shift of labor and capital from import-competing industries to expanding, newly competitive export industries. The unemployment caused by trade opening up should be temporary, and eventually offset by job creation in other sectors. Output losses due to this transitional unemployment should also be small relative to long-term gains in national income (and lower consumer prices) due to production increases elsewhere. In other words, these adjustment costs should be evaluated in comparison to the costs of continued economic stagnation and isolation that occur without open trade. There is a growing consensus in studies that international trade openness has a positive effect on per-capita income: A 1999 World Bank study by Jeffrey

Frankel and David Romer estimated that increasing the ratio of trade to national output by one percentage point could raise per-capita income by between 1.5–2%.[13]

The amount of cross-border trade has ballooned over the past 50 years, swelling from $310 billion to nearly $6 trillion and accounting for more than 20% of global output according to the World Bank. Indeed, trade—which grew twice as fast as global output in the 1990s—will continue to drive economic specialization and growth. It is also important to note how trade and comparative advantage have shifted the global economy and labor pools. Just as the U.S. labor pool shifted from farm to factory during and after the Industrial Revolution, there is now a similar global shift. The world's economy is becoming more sophisticated, segmented, and diversified, moving from basic agricultural commodities and goods to more specialized items and services. This process continues to drive trade and growth as more and more of the world's people become a part of its cycle.

THE GLOBAL BUSINESS OF WELLNESS

Everyone wants to live a longer and healthier life—it's a seemingly universal value. It should come as no surprise that as people grow wealthier, their health needs evolve, whether it be paying for child vaccinations, getting routine checkups, purchasing vitamins and dietary supplements, working out at a gym every week, getting face lifts or hip replacements, injecting Botox for wrinkles, having laser eye surgery, or taking early warning tests for a variety of diseases. All over the world, growing investments in managing human health amounts to trillions of dollars.

Health and "wellness" are inextricably bound up in a country's economic fortunes: With a healthier population, there are better chances of success. And for many Biological countries, gaining access to even the most basic healthcare is tremendously important. In places like Tanzania, annual per-capita basic healthcare expenditures is about $8 versus more than $2500 in the U.S. (not taking into account discretionary "wellness" purchases). But when they reach life expectancies of 60 years and higher, people want to live even longer and better, and will spend money to do so.

While one might expect the amount that people spend on healthcare to shrink as a percentage of income as they grow more affluent, this is not the case! Why? Because with wealth, people want to extend and enhance their lives as well as those of their children. They want basic healthcare plus extra services to help prevent disease down the road. In the U.S., $1.4 trillion is devoted to the *curative* healthcare industry—to reacting to illness and finding cures—which is about 14% of the American economy.

Wellness is an increasingly important need in wealthy Material and Experiential societies where people highly value both feeling and looking well. For example, more than 3 million Americans will undergo some form of cosmetic surgery in 2003. Experientials attend three-week yoga/spa retreats and have mud baths, acupuncture, and massage treatments. People take nutritional supplements and spend extraordinary amounts on the "right" foods and beverages. Today, over 50% of Americans take vitamins. They pay big bucks for personal trainers and dietitians. Health clubs in the U.S. grossed more than $14 billion in 2001, and the U.S. diet industry tallied more than $33 billion.

One could also look at the explosive growth of life-enhancement drugs such as Claritin and Allegra (for allergies), Propecia (hair loss), Viagra (male virility), Fosamax (bone builder for osteoperosis), Celebrex (arthritis), Vasotec (high blood pressure), Zocor and Lipitor (reduce cholesterol), and Prozac (antidepressant), among others. Such wellness drugs generate more than $100 billion in U.S. sales each year and have great export potential. As generic versions become available in the coming decades, today's relatively high prices will deflate dramatically and open up their availability to more Material and even Biological populations.

As people's lives grow longer, we can only expect more spending on health and wellness all around the world. One author estimates that by 2010, $1 trillion will be spent in the U.S. alone on "wellness" goods and services.[14] However, the growth opportunities for pharmaceutical and medical technology companies may be greater in exporting to the billions in developing Biological and Material places. Indeed, wealthier countries have huge comparative advantages in this higher tech sector in terms of research, development, and intellectual property.

ACCELERATED FINANCE

It would be nice to think that human capital and free trade theories alone could fuel this great surge in living standards. But remember, the real reason businesspeople try to develop cheaper goods and services is to generate excess profit, or surplus capital, that can be reinvested and grown into even more money. This incentive should not be underestimated. The activity of financiers to gather surplus capital and channel it into new commercial opportunities for even greater wealth accumulation and better living standards is a powerful element in the prosperity process.

What exactly is finance? At the risk of oversimplification, it can be defined as a system that efficiently gathers excess capital and redistributes it, fairly scientifically, to the investment opportunities that have the best chances for success. It is a philosophy that tries to balance the returns to investors with those of the users of the capital. It is supported by a web of institutions—banks, insurance companies, pension funds, mutual funds, stock exchanges, among others—that pool money, invest it in projects and companies in a diversified fashion, and measure the success achieved. It is further supported by an enforceable legal system that governs how such capital can be gathered and invested to safeguard against theft and fraud.

Finance is a vitally important, yet little understood piece of the wealth equation. The historian Hernando De Soto has focused on this point in his book *The Mystery of Capital: Why Capitalism Triumphs in the West and Fails Everywhere Else*. In explaining why some countries are "rich" and some are "poor," De Soto emphasizes the need to establish and normalize the legal infrastructure to convert assets from "dead" into "liquid" capital. In high-income countries like the U.S., Germany, and Japan, standardized private property laws allow us to mortgage a house to raise money for a new venture, permit the worth of a company to be broken up into so many publicly tradable stocks, and make it possible to govern and appraise property with agreed-upon rules that hold across neighborhoods, towns, or regions. This invisible infrastructure of "asset management"—so taken for granted in the West (even though it has only fully existed in the U.S. for the past 100 years)—is necessary to make capitalism successful, insists DeSoto. Even though this financial structure is primarily a legal one, he argues that the process of making it a normalized component of a society is more a political, attitude-changing challenge than anything else.

Following this line of thought, imagine a place where no finance exists. Let's say a man owns a house worth $20,000 and he rents it out each year for $3,000, which is a 15% return on his money. If an institution like a bank lends him $15,000 against the house for a 10% interest rate, he could free up $15,000 for more investments, and leave only $5,000 invested in the house. After the man pays the annual interest of $1,500 to the bank, he nets a profit of $1,500 on only a $5,000 investment in the house—a 30% return on his capital versus 15% before finance. Then, assume that he takes his freed-up $15,000 and buys three more houses with bank financing, and rents them using the same figures. The man now nets $1,500 per house, or $6,000 total—versus only $3,000 when he owned only one house and had no mortgage. Plus, he owns three more houses. While his situation seems better, think about the people from whom he bought the three new houses. They now have $60,000 and can reinvest the money into whatever assets they want, whether it goes into a bank, more buildings, a stock or bond, or starting a new business. This is just a glimpse into what can happen when well-conceived, well-regulated finance is implemented within an institutional framework that safeguards property rights.

In advanced countries like the U.S., the home mortgage sector is incredibly sophisticated. Americans take it for granted that they can buy homes with only a fraction of a house's purchase price—often with 20% down, but sometimes with much less, or even nothing. The process works like this: A customer goes to a bank (or logs onto an online mortgage company), fills out an application, hopes to get approved, and then gets the money at closing to pay the seller (who often takes the money to pay off an outstanding mortgage). However, most mortgages are not held by banks until they're paid; they are typically bundled and resold as bonds that pay interest coupons to investors. In fact, the U.S. government supports this with home-lending organizations like Fannie Mae and Ginnie Mae. Let's say a mortgage pool pays, for example, an 8% average interest rate. Through Ginnie Mae or Fannie Mae, the U.S. government guarantees all the mortgage payments, and then resells the pool of mortgage-backed bonds in the market at an interest rate of maybe 6.5%. Insurance companies, mutual funds, university endowments, pension funds, and other long-term investors then buy those 6.5% bonds. In fact, some people who mortgage their houses ultimately buy the bonds into which their own mortgages have been pooled.

This mortgage system is an extraordinary example of how finance supports wealth creation. Institutions like insurance companies and pension funds gather money to invest and invest to offset long-term liabilities: insurance policies and pension benefits they must pay in the future.[15] An American wants a house and needs 30 years to pay the loan off. There are banks that help analyze the borrower's ability to pay and understand how to pool the loan with others into bonds. There are investment banks that specialize in distributing such bonds. There are government policies in place to encourage home ownership by guaranteeing certain bond payments, as well as providing tax incentives (though mortgage interest deductions). In the U.S., based on this financial engineering, an enormous homebuilding industry has been created, including architects, title companies, real-estate developers, construction companies, landscaping companies, utility companies, lawyers, surveyors, engineers, etc. This is why home ownership in the U.S. is more than 68% in 2002, and why homebuilding and real estate comprise more than one-fifth of U.S. domestic output and employ more than 20 million people directly and indirectly. Because of America's hyper-sophisticated financial system, including residential and commercial mortgages, trillions of dollars are freed up for many other purposes.[16]

Mortgages are just one example of the astounding depth and sophistication of financial markets in advanced economies. Capital is available through mortgages, but also from banks, insurance companies, mutual fund companies, venture capitalists, and credit unions, to name a few sources. Virtually everyone has access to some form of credit, even if it's just a credit card or the ability to get telephone service and pay after receiving a bill. This frees up huge amounts of capital, promoting further investment, innovation, and consumption, and spinning the virtuous cycle of wealth. Such refined financial infrastructure is a major difference between advanced and developing countries, and it is critical in promoting further investment and wealth creation.

DeSoto notes that in developing countries, there are literally trillions in "undocumented" assets that have not been utilized in the wealth creation process. First, much of developing countries' economies are unreported and cash-oriented, or what is termed "informal." This means capital is often tied into goods or saved under the mattress. Second, people may own homes and assets, but have no legal title to them. DeSoto argues that in some places like Mexico, 78% of the population operates in this informal arena, and perhaps 90% in Egypt. Undocumented Mexican buildings, equipment, and enterprises might total more than $300 billion (or more than 50% of annual output), and Egypt may have $240 billion in "unofficial" assets—multiples of stock market capitalization in both countries.[17]

Banking and debt markets provide a wide range of capital for an economy to grow, but stock markets are also critical to fueling comparative advantage and free trade: They function as an arena for companies to raise money to become better, more efficient operators. How important are stock markets? In a word: *very*. Around the world, *trillions* of dollars are invested in them. The underlying value of stock markets has increased globally from $400 billion in

1950 to approximately $25 trillion by 2000.[18] From 1990–2001 in the U.S., the primary—or initial public offering (IPO)—market raised over $434 billion for more than 5200 companies. Keep in mind that this money was for private companies that had never been publicly listed. For companies that were already publicly traded, the U.S. stock market helped raise *more than $650 billion* in secondary stock offerings for more than 4500 other companies. What do these companies do with this money? Basically, they continue building human capital and strengthening comparative advantage: reinvesting in research and development, building new and expanding old businesses, making acquisitions, acquiring new technology, etc. Having mechanisms to access such capital fuels an economy's ability to keep creating wealth.[19]

Yes, a big, liquid stock market is central to the wealth story. A study by Ross Levine and Sarah Zervos of the World Bank, using data on 49 developing countries from 1976–1993, further supports the notion that economic growth and financial marketization are tightly linked. This analysis suggests that liquidity—as measured by the volume of stock trading—is positively and significantly correlated with current and future rates of economic expansion, capital accumulation, and productivity growth. A liquid stock market attracts a wider audience of investors by reducing the perceived risk of holding stock. Zervos and Levine note that companies in liquid stock markets are often regulated by bodies that require timely disclosure of financial information, a factor which often makes local banks more inclined to lend to those listed companies. In addition, these economists have found that the ratio of local bank loans to output has also risen in line with local stock market turnover. The economic results of greater stock market liquidity are striking: For example, had Mexico's *bolsa* been as liquid as Malaysia's stock market in 1976, its economy would have grown by an additional .4% per annum for 17 years.[20]

Figure 3–3 illustrates how stock markets in the wealthiest countries tend to be the largest not solely in terms of nominal market capitalization, but also per capita as a percentage of the national economy. That is, the wealthier the country, the more important the stock market is to the economy. This is an intuitive concept, since richer countries have more excess capital that needs to be reinvested.

Once liquid stock markets are in place, other "feeder" forms of finance can develop, like venture capital. Such forms of private, untraded equity help grow smaller companies that are not traded on

Figure 3-3   Financial development versus economic development market cap/head versus GDP/head, 2000E (U.S. dollars in billions).

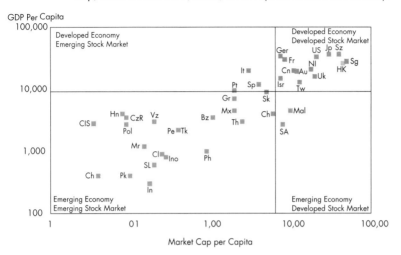

Aus Australia, Bz Brazil, Ch Chile, Chin China, CIS Russia, Cl Colombia, Cn Canada, CzR Czech Republic, Fr France, Ger Germany, Gr Greece, HK Hong Kong, Hn Hungary, In India, Ino Indonesia, Isr Israel, It Italy, Jp Japan, Mal Malaysia, Mr Morocco, Mx Mexico, Nl Netherlands, Pe Peru, Ph Philippines, Pk Pakistan, Pol Poland, Pt Portugal, SA South Africa, Sg Singapore, SK South Korea, SL Sri Lanka, Sp Spain, Sw Switzerland, Th Thailand, Tk Turkey, Tw Taiwan, Uk United Kingdom, US United States, Vz Venezuela

stock exchanges—think of them as "minor league" companies hoping to make it to the "big leagues." These minor-leaguers could be an aspiring biotechnology firm working on gene therapies for terminal illnesses, or a software developer that focuses on online security, or a retail store specializing in outdoor sporting goods—the possibilities are endless.

With a highly tested and efficient stock market, the American venture capital community, for example, has hammered out unparalleled practices and mechanisms for channeling capital to privately held companies with potential. As of 2001, more than $288 billion was invested in venture capital funds, as well as billions more invested directly by big corporations into privately held businesses.[21] How do such investors in venture capital get repaid? Through a variety of methods: perhaps via the IPO market as mentioned above, possibly through dividends, or maybe by selling out to a publicly traded company. For example, when a corporate employee saves some retirement money in the company's pension plan, the plan's fund manager may invest a small piece of these savings in a venture fund with interests in a Silicon Valley software company. That company takes the money, develops new products, and grows sales. If successful, that company can now either sell a piece of itself through an IPO to raise capital for further growth, or maybe a larger company like Microsoft buys the company and helps it grow. In any event, venture capital greatly helps develop a country's human capital and comparative advantage.

The institutional underpinnings of financial markets are key to growth and progress. Capital is required to take risk and make investments; not only in financial markets and companies, but also in the human capital important to innovation and production. In testament to this, in the late 20th Century we began to see many countries around the world seek the right mix of reform, safeguards, and openness to attract capital and build efficient financial markets—including former socialist-oriented powers like Russia and China. Policy and institutional reform leads to financial market formation and greater access to capital, which in turn promotes even greater reform, deeper markets, and economic growth. This is a virtuous cycle of financial reform and growth that has been unifying the world's capital markets. Well-functioning markets ensure that capital is used in the most efficient and productive ways to maximize output.

Today, more money is flowing around the world than ever before and the composition of that capital has changed. International capital flowing into developing countries was once primarily in the form of loans and multilateral aid. In 1980, nearly 75% of First World's investments in emerging markets was loan-based. But now, more countries are able to attract diverse and stable financing.[22] Through a variety of marketization efforts, by 2000, loans dropped to less than 25%, with the remaining money flowing into stock and bond markets, export credit, and foreign direct investment (FDI, investment in property, plants, and equipment overseas). By 2002, the major credit agencies had expanded sovereign ratings coverage to more than 50 developing nations. This healthy composition of capital flows illustrates the steady political and economic progress that has been made, and continues to be made, in developing countries around the world.

Greater financial flows obviously lead to greater stock market capitalization, an indicator of a market's depth. Developed stock markets like the U.S. have capitalization values typically greater than annual national output. For most developing nations, capitalization is much smaller, less than 50% of output, but growing. According to the World Bank, in 1985, emerging stock markets had a capitalization of $171 billion. By 2000, thanks to privatization and market reform, that number was nearly $3 trillion. In the same period, the value of trading (liquidity) increased from less than 30% per annum in turnover to more than 150%. By promoting savings and liquid markets while involved in trade and comparative advantage, countries can continue to "marketize" and grow.

WEALTH AND EXCESS

The wealth creation process is not perfect. Free markets can breed unacceptable excesses. Well-developed financial markets are immensely important to increased living standards, but they have also been known to destroy wealth, too.

On the consumer level, developed financial markets often translate into easy credit. Many Amricans routinely receive in the mail pre-approved credit card applications with high spending limits, and retailers and manufacturers are forever offering us credit in efforts to entice us to buy more goods. While credit-driven consumption has benefits—such as the mortgage example demonstrates—easy money can lead people to spend recklessly beyond their means. In America, for instance, managing household debt has almost become a national pastime. Indeed, average American household credit card debt is approximately $8,523, the highest in the world.[23] During economic crunches, such debt may result in a rise of personal bankruptcies. In normal times, it may simply lead to stress and "Affluenza," the buzzword describing the anxiety of keeping up with the Joneses.

Then there are the public excesses in the financial world. While Adam Smith's invisible hand of self-interest propels most of humanity to work and toil honestly for greater wealth, many still try to rig the system, and there are many greedy investors who unfortunately fuel the fire with wishful thinking, betting to get out before a collapse. Financial bubbles and scams have littered history: Tulipomania in early 17th Century Holland (then the world's richest country), the South Sea Company scheme in early 18th Century England (then the world's richest country), the infamous Ponzi in the 1920s, the Savings and Loan debacle or Japan's $22 billion Madame Nui toad scandal in the 1980s[24] (when Japan seemed like the world's richest country), Long Term Capital Management's meltdown, and the Internet craze of the late 1990s, just to name a few.

The recent corporate malfeasance embodied in names like Enron, Adelphia, Tyco, and Worldcom—in which accounting gimmicks were used to inflate earnings—is another example. Managers of public companies, with large stock options and vested equity interests in their companies, are motivated to raise stock prices, not only for themselves but for their shareholders as well. That's not a crime. In fact, that's what all shareholders are betting on: CEOs increasing earnings legitimately and creating greater value. However, it is a crime to manipulate a stock's price through phony revenue tricks, omitting or reclassifying certain expenses, or using complicated financing schemes that a Harvard MBA can't even understand. But remember, this is not a new development. Greed and dishonesty have been with us forever, and it certainly shouldn't be seen as a reason to halt the global wealth creation process.

The excess or bubble phenomenon is not limited to wealthy countries. There were several pyramid schemes in the former Soviet Union shortly after it dissolved in the early 1990s, including Russia, Romania, and Albania. But financial markets tend to survive schemes, frauds, and excesses. Readjustments, prosecutions and penalties, and increased regulation can all be employed to bring virtue back to finance.

THE CULTURE OF WEALTH CREATION

Wealth creation is arguably as much a result of cultural attitudes as economic forces. Many theorists have hypothesized that certain cultures have a predisposition to prosperity; perhaps Max Weber started the debate with his observations on Protestant attitudes.[25] Lawrence Harrison has recently expanded the discussion by examining a range of modern countries, and has found that cultures predisposed to wealth normally incorporate three attitudes: that rationality is the tool with which the world can be manipulated and wealth created; that education is key to such rational thinking; and that forethought, savings, and planning for the future should be encouraged.[26]

But there are cultures that refuse to accept advancement, economic and otherwise. While it may not be politically correct, Harrison builds a convincing case in his descriptions of "progress-prone" versus "progress-resistant" cultures. He cites a typology developed by Argentine sociologist Mariano Grondona: "The progress-prone society is characterized by an ethical system based on responsible self-interest and mutual respect. In the resistant culture, morality seeks perfection (altruism, self denial), which exceeds the bounds of human nature and becomes utopianism." Harrison notes the differences between cultures prone or resistant to progress in the Grondona typology:[27]

1. Life in progressive societies is something that individuals control and shape; in resistant cultures, life is beyond one's control.

2. Optimism is nurtured in the progressive culture. In the resistant culture, survival is the goal and pessimism the mood.

3. Religion explains and justifies success in the progress-prone society, whereas in the resistant society, it explains suffering.

4. Wealth is created through initiative and hard work in progress-prone societies, versus wealth as something that exists finitely in the resistant culture, and life is a struggle to acquire it or redistribute it.

5. Competition in the progressive society promotes excellence and efficiency in a positive way, versus the resistant culture where competition is seen as aggression that threatens stability and solidarity because it nurtures envy.

6. Economic justice in progress-prone societies demands savings and investment for the benefit of future generations; in the resistant society, economic justice demands equitable distribution for the current generation.

7. In the progress-prone society, labor is a moral duty, intrinsically bound with self-expression and satisfaction. In the resistant culture, work is a burden, a necessary evil.

8. Dissent is a key component to a progressive society; it encourages innovation, progress, and reform. In the resistant culture, it threatens stability.

9. Education nurtures inquisitiveness and creativity in the progressive society; in traditional, resistant societies, it transmits orthodoxy.

10. Rationalism, pragmatism, empiricism, and utilitarianism are highly valued in the progressive culture and threaten the resistant culture, where tradition, emotion, and chance are often more underscored—with stagnating consequences.

11. A forward time bias and a faith in manipulating the future are central to the progressive society, whereas the resistant society dwells on the past, with the future being one of fatalistic destiny.

12. The world is a setting for action, achievement, and optimism in the progressive society. In the resistant society, the world is dominated by irresistible forces (God or the Devil, multinational corporations, etc.), which lead to a more anxious, pessimistic world view.

The obvious economic differences between developing and industrialized countries reveal as stark a difference in mindset. While Grondona was basing much of his theory on his own Latin American experience, there are others around the world who make similar arguments. Daniel Etounga-Manguelle underscores regressive tendencies in Africa whereby many "societies condition their members to accept uncertainty about the future, taking each day as it comes versus being acculturated to conquer the future."[28] He adds:

> In traditional African society, which exalts the glorious past of ancestors through tales and fables, nothing is done to prepare for the future. The African, anchored in his ancestral culture, is so convinced that the past can only repeat itself that he worries only superficially about the future. However, without the dynamic perception of the future, there is no planning, no scenario building; in other words, no policy to affect the course of events."[29]

Harrison also cites anthropologist George Foster's similar "universal peasant culture" that categorizes many pre-industrialized, agrarian-oriented societies in Africa, Asia, Latin America, and the Middle East:

> Broad areas of peasant behavior are patterned in such a fashion as to suggest that peasants view their social, economic, and natural universes—their total environment—as one in which all of the desired things in life such as land, wealth, health, friendship and love, manliness and honor, respect and status, power and influence, security and safety, exist in finite quantity and are always in short supply, as far as the peasant is concerned. Not only do these and all other "good things" exist in finite and limited quantities, but in addition there is no way directly within peasant power to increase the available quantities.[30]

While Harrison believes such a way of life is actually a cultural pathology, I would say that it is rooted in pre-industrial, agrarian experience. For the peasant, with limited exposure to advanced capitalism, wealth is increased by luck (such as a bumper crop) or maybe theft (either true larceny or forms of corruption such as government kickbacks, etc.). The concepts of technological advancement, free trade and comparative advantage, and modern finance are less understood in agrarian countries (or have only been introduced recently). Also, keep in mind that most of the developing world was largely illiterate until the last 40 years. So it is not surprising that "resistant" cultures have continued for so long.

STOCK MARKETS, EQUITY CULTURE, AND WEALTH

How much is a country's socio-economic future tied to its stock market? How much of a country's psyche is tied to its financial market? In my experience, a great deal. A nation's outlook and sense of the future is intimately mirrored in its markets: the type (bond or equity), the depth (the size and number of investors), and the performance. When you live in a well-to-do country like the U.S., where the stock market is roughly the size of annual gross domestic output, it's easy to note how people's outlooks are often shaped by and mirrored in the state of the stock market. In the 1970s, only one in six Americans owned stock; today, it is one in two. America is the premiere "equity culture" around the world, and its attitudes reflect the wealth that has accrued over the last 2–3 generations.

Just a few decades ago, stock prices reflected "book value," the value of a company's hard assets. But in the past few dozen years, stock prices have been valued by price/earnings ratios (p/e), which are based more on future possibility than current reality. The underlying reason: If people are optimistic about the future, they will pay more for a stock today. The 1990s were, perhaps, the culmination of this thinking as p/e's soared to 100+ on the NAS-DAQ. And people had a lot to be optimistic about: Communism had fallen, making America's arch enemies new economic partners; global trade was increasing twice as fast as the global economy; unemployment was falling; and, computer geeks in Silicon Valley made anything look possible.

All expectations manifest themselves in the stock market, creating an "equity culture." With average incomes among the highest in the world, Americans have grown (fortunately or unfortunately) to live daily with volatility and risk, having largely benefited from such an attitude in the 20th Century. America, in many ways, exemplifies Experiential, future-biased optimism. The abundance of opportunity and freedom commensurate with such wealth is also a self-reinforcing, optimistic attitude; in such a society, tomorrow will always be sunnier day, even in the face of downward trends. Most people believe over time the markets will be higher. No doubt, this "equity culture" feeds the stock market, America's ultimate expression of optimism. Sure, there will be down periods, out over the long run, optimism has produced handsome returns.

This equity culture does not exist everywhere, particularly in early-stage developing countries. In the early 1990s, stock markets were first created in the newly freed states of the former Soviet Union. Most citizens, for example, were given privatization vouchers to exchange for stocks, but sometimes traded them for vodka and cigarettes. Coming out of the depressing Soviet era, no one knew what they were worth or could dream of "forward earnings"; the previous bleak period led to an exceptionally discounted view of future potential. In those economically insecure countries, savers actually preferred bonds and bank deposits as forms of investment—with a predictable cash flow and a return of principal.

But around the world, particularly in some of the newly rising Asian countries, such equity culture has caught on. Places like Taiwan, Singapore, and South Korea have exceptionally well-capitalized stock markets. Already young people in these Asian economies are convinced that their lives can be better than their parents', which were better than their parents', and so on. This may be one of the reasons why many Asian markets and economies in crisis in the late 1990s rebounded quickly in the new millennium.

ABUNDANCE REINFORCES ABUNDANCE

Grondona's typology actually says an equal amount about why wealthy countries can continue to grow stronger over time. Look at the U.S., the archetype for the wealth catalysts and culture we've been discussing. Contrary to the developing world's pessimism, in America, "the abundance mentality starts with the unconscious premise that there exists, at all times, close by, a happy hunting ground, a valley where acres of diamonds are theirs for the picking," says David Brooks, author of *Bobos in Paradise: The New Upper Class and How They Got There*. Brooks continues, "In the land of abundance, work is worth it because it is often rewarded. In the land of abundance, a person's lower-class status is always temporary. If the complete idiot next door has managed to pull himself up to the realm of Lexus drivers, why shouldn't the same thing happen to you?"[31]

It is clear that a few successful generations of material improvement can shape such optimism. If such processes legitimately create an ample Material middle class, which they have in the U.S. and in many other countries, such sentiments become embedded in the culture; in fact, they become intrinsically tied to the national psyche. As Brooks notes, "The great power of [the wealth creation process and resulting] abundance is that it takes dreams that are aristocratic in nature and makes them democratic in possibility. There's so much bounty that the life of ease and refinement is not just confined to the well-born and well to do. There are plenty of heavens to go around, for *Reader's Digest* readers as well as *Vanity Fair* readers."[32] With opportunity just around the corner, wealth culture creates a risk-taking state of mind, which in turn helps reinforce further prosperity.

There are societies that developed modest financial wealth without the three catalysts of human capital, comparative advantage and trade, and finance, but such places often fail to develop what Grondona would call a "progressive" culture. The best examples are several members of the Organization for Petroleum and Economic Cooperation (OPEC) that have seen output per capita rise with oil prices (which have climbed 10-fold since 1973). Output statistics have expanded largely through higher energy prices—a "bumper crop" of sorts—owing very little to domestic productivity and improved human capital. Indeed, the wealth created in some of these countries—where oil is some 75–90% of the economy—seems to actually strengthen a "resistant" culture. The visible wealth is typically controlled by a small percentage of the population, possibly a ruling family, as in Saudi Arabia, or a political party whose power is rooted in force, as in Nigeria. The wealth created is spread often through systems of patronage and cronyism, and is not available to the average citizen. Local markets are often distorted or nonexistent. This explains how wealthy Gulf oil states, for example, can have relatively high economic output but still have regressive cultures that are similar to those of poorer countries.

WHEN WEALTH IS NOT WEALTH: THE CURSE OF COMMODITIES

There are many countries around that, on the surface, seem rich through their natural resources. However, don't immediately equate "commodity rich" with the "wealth" we've been discussing. There's a big difference between generating income by pumping oil out of the ground versus cultivating prosperity through the three wealth catalysts of human capital, trade, and finance. In fact, it has been suggested that natural resources are actually an impediment in developing countries, smothering democratic trends and collective prosperity, what author Amity Shlaes calls "the commodity curse." This seems particularly true of oil-rich countries in the Gulf, along with some countries in Latin America (Venezuela, Ecuador, Colombia), Africa (Angola, Nigeria), and other assorted places in Asia and the former Soviet Union. It also pertains to almost any country that depends on one or two export commodities for most of its economy.[33]

The idea of Shlaes' "commodity curse" may be economically counterintuitive, given that valuable natural resources can be the basis for some of the wealth creation concepts discussed, that is, free trade and comparative advantage. However, commodity wealth manifests itself differently in nations where democracy, education, and private property have yet to be valued widely.

Think of it this way: Whoever controls the oil field or the gold mine in a developing country often controls the nation. In developing non-democratic countries, commodities are often under state rule. Historically, this has led to centralized, insular policies (including import substitution, tariffs, etc.) versus diffused democracy and market-driven economics. In this respect, nationalized assets have a way of stunting economic, political, and cultural maturation. In some ways, they embody Foster's "peasant culture" and Grondona's "resistant" tendencies because the dependence on commodity prices almost always precludes the effort to develop human capital, a key ingredient to successful comparative advantage and free trade.

Corruption is often prevalent where a country's cash flow is controlled by the state. Why, for example, should a government in control of a cash cow ever develop competitive sectors? That would simply undermine its power. For regimes dependent on commodities, a few good "bumper crop" years are enough to suppress the implementation of serious reforms. Indeed, such regimes have little interest in raising living standards, boosting education, or cultivating any optimistic, wealth-oriented values. As Shlaes notes, this may be at the root of peasant culture: "The commodity curse thesis does a lot to explain why so many Middle Easterners do not seem eager to hammer swords into ploughshares, or trade Kalashnikovs for Windows XP. Subjects of Saudi Arabia or the youth in Iran have little hope of collecting huge material rewards in their own lifetime. That is why some embrace Islam's paradise, Koran school and suicide hijacking."[34]

The economic success stories of the last 50 years—Japan, Hong Kong, Taiwan, Singapore, and South Korea, and now China and India—have fairly small endowments of natural resources and so have been forced to rely on literate, skilled labor to raise living standards. They've realized the importance of stable, unlimited human wealth versus limited commodities under the ground. As Shlaes adds, "It is no accident that Israel, with not much more than Dead Sea salt to sell, has turned out to be the Middle East's only democracy and a technology exporter."[35] And some developing economies that do have resources, such as Mexico, have made strides to diversify income away from one source. Since the early 1980s, Mexico has shifted its economy from approximatly two-thirds oil-related, one-third diversified, to two-thirds diversified, one-third oil.

Commodities may be a start to help modernize an economy, but an overdependence on them often leads to a failure to develop the greatest long-term asset for a country: human capital. This is a resource that can increase every year, and will not dwindle with use.

Our three wealth catalysts—human capital, trade, and finance—have proven to be invaluable for growth and prosperity. However, how these catalysts are nurtured in countries will ultimately determine long-term success. Culture shapes wealth, and wealth shapes culture; the process is symbiotic. Both feed off each other in a mutually reinforcing manner. Societies need an optimistic, risk-taking, trusting, goal-oriented outlook to achieve wealth, and wealth, in turn, reinforces this cultural predisposition. The more demonstrable successes that occur in the wealth creation process, the more likely resistant cultures will be to accept these underlying principles as the rules of society and begin to spin their own virtuous cycles of prosperity.

4
Wealth and Government:

Voting with Our Pocketbooks

Government is a contrivance of human wisdom
to provide for human wants.
Edmund Burke (1729–1797)

The forces that create prosperity cannot exist without a supportive environment, and that environment is determined by government. Depending on philosophy and policy, government can foster wealth creation or stifle it. Most politicians today understand the wealth catalysts of productive human capital, free-market economics, and sound financial infrastructure. But *how* these elements are cultivated, strengthened, and refined remains the subject of contentious debate for many in Biological, Material, and Experiential-trending societies; that is the focus of this chapter.

As wealth has changed individual values, people have sought to have those values reflected in their political institutions. Modern turbo-wealth creation requires a flexible, accountable government that can react not only to domestic needs, but also to international pressures, particularly as global integration occurs. Indeed, while the 20th Century was remarkable for the pace and breadth of economic progress, it was also marked by historic political transformations: the civil rights protests in the U.S., the dismantlement of the Soviet Bloc, China's Tiananmen Square protests, and decolonization and democratic elections in Africa and many other developing countries. In the face of economic progress around the world (beamed into homes via TV), many of these recent political reconfigurations have arisen when people demanded a better life—or at minimum, the opportunity to improve life—from their governments.

Until quite recently, political change has been slow and lumbering. Until the 20th century, most governments' legitimacy was rooted in birthright (Egyptian pharaohs, Roman emperors, royal families of Europe and Asia) or an occasional theocracy, and not easily challenged. Many aspects of government in advanced societies today— free elections, separation of church and state, taxation for public policies, etc.—are fairly modern developments. Before the wealth surge of the last few generations, government served largely to maintain social order in Biological societies. Few governments saw their role as a provider of prosperity; the possibilities for such progress simply didn't exist. Only in the last century have the democratic and secular principles that are intrinsically bound with wealth creation become more dominant.

As Figure 4–1 illustrates, much of what we think of as "government" —legal frameworks and democratic participation—has only truly evolved in the last 200 years, intertwined tightly with the run-up in wealth. The acceleration of democratic movements is exceptionally pronounced in the last 50 years throughout the world.

Figure 4–1   Wealth and government trends, 2000BCE–2000CE.

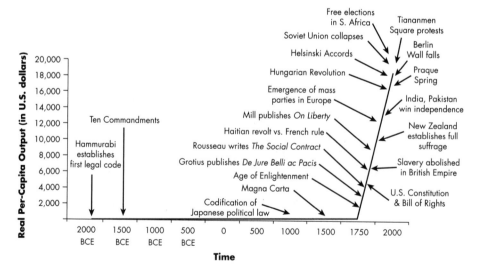

In recent decades there has been a discernable worldwide shift toward a more hands-off governing style, at least in terms of the economy (Figure 4–2). This is true from Latin America to East Asia and from Africa to Europe. The reasons are fairly simple: Free-market economies have been the most successful at generating wealth and improving living standards. Moreover, open economies have attracted more foreign capital to fuel further growth, since money and business are drawn to where they are least restricted. Data from the 2002 *Freedom in the World* report show us how and why governments are responding: "free" countries grow the fastest and account for the vast majority of the world's wealth—87% in 2000 compared to 7% for countries considered "not free." The same story is told by the *Index of Economic Freedom*, which defines economic freedom as "the absence of government coercion or constraint on the production, distribution, or consumption of goods and services beyond the extent necessary for citizens to protect and maintain liberty itself."[1]

It is little wonder then that many governments have been trying to implement wide-ranging policy changes to attract capital, modernize production capacity, and foster greater human capital and productivity. Despite this global focus on policy and economic reform, the process is neither universal nor consistent. Countries in the Biological, Material, and Experiential developmental phases each are capable of differing degrees of progress and possess varying policy tools through which to implement change. In lower income, Biological-oriented countries, the primary purpose of government is to provide stability, a low-rung Maslow need. Still preoccupied with

Figure 4–2   Free countries grow the fastest and are the wealthiest.[2]

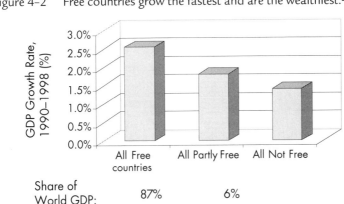

Source: Freedom House.

the more fundamental concerns of feeding and housing their populations, Biological governments are consumed with fulfilling basic survival needs and are not well-suited to implement rigorous structural and economic reforms. With limited financial capability and human resources diminished by poor health and education, they struggle to meet the needs of suffering populations today while trying to build wealth-generating capacities for tomorrow.

However, for countries entering the Material phase, governments can become promoters of prosperity and opportunity. Many nations entering the Material phase over the past few decades have undertaken policy prescriptions such as trade liberalization and offering export incentives, opening financial markets and domestic transparency, and infrastructure investment and human capacity building. These policies have been found to be far superior to the strong statist protectionism of countries such as the former Soviet Union, pre-reform China, and some parts of Latin America. With growing wealth, the Material state's role shifts towards a *laissez-faire*, regulatory position. This is the current condition of much of the industrial West and increasingly of some of the world's fast-emerging economies in Asia. The world now contains more than a few examples of countries that have "made it" by combining the right blend of openness and economic reform, propelling over two billion people to record living standards.

As populations progress through the Material phase and attain a higher level of economic, social, and physical security, they expect government to recede further into a non-interventionist role. Later-stage Materials and Experientials—armed with better education and financial resources—also begin to use the political process to further individual interests that go beyond pure economic policy.

For those upwardly mobile in rarified upper-Material or Experiential communities, global governmental trends may not seem immediately relevant. However, wealth trajectory of successful nations is predicated on the ongoing process of lowering production costs and opening new markets, often in countries whose economies are a few steps behind. Enduring prosperity requires more and better workers globally, as well as more consumers, more borrowers, and more savers. That means that political stability, global security, and trade-friendly policies are of universal interest. It may be even more important for privileged Westerners, sometimes perceived as being oblivious to the plights of less prosperous people around the world. The wealth creation process and subsequent value and policy shifts certainly affect national and international security issues, whether directly in traditional defense plans and spending or in more modern, indirect situations such as cross-border terrorism or UN peacekeeping efforts. For example, the values of Middle East governments have obvious ramifications for those in Asia, Western Europe, and the U.S. since so many economies are entangled with the region's oil reserves. Government policies toward weapons of mass destruction, as another example, clearly have grave global impacts whether they're in India, North Korea, China, Europe, the Middle East, or the former Soviet Union. Further, there is growing evidence that public policies toward the environment reverberate globally. Decisions to accelerate deforestation in the Amazon, for example, or to expand national highways in Asia, or to subsidize certain farm products or energy sources versus others in the U.S., can and do have long-term implications for billions around the planet.

WEALTH AND CORRUPTION

Corruption distorts wealth creation and undermines the faith in and effectiveness of government and public policy. In both the private and public sectors, corruption leads to the misallocation of resources based on sound economic principles. One can see how state-centralized economies—versus those diversified and diffused in private hands—could be more prone to corruption.

Corruption takes many forms. In wealthy countries, beyond obvious kickbacks and briberies, it may arise in a subtler manner: cozy business relationships, mismanaged conflicts of interest, poor information disclosures, etc. Corruption clearly exists in wealthy countries, and can have a detrimental effect on local and national economies as the U.S.'s Enron and Worldcom scandals amply demonstrated. But the damage may be greater in poorer Biological societies where lives hang in the balance and resources are scarce. In such places, building sound domestic integrity in institutional life may be the greatest long-term accelerator of wealth creation. Governments that fail to implement or enforce anti-corruption laws face challenges in growing capital, allocating it to the most optimal sectors, and spinning the virtuous wealth cycle. Corruption also helps reinforce Grondona's pessimistic, progress-resistant culture.

Transparency International (TI) was formed in 1993 to expose corrupt practices around the world. One of TI's key contributions is its Corruption Perception Index (CPI), the only one of its kind that annually ranks countries' corruption environments. As Peter Eigen, Chairman of TI, notes, "Political elites and their cronies continue to take kickbacks at every opportunity. Hand in glove with corrupt businesspeople, they are trapping whole nations in poverty and hampering sustainable development. Corruption is perceived to be dangerously high in poor parts of the world, but also in many countries whose firms invest in developing nations... From illegal logging to blood diamonds, we are seeing the plundering of the earth and its people in an unsustainable way."[3]

TI ranks 102 countries, of which 70—including many of the world's poorest—score less than 5 out of a perfect 10. Countries perceived as very corrupt include Indonesia, Kenya, Angola, Madagascar, Paraguay, Nigeria, and Bangladesh, all which score less than 2. Countries with low levels of perceived corruption are predominantly rich Material and Experiential-trending: Finland, Denmark, New Zealand, Iceland, Singapore, and Sweden. However, low income does not always mean corruption. Botswana, for example, has consistently ranked as one of the least corrupt despite its very modest income.[4]

Over time, TI's influence may grow, similar to Amnesty International's in the human rights arena. The world community should exert pressure on corrupt governments to reform, for the sooner corruption can be controlled, the faster the wealth process can accelerate and provide for the neediest.

DEMOCRACY AND DEVELOPMENT

The rise of democracy in the world has been intrinsically tied to the economic shift toward a free-market system. While democracy may not be an endpoint (nor inevitable for all countries), the late 20th Century witnessed a pronounced shift toward greater global democratic governance (see Figure 4–3). One resonating symbol of this is the image of German students on the Berlin Wall—pick axes and hammers in the air—dismantling the concrete divide between democracy and authoritarianism. Now, close to two-thirds of the world's populations live in societies that are democratic or are moving toward democratic regimes, versus less than 5% in 1900.[5]

In his analysis of recent Communist state transitions, Fukuyama noted that not only were citizens motivated by economic reasons—they wanted living standards on par with those around them—but they also wanted certain social rights. People wanted to create a political system that fostered universal recognition, or greater self-determinacy; in many cases, that system is democracy.[6]

Figure 4-3   Comparative percentages of democracies in the 20th
              Century: Democratic governments elected by *universal*
              suffrage, 1900–2000.[7]

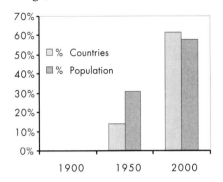

Figure 4-4   Different types of regimes, worldwide, 1900–2000.[8]

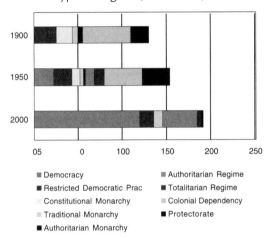

The links between economic security and democracy have been well-documented, though the exact relationship is often in question.[9] All modern democracies are essentially open economies, but not all market economies are democracies. John Mueller notes:

> While democracy may not be necessary for capitalism, democracy probably does benefit capitalist growth. It does so by furnishing property owners some potential remedy against governmental confiscation, by establishing the rule of law, by routinely encouraging an openness and transparency of information, by allowing *all* interest groups (rather than a subset of them) to attempt to influence government policy, by removing defective leaders, and at least in recent years, by furnishing an atmosphere of stability and predictability.[10]

With increasing economic security, there has been a discernable global trend away from totalitarianism toward popular participation (Figure 4–4). The world, then, is moving towards more participatory regimes in which people have a say in the forces that shape their world. Inglehart adds:

> Economic development seems to bring gradual cultural changes that make mass publics increasingly likely to want democratic institutions and be supportive of them once they are in place...development tends to make mass publics more trusting and tolerant and leads them to place an increasingly high priority on autonomy and self-expression in all spheres of life, including politics, and it becomes difficult and costly to repress demands for political liberalization. With rising levels of economic development, cultural patterns emerge that are increasingly supportive of democracy, making mass publics more likely to want democracy and more skillful at getting it."[11]

This process toward democracy is neither seamless nor simple. History has shown that power is not relinquished easily. The transformation of governments often has been violent, and there are still millions of poverty-stricken people who live under strict, authoritarian regimes. But when democracy and capitalism catch on, noticeable improvements are registered in voter participation rates. For example, between the 1958–1962 and 1998–2002 periods, voter participation gains were made in most parts of the Biological world: in Bangladesh (from 55% to 75%), Egypt (from 40% to 48%), Honduras (from 63% to 82%), Turkey (from 81.5% to 87%), and Ghana (from 50% to 61%), among others.[12]

WOMEN AND GOVERNANCE

Even in countries where suffrage laws may be on the books, women's political rights and participation are not necessarily guaranteed. This is glaringly evident in Biological societies where women are often less enfranchised in the overall economy. Women continue to be politically under-represented in virtually every country in the world, with the Inter-Parliamentary Union reporting that women hold less than 14% of parliamentary seats in all areas but Scandinavia (one of the most Experiential-trending regions in the world).[13] But, conditions are improving. The percentage of women parliament members increased four-fold in the world from 1945–1995: from 3% in 1945 to 11.6% in 1995.[14]

After a generation or two of increasing status, women in Material societies have gotten a larger share of the world's economic pie. Tied to this economic might is social and political clout, increasingly exercised at the voting booth. In male-dominated India, for example, female voter turnout grew from 47% in 1962 to 58% in 1998. And some countries have implemented quota systems to encourage and foster female political participation. In 1991, Argentina passed legislation to introduce a quota system in national elections where 30% of all candidates needed to be women.[15] In Tanzania, 20% of national and 25% of local government seats are actually reserved for women.

In the wealthiest societies, women are increasingly involved in the highest levels of governance. In 1999, Sweden became the first country *ever* to have more female government ministers than male. While the global political picture remains largely male-dominated, the gradual integration of women into the economic fabric of each country bodes well for political participation. We are only a few generations into the wealth generation process, and it is only a matter of time before women have equal representation in government.

BOTTOMS UP

Most Biological countries hope to move beyond dependence on agriculture and/or mineral extraction and into low-wage manufacturing (much as the successful East Asian countries have done in the past 40 years). But in such countries, where people often live on $3 dollars a day or less, money goes to basic services versus middle-class luxuries. People are rightly more concerned with their next source of calories than with 400 channels of satellite TV. There are 2–3 billion people on earth whose daily goals are eating enough, drinking clean water, and avoiding diseases like malaria. To create wealth, governments of such countries must first address domestic issues of health, education, and destabilizing civil strife.

Unfortunately, in many places, Biological governments are not capable or willing to take the steps necessary to build domestic capacity, to educate the population and provide the infrastructure essential to economic well-being. Often, governments do not even provide the most basic necessities. Keep in mind that cultivating human capital—building healthy, educated populations—can easily take a generation or two—much longer than any government can stay in power.

This raises difficult and complex questions as to whether governments should use scarce resources to help their citizens get through today or plan for the future. Tragically, a physically and psychologically weak citizenry—underfed, undereducated, and often fearful—doesn't have the cumulative strength to shape government opinion or policy. Maslow's bottom-rung physiological needs unfortunately undermine wealth creation tendencies, promoting what Inglehart calls "survival" values, which encourage conformity and order under strict religious or authoritarian regimes.[16] Many of the world's poorest countries are also the most authoritarian, with leaders and governments that tend toward absolutism: Think of the Taliban in Afghanistan, Kabila in the Congo, Mugabe in Zimbabwe, Lukashenko in Belarus, or Kim Jong Il in North Korea. Without appropriate leadership, countries can be doomed to cycles of violence, upheaval, and autocratism that disrupt economic progress.

WEALTH, POVERTY, AND WAR

Does wealth reduce cross-border wars? Surprisingly, there is ample evidence to support this notion.[17] For much of history, conquest for land, raw materials, and slaves was the sole method of wealth acquisition. However, when wealth can be *created*, in part through free trade between nations, one motivation for warfare is eliminated. As author John Mueller notes, trade brings "the economic advantages of conquest without the unpleasantness of invasion and the sticky responsibility of imperial control. Thus, war is unlikely if countries take prosperity as their chief goal and if they come to believe that trade is the best way to achieve that goal."[18]

With newfound productive potential and some loose change in their pockets, people want more: more freedom, more products, more convenience, and more comfort.

It is interesting to see that Germany and Japan have become some of the best trading partners and ideological friends of the U.S., UK, and France—former foes in World War II. Cross-border rivalries formerly waged on battlefields are now waged largely in the marketplace. That's why there are few cross-border armed conflicts among the wealthiest countries in the world.

Conversely, poverty can often lead to armed eruptions, both inside and beyond a country's borders. As a recent UN development report noted, "Without peace there may be no development. But without development peace is threatened." A snapshot of the globe shows us that the world's hot spots—with some 40+ conflicts in motion today—are almost invariably in the poorest Biological countries. And a quick glimpse at the past decade reveals more instability in regions where poverty and inequality dominate. In the 1990s, countries such as Angola, Afghanistan, Sudan, Sierra Leone, Haiti, and Zaire—all among the poorest— were in varying degrees of crisis.

The UN identifies a number of factors that may signify a potential for armed conflicts (either between or *within* a country): ethnic conflict and discrimination; poverty and economic inequality; misspending on military goods; lack of resources; and political instability. While poverty may not be the sole cause of war, there is little doubt that the connection is strong. Interestingly, political freedom may also be a factor in the discussion: Serious famines rarely occur in independent, democratic countries with a free press. The UN points out that some poor countries like Botswana and Zimbabwe with participatory governments have, until now, been able to prevent famines (although Zimbabwe's farm confiscation policies and democratic back-treading have seriously raised the possibility), whereas countries like Sudan, Ethiopia, and North Korea—where authoritarian governments rule—have not.[19]

For the hundreds of millions currently caught in the cycle of civil strife, poverty, and hunger, meaningful economic and social progress is tragically thwarted. Moreover, in Biological societies, security and massive defense spending often trump human needs. In sub-Saharan Africa, the portion of the region's GDP devoted to military spending rose from 0.7% in 1960 to 2.9% in 1994 despite widespread poverty. Over 216 million people live in poverty, 120 million adults are illiterate, and 350-odd million have no access to healthcare, yet the region's military expenditures are over $8 billion. The picture is the same in South Asia, where annual military expenditures exceed $14 billion and almost 600 million people live in poverty.[20]

The cycle of poverty is not unbreakable. There is ample evidence showing how forward-thinking governments—even those in poor countries—can seed more prosperous futures through policy choices. South Korea, the modern East Asian powerhouse, was once a poverty-stricken country of little economic muscle. Just three decades ago, South Korea's GDP was comparable to the poorer countries of Africa and Asia. Today, South Korea's GDP is 7 times India's and 13 times that of neighboring North Korea's, and already close to some of the economies in the European Union (EU). During the same period, South Korean literacy rates rose from 33% to 90%. This success was achieved through a government system that fostered industrial development and growth, which included directed credit, sponsorship of specific industries, and a strong labor effort.

As the case of South Korea aptly demonstrates, a key factor in a country's ability to move from Biological survival status to a more dynamic and stable economic system is government policy: A central authority must play a role in facilitating commerce. It is a role that continues as people move beyond filling basic needs, when incomes reach, say, the $1500–2000 GDP per-capita figure. With newfound productive potential and some money in their pockets, people want more: more freedom, more products, more convenience, and more comfort. They want cleaner water and affordable electricity. They want telephones. They want to take the bus instead of walking to work. They want paved roads, schools for their children, and hospitals for their parents.

Just as government policy can accelerate economic growth, bad policy can smother it. For Communist and other statist economies, it was believed that a strong, central state with complete control over production and consumption could fill people's needs by providing them employment, housing, and state-produced goods—just a step above the Biological needs. In the former Soviet Union and Communist China, government spending consumed as much as 70–80% of GDP in the 1980s.[21]

The Soviet experiment failed.[22] The reality was that people's needs were *not* being satisfied: USSR citizens were often living barely above survival levels and they wanted more. They wanted a choice of goods; they wanted not just government-issued bread, but choices between wheat and rye, and they didn't want to wait on line for hours. Above all, they wanted the opportunity that the state system had denied to them. They wanted a government that would promote their needs and help them move up through the cycles of consumption as those in wealthier countries had done.[23]

INTERNATIONAL ASSISTANCE: FILLING THE BIOLOGICAL GAPS FOR GREATER HUMAN CAPITAL

While there has been monumental socio-economic progress in the last 50 years, there are still many societies in crisis. According to the UN *2001 Human Development Report*, there are still about one billion people without access to improved water sources and even more without basic sanitation. Over 325 million children in developing countries are not able to attend primary or secondary schools, and there is a woeful shortage of serviceable roads and communication services, particularly in geographically isolated communities.

It is little wonder that many poor Biological citizens have a hard time competing in the global economy; unfortunately, there are 1–2 billion people who probably cannot succeed on their own. However, as more wealthy societies understand global economic interconnectedness, international aid organizations are assisting in many cases where Biological governments are failing. International aid has become a lifeboat for many troubled countries, offering support, guidance, and sometimes outright governance to struggling nations.

The technology and know-how to solve many problems in the developing world already exist and are relatively inexpensive. For example, malaria, the potentially deadly disease spread by mosquitoes, afflicts some 500 million people in developing countries and kills nearly 3 million each year. In addition to these tragic deaths, the disease leads to huge losses in productivity when workers are absent due to illness or caring for sick children. According to development specialist Jeffrey Sachs at Columbia University, countries like Tanzania could be *twice* as wealthy if malaria was controlled. Similar production losses are linked to chronic diarrhea, a serious concern for 1+ billion people with poor drinking water and sanitation. Solving these simple afflictions is not like curing cancer; often, $5 per capita would help improve public hygiene and sick rates dramatically.[24]

Executing these seemingly simple solutions, however, is not always easy and not all foreign aid gets to the needy. There are repeated stories about donated food and medicine getting lost, spoiled, or stolen. According to one study, for every $100 spent on drugs by African governments, only $12 effectively reached patients; the rest was squandered through inefficient procurement (including kickbacks), poor storage, or poor prescriptions. Sometimes, if a recipient country lacks the ability or knowledge to allocate aid resources, funds simply get misspent. There are numerous examples of countries spending, in all good faith, 20% of a health budget on immunizations when vaccine-preventable diseases may only account for 5% of a country's "disease burden" (i.e., how many years of life are lost due to specific maladies). International aid organizations must provide the know-how, as well as the funds, to help these needy populations effectively.[25]

In addition to governmental aid and international charities, the private business sector is filling some gaps that Biological governments cannot or will not fill. In South Africa, for example, some of the largest employers—including the Anglo American mining group—have begun to provide free AIDS drugs to employees diagnosed with the disease. Besides the positive press coverage companies receive for providing such drugs, there are also economic benefits: Healthy workers can keep working, while sick ones cannot. In certain countries where 10–30% of the population may be at risk of contracting AIDS, such healthcare assistance may become a necessary cost of doing business there.

These developments are significant because they represent a growing acceptance of international and private-sector cooperation as a norm in modern governance, certainly with struggling Biological societies. The benefits of increased international assistance can be destiny-changing: $100 billion per annum more in financial aid from the wealthiest 20-odd countries—or less than 1% of their annual economic output—could actually provide $50 a year to 2 billion of the world's Biological citizens. Imagine what this $50 could do in places like Tanzania, for example, where current annual health spending is only $8 per capita. When confronted with lost global economic output due to childhood diseases (like malnutrition, pneumonia, measles, and diarrhea) and controllable infectious disease (such as malaria and AIDS), additional aid should be seen as a small price to pay for greater global security, stability, and continued prosperity. According to a World Health Organization commission, for every $1 of additional health aid, the world would receive $6 in added economic output from the healthier population.[26]

LIVING IN THE MATERIAL WORLD

Material-oriented governments have generally acknowledged that economic growth and international connectedness are essential components of national progress, and they shape policy in those directions accordingly. Governments in the Material phase encourage institutions and regulatory frameworks that facilitate economic progress, and as Fukuyama would suggest, that augment social status and personal esteem.

There is a new and remarkable value that people expect their governments to help them obtain what other countries have.

Governance tends to move toward democracy in Material countries as more and more people are empowered by the economic changes and demand greater recognition and say over their futures.

In the late 1970s and 1980s, Japan—and then the East Asian tigers of South Korea, Taiwan, Hong Kong, and Singapore—became globalization's best Material success stories. Their governments followed development strategies based on world economic engagement combined with rigorous domestic policies to promote stability and capacity. Policies were based on market principles and fiscal discipline to encourage greater investment in export sectors and human capital building. As wealth accumulated, consumption and demand increased, leading to greater access to capital and a deepening of the export sectors. These changes, in turn, prompted greater growth.

This example resonated around the world, particularly in countries that had, until then, been following the Socialist-oriented "import substitution" policies of tight domestic protection and isolation from the world economy.[27] Suddenly, there were examples of countries that had, contrary to all expectations, been able to engage in the global economy and grow. Citizens in Biological states, in a fundamental shift of their view of government's role, began to demand that their governments provide similar advances. Using East Asia as an example, many developing nations undertook massive policy reforms in the 1990s. They reduced tariffs, removed distortions in exchange rates, liberalized financial markets, and trimmed fiscal deficits.

Of course, this was and is not an easy path to follow. In theory, governments know what to do, but policies are often too tough to implement, and may not always lead to immediate results. Each country must find its own blend of liberalization and reform, and as recent history has shown, there are no guarantees of obstacle-free success. For a long time, the Washington Consensus, as espoused by the IMF and World Bank, was considered the ultimate formula for development: Based on East Asian successes, the Consensus focused on regulatory reform and liberalization in domestic economies. However, following the Asian financial crisis in 1997, this theory came under increasing attack for its short-sightedness regarding oversight and pace. It is now widely thought that East Asia may have tried too much too fast under pressure from the international financial community. Deregulation in important sectors occurred faster than domestic reform, leaving opportunities for abuse and corruption.

Despite cyclical downturns and adjustments, the growth story of the Asian economies—from Japan's monumental rise in the late 20th Century to China's current ascent—continues to provide a real incentive for countries around the world to implement economic policy reform. Similar success stories are being written for more than a dozen former Soviet economies—including Poland (one of the fastest growing European economies in the 1990s), Hungary, Czech Republic, Latvia, Lithuania, and Estonia, among others.

These countries have all achieved investment-grade credit ratings, impressive growth, and economic integration with the rest of Western Europe (some are even members of NATO) in less than 10 years since the fall of the Soviet Union. Indeed, the essential purpose of a Material government seems to be to move people beyond necessity and help them make choices that create wealth.

Many Latin American economies got a second chance at progress with the Brady Plan in the 1980s, as it was rightly believed that economic disasters in these countries would negatively affect the West. The Plan helped restructure unbearable debt burdens that had stifled these economies, and in return, called for concerted trade reform and financial liberalization as well as strict domestic financial discipline. Privatization and free-market policies ensued. According to the World Bank, between 1992 and 1996, Mexico alone privatized at least $22 billion in assets by selling state-owned banks, mines, and utilities. It is generally considered that Mexico's divestitures, plus a focus on exports through its *maquiladora* assembly program, helped the country diversify its economy away from oil and solidify the country's hard currency capabilities in less than 10 years. These policies were further strengthened by the ratification of the North American Free Trade Agreement (NAFTA) in 1993.

Privatization has perhaps been the most dramatic factor in de-linking government and markets. Nowhere was the divestiture of government-controlled industry greater than in Latin America, where numerous enterprises that had been nationalized in the 1960s and 1970s were auctioned off to the private sector. Privatization has now occurred in more than 100 countries worldwide, and global output attributable to state-owned enterprises has fallen to less than 6% from over 10% in 1979.[28] Privatization is crucial to developing economies because it promotes the attraction of foreign capital and more efficient allocation of resources. By improving a country's ability to interact with the rest of the world, privatization and trade openness generally have a positive effect on per-capita income.[29]

Despite failures and obstacles, many of the world's governments are trying to establish efficient institutions to promote economic activity. The idea of a fully functioning free-market economy has generally supplanted the notion that government can be the key economic provider for its citizens; government should provide the scaffolding for markets without direct involvement. But, the political maturation of Biological to Material countries goes well beyond implementing and safeguarding free-market principles. Along with economic expansion comes a broadening of individual rights and democratic ideals common in the U.S. and other wealthier countries: free speech and an uncensored media, due process of the law, and a codified respect for diversity. These rights and policies can be integral to a country's worldwide acceptance as a modern economy and trading partner. For example, Turkey, an enormous country of nearly 70 million (of which 12 million are Kurds, a minority with distinctly second-class rights), is bidding for membership to the EU. In 2002, the country's parliament approved sweeping laws to modernize Turkey's political and social infrastructure, including outlawing the death penalty (except in cases of war); making slavery a capital offence; granting the European Court of Human Rights the power to order retrials in Turkey; lifting a variety of bans on Kurdish media broadcasts and teaching the Kurdish language; lifting censorship of foreign TV broadcasts and allowing public protests; and removing restrictions on non-Muslim religious foundations.[30]

CHINA'S SLOW BUT HARD RIGHT TURN

China is undergoing the world's most widely watched economic and political transformation. Within 50 years, the behemoth has turned from an almost completely closed, central-command economy to a rapidly expanding powerhouse with growth prospects that exceed those of most of the world for the foreseeable future. In 1956, 96.3% of China's farms were collectivized.[31] Industrial production was managed entirely through government quotas, and regional development policies advocated complete self-sufficiency. These policies were based on Mao's belief that growth was possible without industrialization.

Like similar plans in the former Soviet Union, these philosophies ultimately failed. Farm collectivization begun in the late 1950s cost the Chinese economy as much as 15–20% of total industrial output during the 1960s and 1970s.[32] Since then, the Chinese government has undertaken a series of reforms to promote economic growth and greater openness. One of their first moves was to establish special economic zones with incentives for industrial development and export-intensive manufacturing. The state has closed factories, restructured state-owned enterprises, and opened up the economy to foreign investment. China's recent accession to the World Trade Organization (WTO) is perhaps the ultimate sign of its reform efforts. While the state continues to play a significant role in social and economic development, it is relaxing restrictions and releasing more and more of the economy to external, non-state forces.

The changes are manifest in the workforce: In 1950, 84% of the population worked in agriculture. By 2000, that number had been halved. Now, more and more Chinese work in urban, coastal service centers, and as a result, there is a rapidly growing middle and upper class filled with professional engineers, lawyers, and businesspeople. There are now thousands of multimillionaires in China (perhaps millions), and many are no longer afraid to tout their money, or their political and economic interests.

The question for the Chinese government now is whether growing affluence and choice translate into social and political dislocation. It is a realistic concern, particularly as, over the past 20 years, China has shifted from one of the most egalitarian economies to one of the most unequal. To stave off some disparities, the government recently decided to accept capitalists into its ranks, folding the emerging business class into the ruling elite.

But the future is by no means certain. While the Chinese government boasts of a middle class that will become larger than the entire American population within two generations, it still must grapple with the potential loss of political control of citizens whose demand for self-determinancy grows stronger with wealth creation.

In response to these popular demands, many early-stage Material governments create massive social and economic safety nets, similar to the "welfare states" that arose in the U.S. and Europe as the result of rapid economic growth and deregulation in the early 20th Century. It is true that market economies tend to develop unevenly because society is organized in terms of relative efficiencies. As a result, governments must address the conflicting needs of promoting expansion and taking care of those who are left behind. At the beginning of this century, public spending in countries classified as "welfare states" was only around 10–15% of their national incomes. Now, in many countries, it is around 50% or more.[33] In the U.S., mandatory spending for government entitlement programs[34] has grown significantly as a percentage of national GDP, and now accounts for almost 75% of the government's expenditures, up from about 45% in 1965.[35]

While late-stage Materialists do not necessarily want the government to stop providing these basic services, they may disagree about the way they are being distributed. In these wealthier countries there is a growing tendency toward community involvement rather than federally mandated reform. Recent limitations on government assistance and "workfare" programs in the U.S. are evidence of this trend as is the rise in educational reform initiatives such as charter schools, vouchers, privatization, and busing. Advanced Material populations tend to have less faith that their governments will appropriately allocate tax revenues and perceive huge government bureaucracies to be wasteful. While governments continue to provide safety-net services, they are increasingly disentangling themselves from industry and the economy. In the last few decades, the U.S. has deregulated telecoms, airlines, and some energy and power industries.[36]

In 1999, an ICR/*Washington Post* poll asked: Would you say you favor a smaller federal government with fewer services, or a larger government with many services? Fifty-eight percent of Americans indicated that they would prefer a smaller government. These sentiments were mirrored in Canada. In a national survey, the Conference Board of Canada found that "values have changed" in Canada over the past 20 years. Canadians no longer trust their government as much as they used to and place an increased premium on accountability. Canadians are also less supportive of governmental social programs other than universal healthcare.[37]

This increasing demand for non-intervention has had profound meaning for the types of policies advanced Materialist governments can implement. In Biological and early-stage Material countries, fiscal policy is the primary tool. These governments spend to build roads, schools, hospitals, and the infrastructure that puts people to work and greases the wheels of commerce. Large public projects create jobs, improve basic services, and can directly impact the lives of citizens by providing greater access to opportunity. People in Biological and Material countries look toward large government expenditures to boost their own personal incomes and well-being. Think of Franklin Delano Roosevelt and the New Deal during the Great Depression: Concerted government programs were implemented to generate employment, fire up the domestic economy, and safeguard the public from corporate excesses.

But for later stage Material states, such large fiscal expenditures and public works policies, in many respects, may no longer be necessary except in dire times. On one hand, the infrastructure for economic efficiency is largely in place. On the other hand, when things go economically awry, people want a quick fix—not the slow and long-term trickle of fiscal policy. Instead, these governments are turning more and more to monetary policy—decisions that affect money supply, interest rates, and foreign exchange rates—as the remedy for economic woes.

This creeping shift from fiscal to monetary policy is perhaps the most important change in economic management as governments adapt to the changing needs and values of their constituencies. Monetary policy is more powerful in wealthy economies because individuals and corporations are directly vested in the wealth creation process: A majority own some assets—stocks, bonds, houses, etc.—the success of which is directly related to interest rates and money supply. Wealthy societies are also built on liabilities—debt— much of which are also linked to interest rates. Lowering interest rates, for example, can reduce debt payment and free cash for additional consumption or investment. When the economy slackens, people quickly look toward interest rate policy for an immediate remedy. This is why U.S. Federal Reserve Chairman Alan Greenspan became a household name, not only in the U.S. but around the world: The policies he represents have become the *tour de force* of the Experiential-trending economy. When markets and the economy either heat up or slow down, all eyes fall on the Fed Chairman to tinker with interest rates like a thermostat to create the optimal temperature. Monetary policies are geared to shape financial and economic activity directly: raising interest rates to curb excessive growth, lowering them to promote borrowing. In turn, decisions by central banks to devalue, stabilize, or revalue a currency can have direct impact on comparative advantage and trade patterns, both direct wealth creation elements. Moreover, monetary policies are intended to promote *confidence*, that is, to show that the government is watching the world and markets, and can assist from the sidelines to help spur growth.

MONEY AND GOVERNMENT: THE NEW INTERRELATIONSHIP BETWEEN MONETARY REGIMES AND POLICY-MAKING

A sophisticated, multi-dimensional global economy has created more and better opportunities that have forced Biological and early Material governments to cede power over policies and arenas they once controlled. The process is not necessarily smooth, but it is perhaps one of the most significant developments of the modern global economy.

The process also happens in countries that are more economically advanced. The EU, for example, is perhaps the ultimate modern example of national concerns giving way to international cooperation. When trading in their own lira, francs, and deutschemarks for the new Euro, citizens of the EU gave up much more than their own individual bank notes—they also gave up unprecedented levels of national autonomy. Because currency is more than just a symbol of national sovereignty; it is also a piece of it.

Without the ability to mint money, a country becomes more and more entangled with other countries, and has less power to control its own fate. This happened in the mid-1990s when many Asian nations found that their dollar-pegged currencies hampered trade performance because the dollar grew stronger as the Japanese yen grew weaker.

Or take the unfortunate case of Argentina. In the early 1990s, President Carlos Menem adopted currency convertibility for the peso, essentially fixing the exchange rate to one-for-one with the dollar. The system, Menem insisted, would help Argentina modernize by "hitching its wagon to the front of the train" of the global economy. As a result, inflation was checked and confidence boosted. Foreign investment flocked into the country, state-owned businesses were sold off, and inefficient local businesses were closed.

However, by dollar-pegging, Argentina relinquished its ability to use monetary policy to stimulate its economy. Moreover, if the bulk of national debt is dollarized (as in Argentina's case), then it increases the risk of default, since these countries cannot print more dollars to pay the hard currency debt off. Therefore, unless they can run an extremely tight ship at home, pegged currencies (and their countries) are at the mercy of the markets.

As the global economy slowed, Argentina fell into crisis. Its only option was to influence fiscal measures: In 2000, they slashed public-sector employee wages by 10–15%. In the fall of 2001, the country's Finance Minister increased tariffs, provided subsidies for exporters, altered taxes, and finally had to place a withdrawal cap of $250 per week from accounts to stave off a run on the banks. None of these measures had the appropriate effect and the country spiraled into default.[38]

The problems for the Eurozone, the latest experiment in currency linkage, are even more complex than those for Argentina's dollar peg. The fact that 10 countries have adopted a common currency without a unified government raises important sovereignty issues. Throughout recorded history, a big role of government has been currency management and control, but that has now changed. The countries of the EU must now coordinate policies and fit certain targets to maintain the strength and viability of their common currency. They have banded together in an effort to capture greater wealth.

The Euro represents the ultimate power of economic determinism. The countries of Europe, after generations of war and conflict, decided to put their differences to rest and join together to create an economic powerhouse: a union with a capacity far greater than the sum of the individual countries. Each government has ceded huge economic and financial controls to centralized bodies to get richer collectively.

TRENDING TOWARD EXPERIENTIAL POLITICS

There are now segments of wealthy industrial and service countries that are moving from the Material toward the Experiential phase of governance. These strata are, even in a country as wealthy as the U.S., relatively small—perhaps 10–15% of the population. However, the political attitudes and behaviors of this minority are still worth examining because this group is uniquely empowered, both economically and socially, to participate in the political process and effect policy change. In addition, concerns voiced by Experientials often hint at trends that will later develop in the broader Material population.

Obviously, much of the Experientials' power is derived from financial clout. With higher incomes, this group typically pays a disproportionately large percentage of taxes in their respective countries. For example, in the U.S., the top 1% of taxpayers (those with adjusted gross incomes above $250,000) pay more than one-third of all federal income taxes.[39] The top 25% (with incomes above $48,000) pay 82%. The top 50% of taxpayers (having incomes above $24,000) pay 95.7%, meaning that U.S. taxpayers in the bottom 50% income bracket pay just 4.3% of federal income taxes (see Figure 4–5).[40]

No doubt in partial response to their higher tax burden, Experientials tend to vote more than lower income groups. In recent U.S. presidential elections, 70+% of eligible voters whose total family income was $50,000 or more reported voting, compared to less than 40% of those with incomes under $10,000. Sixty-four percent of homeowners said they voted, compared with only 42% of renters. On the age front, 70% of those aged 55–74 (a high-income group) voted compared to approximately 35% of 18- to 24-year-olds (one of the lowest income groups). Education is also a factor: Those with bachelor's degrees were nearly twice as likely (74%) to have voted as those who had not completed high school (39%).[41]

Figure 4-5   Tax concentration in the U.S., 1981–1997.

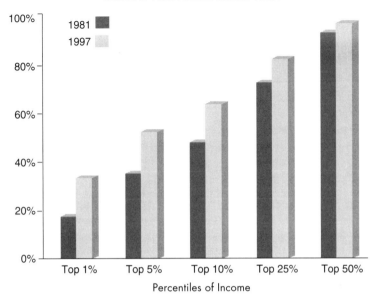

Shares of Total Federal Income Taxes

Source: Internal Revenue Service.

The high political participation of Experiential populations is more striking when compared to the general trends in advanced Material countries, where voter participation has shown steady declines in recent decades. In 1960, 63.1% of the voter-eligible population cast ballots in the U.S. presidential and congressional elections, versus 46.6% and 49.3%, respectively in 2000.[42] Similarly, in Japan, parliamentary elections declined from 73.5% in 1960 to 60.6% in 2000.[43] In the UK, from 1959 to 2001, rates fell from 77.5% to 57.6%.[44] Even in a newly Material country like South Korea, voting rates dropped from 76% in the 1958–1962 period to 57% in 1998–2002.[45]

These tax and voting trends may suggest that mature Material countries, those two or three generations into mass prosperity, may have succeeded sufficiently that majority segments are content with their existing political systems. Free-market policies are taking care of their needs, and most social rights have been codified (if not routinely enforced) at the cost of an acceptable level of taxation.

Experientials are not only influencing policy by voting more. With their excess resources, Experientials are also attempting to promote their own personal, social, and economic values by seeking out and supporting groups that reflect those agendas, and these groups wield substantial power and influence over government. In America, for example, 608 political action committees (PACs) were registered in 1974; by December 1995, the number of PACs totaled more than 4,000.[46] The range of interests they promote are vast, and include groups like the National Rifle Association (NRA), the Sierra Club, the National Organization for Women (NOW), and the American Association of Retired People (AARP, with 35 million American members). Also growing in prominence are new political movements like the Greens and the Right to Life Party, among others.

EXPERIENTIAL POLITICAL MOVEMENTS

While the U.S. is dominated by two main political parties (some would argue, two parties that have largely converged in core philosophies in the last couple of decades), there are new political movements sprouting up every day. Around the world, most countries have multiple parties and often governments are formed as coalitions of disparate political factions. Occasionally, Americans see visible alternatives to Democrats and Republicans in some elections, such as Ross Perot of the Reform Party. There are occasionally other parties seen in ballot boxes on elections days, some with single-issue agendas: Liberals, Right-to-Lifers, Socialists, Labor, Marijuana Legalization, etc. While few will ever grow into meaningful political forces, there are two Experiential-feeling groups that warrant some attention.

In the U.S., one extreme Experiential ideology is espoused by the American Libertarian Party (ALP). Founded in 1971, the party currently holds more than 300 elective offices, more than twice as many as all other third parties combined. In 2000, the ALP ran more than 1,430 candidates, also more than twice as many as all other third parties combined. The party's core philosophy is that government should be small and minimal, and the less involved in our lives, the better. As Thoreau noted: "*Government is best which governs not at all.*"

The ALP is committed to individual liberty and personal responsibility; a free-market economy of abundance and prosperity; and a foreign policy of non-intervention, peace, and free trade. In short, Libertarians believe that almost all goods and services should be available through private means. In that way, people can talk with their dollars and make decisions about what is and is not available through market mechanisms.

For a Libertarian, taxes are tantamount to theft. National services such as education, welfare, and transportation should be privately operated. For Libertarians, the waves of privatization and corporatization over the past decades have not gone far enough: The state should sell off everything and let markets do the work.

While the Libertarians reflect the rugged, individualistic side of American Experiential politics, a larger global movement has been embodied in the Green Party. Originally conceived around environmental issues, the Green Party was formed in 1972 in New Zealand. Since then, the Greens have grown into a vital international network of parties and political movements that have expanded beyond conservation to include non-violence and social justice in their platform. Greens believe that, for sustainable, long-term development, certain trends in global consumption, population, material inequity, and environmental degradation must be halted and reversed. To promote equality, the Green Party supports democratic, transparent, and accountable governments at both the local and national levels.

The goal of the Green party is not to maximize world GNP, but rather to better humankind's long-term "wealth." In the broader sense of the word, it wants sustainable, equitable, growth. While not yet popular in the U.S. (although the Greens' candidate for president in 2000, Ralph Nader, is very well-known), the party now runs for public elections in over 70 countries around the world. No longer just part of the political fringe, the Greens are currently part of national government coalitions in Germany, France, Belgium, and Mexico.

The philosophy of the Green Party is fairly inclusive; it even allows room for environmentally unfriendly actors. Multinationals may still run their factories at 100% utilization rates; however, those corporations must also pay substantially higher taxes to compensate for the excessive pollution they spew. In practice, the Greens believe that environmentally degrading behavior can be limited through both regulation and greater efficiency. Laws can be instituted to ensure that environmental cost is included in the prices of goods and services. By incorporating the "real cost" of environmentally harmful actions, corporations will then be motivated to invest in measures to increase resource efficiency.

While Libertarians and Greens seem like polar opposites of the political spectrum, they overlap in one key area: They both support more active and greater responsibility of citizens in all aspects of life. Both reflect an ideal that governments—as entities—cannot effect positive change as much as the individual consumer and corporate patterns of behavior can.

THE STATE IN THE NEW WORLD

As societies advance economically, the power of government may diminish domestically. But internationally, the state remains a very real and important actor. Globalization has led to even more state involvement in international affairs, especially for the U.S. and Europe whose security forces are now spread around the world. As people become more interconnected through technology and economics, instability in one region can destabilize another. This becomes an issue of international concern in a very real and immediate way.

The importance of governmental structure, even an Experiential-oriented, non-interventionist model, is made abundantly clear in times of insecurity and national emergency. In June 2000, just 29% of Americans said they trusted the federal government to do what is right most of the time. Just days after the terrorist attacks of September 11, 2001, over 60% said they trusted the government.[47] Further, people were instantly more willing to give up certain rights and privileges in order to feel protected. A *New York Times/CBS News* poll in December 2001 found that 64% of Americans said they supported presidential authority to make changes to rights usually guaranteed by the Constitution.[48] Inglehart calls this reaction the "Authoritarian Reflex." In the most extreme cases, this sort of insecurity can pave the way to an authoritarian regime as people seek the perceived "strong man" to lead them to recovery.[49]

GLOBALIZATION AND THE LOSS OF SOVEREIGNTY

Is the international flow of goods and services—the globalization of the world economy—making governments slowly obsolete? While it is unlikely that we will see the end of the state as political unit anytime soon, there are transnational actors that increasingly encroach on governments' abilities to act. This is particularly true as more and more of the world recognizes the merits of world trade and capital mobility: To be part of the system, they must abide by certain rules. Over the past 50 years, world trade has swelled from $310 billion to nearly $6 trillion, and accounts for more than 20% of world output.

The WTO demands that governments align tariffs and subsidies with those of their partners. To enter the WTO, China had to open many hitherto protected industries to foreign ownership and competition. By slashing tariffs, the government decreased its own hold and ability to shape the domestic economy. But without opening to global trade, these economies are doomed to stagnate.

Sovereignty's assault is not limited to supra-national institutions like the IMF, World Bank, UN,[50] and WTO. Multinational companies (MNCs) are also important conduits of change. MNCs often side-step their home governments and bargain directly with foreigners. Many countries make large concessions to attract MNCs and their factories. And privatization in many developing nations often provides access for MNCs to buy into new marketplaces. As seen in Figure 4–6, many MNCs are larger than the nations they work with.

This corporate economic muscle can roll over government policy on occasion. Not only do companies side-step government regulators, but they also dictate the shape of policies and reform. There are also private financial institutions—banks, mutual funds, hedge funds, among others—that wield mighty checkbooks in the markets. They have their own interests regarding countries' fiscal and monetary behavior. When such investors grow skittish, their mobile money can be yanked from countries very quickly, creating a stampede that, in itself, often forces countries to alter policies.

And let's not forget about the increasing number of special interest groups that act across national boundaries. Environmental groups like the Worldwide Wildlife Foundation (WWF) and the Sierra Club rank high on the list of organizations working outside of traditional political channels to effect change, along with a variety of human rights organizations such as Amnesty International.

Figure 4–6   1999 comparison of countries and corporations (GDP and sales are in millions of U.S. dollars).[51]

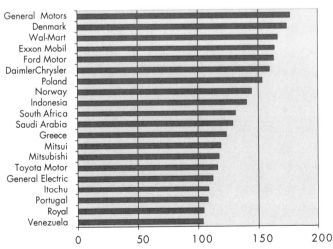

But countries still hold a few cards. In the fall of 2002, the Chinese government, for example, challenged global pharmaceutical companies to lower prices on AIDS drugs or they would allow generic versions to be produced and distributed in their country: They won the price concessions. We have also seen countries occasionally implement expropriation policies on MNCs or implement capital controls, while others sometimes default on debt obligations—interesting examples of flexing sovereign muscle (though not always to a country's benefit). While sovereignty cannot be written off completely, foreign influences are attacking it from more angles every day as globalization grows.

POLITICAL CHANGE AND CHALLENGE

It has been demonstrated throughout history, and all over the globe, that wealth creation breeds changes in expectations and capacities of governments. This is true for societies in the Biological, Material, and Experiential-trending phases. In lower income countries, governments struggle with meeting basic needs while setting the stage for future progress. While some have done it with little outside help, many have found that international assistance and pressure can help accelerate progress. With growing affluence, Material societies require their governments to provide institutions and rules to foster capitalism, encourage free markets and trade, assist in and maintain physical infrastructure, and develop human capital for further wealth creation. For the wealthiest strata, government provides support for the expression of the Experientials' individualized ideological agendas.

As wealth creation continues in all phases of development, governments will have to grapple with ever-changing domestic values and lifestyles in the modern world. Dealing with these rapid evolutions while competing in the global economy and managing international relationships will be major challenges for governments in the coming years.

5
Wealth and Religion:

Is God Dead?

Money is the wise man's religion.
Euripides (c. 480–406BCE)

My own mind is my own church.
Thomas Paine (1737–1809)

Roughly a century ago, philosopher Frederick Nietzsche proclaimed the death of God. But rather than dying, God—or at least organized religion—is changing rapidly to cater to Biological, Material, and Experiential lifestyles. It is intriguing that while religion is no longer at the center of most of our lives, there remains a strong need for spiritual expression in the modern world. As wealth has grown, religion has evolved from providing a public structure for daily life to satisfying private, spiritual needs, and its role may be intensifying—rather than withering—with economic progress.

While many have predicted that science and technology would rid the world of religious beliefs and practices, it appears that affiliation with organized religion is still prevalent, in varying degrees, in both wealthy and poorer countries. According to recent surveys, over 85% of the world's population identifies with a formal religion, whether it is Islam, Catholicism, Buddhism, Hinduism, Judaism, or one of many others (see Figure 5–1). Only 2.5% claim to be atheist, and 12.8% non-religious.

Figure 5-1   Most of the world identifies with an organized religion (percentage of the world's population, 1998).[1]

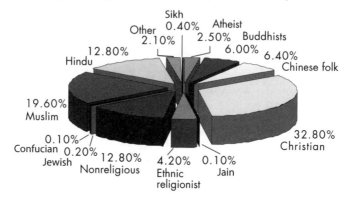

In the U.S., for example, 96% of the population claims to believe in God.[2] But while most Americans claim to be religious, many no longer attend services or actively participate in the religious groups and organizations that permeated life less than a century ago. This trend goes beyond the U.S.; in many wealthier parts of the world, the days when orthodoxy defined social relationships or dictated mores are long gone. Since industrialization and prosperity have taken hold in the West, it is increasingly prevalent for *individuals* to define the scope and meaning of their own spiritual faith and practice, whether it involves singing Catholic Jazz Vespers, going on a macrobiotic Buddhist retreat, or taking a trip to a local psychic.

The evolution of religion is clearly linked to the wealth and value shifts in history. While the trend has been toward greater secularization of many facets of life, this should not be perceived as growing atheism. Adherence to core religious beliefs has not diminished, but rather the form in which these beliefs are practiced has been modified to fit into the wealthier, modern, secular lifestyle.

As Figure 5-2 illustrates, the world's dominant religions are all more than 1,000 years old with few additions since wealth exploded. Most were invented in illiterate times, well before the Renaissance, Enlightenment, and Industrial Revolution. Note that there have been major revisions to these belief systems in the last century, taking into account that life is very different today than in the agrarian world that gave rise to them. As wealth grows and spreads, one would expect even greater evolutions and revolutions in the coming decades.

Figure 5-2   Wealth and religious trends, 1000BCE–2000CE.

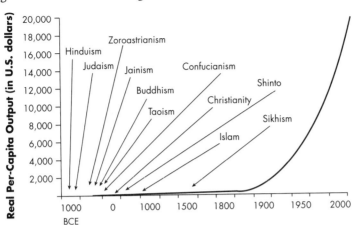

OLD-TIME RELIGION

In the agrarian world, religion plays an important role in ordering life; it is used to dictate virtually everything from political structure to legal authority and economic distribution. As Inglehart notes, during times of economic and physical uncertainty, people seek strict guidelines for behavior. Not surprisingly, in pre-industrialized European society, absolute religious values were imposed to insure order and stability: Charity and sharing were expected of the well-off; economic ambition was stigmatized as "greed"; the poor were taught to accept their place in the social hierarchy; and strict constraints on sexual behavior and the use of violence were in place.[3] People depended on these strict guidelines to make sense of an otherwise inhospitable world.

These religious norms extended into the legal framework. For example, the basic Judeo-Christian tenet "Thou shall not kill" (which has parallels in most religions and societies) attempts to control lawless violence. Likewise, commandments such as "Thou shall not commit adultery" and "Honor thy mother and father" served the purpose of protecting the agrarian family unit, which was once more important to economic and physical survival than it is today.[4]

In pre-industrial societies, one's social station was often determined at birth: noble, priest, warrior, slave, or serf.[5] The essential relationships of life were ruled by unbending standards based on a culture of religion. This strict hierarchy was passed down from generation to generation, socializing the young to conform.[6] Even for the wealthy, there were very few individual freedoms or social mobility. Many cultures went so far as to impose sumptuary laws, which forbade certain goods to certain classes of people (such as various fabrics, spices, and places to live), providing visible, external cues for all social interaction. Until the 19th Century, these laws were updated annually in England.[7]

Today, there are still Biological and early-stage Material societies that remain tied to strict religions traditions, thereby retarding market efficiencies and democratic progress. In countries such as Egypt and Libya, where religion pervades social interaction and political organization, economic progress has been minimal compared to more secular neighbors like Turkey. Some historians have suggested that the dominance of Catholicism in Mediterranean Europe through part of the 20th Century slowed economic progress in countries like Italy, Spain, and Portugal, as compared to countries less controlled by religion such as Germany and those in Scandinavia.

REVOLVING AROUND THE PAST: ISLAM IN THE MODERN WORLD

Islam is the world's fastest growing religion. The number of Muslims has doubled since 1970 to 1.2 billion, and may top 2 billion by 2025, just behind Christianity's 3 billion. Although usually associated with the Arabs of the Middle East, less than 15% of Muslims are, in fact, Arab. Muslim majorities can be found throughout the Middle East, North Africa, East Asia, and the Pacific Islands, with growing segments in Western Europe, the former Soviet Union, and North America.

Despite its surging numbers, Islam and Islamic countries have been slow to enter the modern wealth-culture world. With the exception of Turkey, Malaysia, and a few other non-oil-endowed states, most Muslim-dominant countries remain mired in economic stagnation. Why? Is the religion retarding growth?

Often, a primary hindrance to global economic participation of Islamic countries has been the fusion of religion and government. The Islamic state is a theocracy with rules and power located firmly in traditional religious centers. Ultimately, Islam has total jurisdiction over all aspects of each citizen's life[8] This rigid structure has not lent itself well to participatory democracy nor to self-determination and free will—key components to cultivating human captial. With the exception of several small petroleum export countries, most Islamic states lag in almost all socio-economic statistics.

Further, the modern practice of Islam is unfortunately rife with examples of sexism and oppression: Women are not allowed to attend mosques with men; male and female children are treated differently; and certain family laws allow the husband's rights to supersede those of his wife. Women are not allowed to become Muslim clerics or religious leaders. While some cite similar tendencies in other fundamentalist religious strains (including certain orthodox Judaic and Christian sects), they appear more pronounced and widespread in Islamic societies.[9]

Islamic fundamentalism's attractiveness lies in its promise of spiritual protection against the onslaught of what seems to be an unfriendly world. While Islam may be restrictive of growth and progress in its own ways, it is also a perceived respite from the harsh, competitive world of turbo-capitalism and secularization.[10] With such a world view, it may be difficult for the Islamic community to advance economically. Wealth catalysts such as developing human capital, comparative advantage and free trade, and sophisticated finance can be at odds with strict Islamic life. Human capital can be marginalized by clerical regimes, comparative advantage is often distorted by heavy state intervention by clergy, and finance is stifled by Islam's condemnation of *riba*, or interest, which is the basis of debt and finance. Without some Reformation-style modernization of the religion, the future prospects for Islam's integration into the wealthy world may be questionable.

RELIGION IN THE BIOLOGICAL WORLD

While secularization and prosperity have been mutually reinforcing in many parts of the world, religious-based social and political structures still show tremendous momentum and growth in lower income countries. In fact, religious developments in poorer parts of Latin America, Africa, and Asia illustrate how religion serves different needs and values based on wealth.

Professor Rosalind Hackett echoes Inglehart when she notes that religious outlets in Africa, for example, are thriving "because they help people *survive*, in all of the ways that people need to survive— social, spiritual, economic, finding a mate. People forget how critical that is. In Western academic circles it's very fashionable these days to talk about the value of ethnic identity and all that. But that's a luxury for people trying to feed families. To survive today in Africa people have to be *incredibly* mobile in search of work," and religious institutions "create broad trans-ethnic and trans-national communities, so

Older religions are practiced differently, reflecting the values of the practitioners in poorer countries versus wealthier ones.

that when somebody moves from city to city or country to country there's a sort of surrogate family structure in place."[11]

Even if the broader religion (i.e., Christianity, Islam) is the same, the ways in which these religions are practiced vary widely between poor countries and wealthier ones. Bringing to mind the values that Grondona and Inglehart believe categorize Biological societies, author Philip Jenkins notes: "The Christianity practiced in Africa, Latin America, and Asia tends to be much more rigidly conservative and traditional than that of the North, and its practitioners are often guided by a strong belief in the power of the supernatural to directly shape their lives."[12] In comparing wealthier countries' approach to Christianity versus the growing practice in poorer, Southern hemisphere countries, Jenkins adds, "The most successful Southern churches preach a deep personal faith, communal orthodoxy, mysticism, and puritanism, all founded on obedience to spiritual authority...Whereas Americans imagine a Church freed from hierarchy, superstition, and dogma, Southerners look back to one filled with spiritual power and able to exorcise the demonic forces that cause sickness and poverty."[13]

Even among countries of similar economic development, the evolution of religion is not at all homogenous. For example, Christianity in Latin America doesn't necessarily resemble that of East Asia. It may not even resemble itself *within* Latin America given so many different Christian sects. There are dozens of distinct Islamic groups around the world, with practices in Central Asia differing markedly from those in Africa. Buddhism now claims more than 200 strains, again with tenets and customs in Japan different from those in Vietnam. Then there are hundreds of religious cocktails that combine elements of many religious traditions. Brazilian-based Umbanda (with an estimated 20–35 million followers in 20 countries), for example, mixes native South American beliefs with African religion, pinches of Catholicism, and dashes of 18th Century French philosopher Allan Kardec. All scripture, it appears, is subject to interpretation.

What these religious practices in Biological societies do have in common, however, is that they support and foster the values of the

agrarian world: order, security, stability, and community, particularly where governments are ineffective in these areas. It is intriguing
how traditional formal religions—particularly Christianity and
Islam—have been cross-fertilized and incorporated into these
Biological-stage cultures, producing new variants. The large
Biological populations that are adopting and transforming these
ancient religions may ultimately exert far more control over their
future than traditional congregations.

SLOUCHING TOWARD SECULARIZATION

For industrialization and a culture of accumulation to thrive, the
dominance of religious order must give way. Indeed, a fundamental
aspect of modernization in many countries has been the separation
of church and state. While religious institutions can remain an
important spiritual and moral center for industrializing societies,
new forms of political and social space must be created to promote
the prosperity that industrialization makes possible.

A confluence of radically new ideas and events led to the secularization that marks the modern era. Ideas of the Enlightenment
freed humanity from a belief in the divine right of kings and the
privilege of the aristocracy. New political and economic theories led
to greater faith in free will and individual freedom. At the same
time, greater production and economic progress provided the
incentives for people to experiment with alternate forms of organization. Whereas rulers and other governing elites in Biological societies derived their power from a religious authority, in
industrializing societies, the idea that the bureaucratic institutions
of government existed to promote the best interests of the people
took hold, creating what Weber originally termed "Rational-Legal"
authority.[14] This shift in governmental authority occurred because,
as people gained greater control over their environment, they
placed less emphasis on religious traditions. With more people
improving their lives through market economics, many realized
that they didn't have to wait for an afterlife to be comfortable and
secure. Religion remained an important component of people's
lives, but its authority had shifted away from social order and
toward a more personal, spiritual value. No longer needed to
organize society and dictate behavior, religion became less public,
but no less important.

CHRISTIANITY: THE REFORMATION THAT KEEPS ON REFORMING

The secularization of Christian-dominated societies has been a central element of wealth creation and value transformation around the world since these places ignited the trend. Initially, Christianity was not particularly flexible: People were taught to accept whatever fate they were born into and that access to salvation was only through priests, the ultimate gatekeepers between heaven and hell. However, Christianity gradually secularized. The Protestant Reformation challenged the prevailing church dogmas and provided adherents with a direct link to God, forever altering the relationship between humankind and church. People were given the opportunity to exercise free will and self-determination. Breaking with the past, Protestants condoned economic accumulation and amassed fortunes. It is these factors, Weber argues, that allowed for the Industrial Revolution.

The ideas of the Enlightenment and scientific inquiry further expanded people's conceptions of order, rule, and religion, ultimately culminating in the final separation of church and state during the American and French Revolutions. Christianity has been further modernized through the inclusion of women into the clergy and high church offices in many (though certainly not all) branches. A notable exception is, of course, the Catholic Church, which does not ordain women as priests.

Today, Christianity is the world's largest religion and its reach has moved well beyond the confines of Europe and the New World. At the start of this new century, over 60% of all Christians were from Africa, Asia, and Latin America. Today, the average Christian is under 20 years old, Asian, and has a per-capita income of $600/year.[15] Christianity continues, in many ways, to be a reforming religion changed by its adherents around the world. The fastest growing form of Christianity is Pentacostalism, especially in Africa. In less than three generations, the movement has grown to 520 million, making it the second largest expression of Christian faith (after Roman Catholicism).[16] The *World Christian Encyclopedia* suggests that by 2050, more than one billion people may be affiliated with the movement.

Flexibility has been central to Christianity's success. Millions of people pick and choose certain aspects of the faith and combine them with native beliefs and rituals. In India, for example, Christian clergy wear the costume of the Hindu majority and incorporate Hindu rituals into their services. In Africa, witches and spirits that are part of traditional beliefs are incorporated into the practice of Christianity.[17]

While Christianity has certainly adapted over the centuries, there are still signs of conflict with the modern world. The

Catholic priest sex scandals that became highly publicized in 2002, for example, underscored the view of many that certain aspects of old religions—in this case, the celibacy of priests—may be outdated. It is interesting to note that such scandals have been reported less in Protestant parishes where clergy are allowed to marry and lead relatively modern lives.

The greatest developments in Christianity may yet occur as more Biological populations adopt and adapt the religion. Over time, argue some, these hybrid religions will come to dominate Christianity and its trajectory. As Philip Jenkins notes, "The center of gravity of the Christian world has shifted from Europe and the United States to the Southern hemisphere" because of high fertility rates. "So when American Catholics, for instance, talk about the necessity and the inevitability of reforms (reforms that Southern Catholics would most likely not condone), they do so without fully realizing that their views on the subject are becoming increasingly irrelevant, because the demographic future of their Church lies elsewhere."[18]

The U.S. Constitution institutionalized the separation of church and state based on the belief that a state bureaucracy was ultimately better at organizing society around production and accumulation. Once its success was demonstrated in the U.S., this belief had vast global implications as country after country sought to build non-religious institutions and governments capable of providing opportunity. In Turkey, for example, the efforts of Ata Turk in the 20th Century to separate church and state have led to a rapidly modernizing secular economy, one that aspires to be integrated into the EU and become part of the larger global wealth system.

RELIGION IN MATERIAL-TO-EXPERIENTIAL MIGRATION

Even in the wealthiest countries, where secularization has long been the standard, religion is not fading away, but rather, it is evolving rapidly. As populations have gotten wealthier, their values have changed and the religious institutions formed to support and reinforce those values have often changed as well. In Material societies, the erosion of religious social controls have created a vacuum largely filled by the state. Citizens to look toward their government to provide the economic, social, cultural, and often even moral compass for the nation.

This is a process that continues as countries move through the Material phase. When people feel secure both economically and socially, they are less prone to defer their own interests to a larger authority. As a result, citizens of the most developed nations resist both state and religious authority. This trend has allowed the pursuit of individual expression to supersede all other goals,[19] triggering a simultaneous decline in the importance of organized religion in everyday life and a rise in other forms of spirituality.

In the wealthiest nations of the world, church attendance and strict adherence to the tenets of organized religion have been falling precipitously. According to a University of Michigan international study on faith and values, released in January 2000, church attendance has been declining in the U.S. and many other industrialized nations for decades. The study shows that the percentage of Americans who reported going to church at least once a month dropped from 60% in 1981 to 55% in 1998.[20] Other surveys show that over the past 25 years, church attendance seems to have declined by 10–12%. In fact, when comparisons are made between survey responses and actual counts of members in the pews, it appears as though many people are "misremembering" if they really went to church the previous week; estimates of over-reporting are as high as 50%.[21]

At the same time, there has been a rise in the number of Americans who neither attend church nor claim affiliation with any religion at all. A survey of high school seniors in 1988 revealed that 9% never attended church services. By the late 1990s, this number had risen to 18%. Likewise, the number of Americans who say they have no traditional religious affiliation rose from 2% in 1967 to 11% by the 1990s.[22]

Similar trends can be found in other wealthy countries. In Australia, church attendance fell from 40% in 1981 to 25% in 1998, and in Finland it fell from a low 13% to 11%. Even in the traditionally Roman Catholic country of Spain, attendance fell from 53% to 38% in the same period.

Religion itself adapts, changing to fit the needs of its modern constituents.

Of the 19 industrialized nations surveyed, 15 showed declining rates of church attendance.[23] Since 1980, the Church of England has lost 27% of its membership, with comparable losses in the Catholic Church in England.[24] In response to declining attendance, religious institutions are changing to fit the needs of their modern constituents. In more and more churches, for example, music is upbeat and accompanied by a "praise band." These less formal services have also incorporated modern dance and drama. Many churches are adding mid-week and alternate times for worship rather than the standard Sunday morning service. Modern conveniences—like credit card machines conveniently located in church pews for instant donations—are also sprouting.[25] Many religious groups organize singles events and travel groups—and not necessarily denomination-specific. Many institutions invite lecturers to their houses of worship to discuss matters of general, non-denominational spiritual or secular interest.

These declines in attendance are a result of choice. People do not feel pressured to conform and they enjoy greater freedom to select their religious practices (or lack thereof). It is the ultimate sign that, at least in later-stage Material and Experiential populations, religion has been supplanted as the primary focal point of public life. People beyond the Biological phase do not need the rigorous order that religious authorities once imposed. Further, fewer people report that they find comfort and strength from organized religion or that the traditional church in their country is giving adequate answers to moral issues. The share of the American public who considered organized religion very important in their lives declined from 75% in the 1950s to 56% in the 1980s.[26] Similarly, when asked in the *Human Values Survey* "How important is God to your life?" 13 out of 19 developed countries posted declines from 1980 to 1990.[27]

LESS CHURCH, MORE PHILOSOPHY?

For many Experiential trenders, "religion" no longer needs to be an external structure or organization built around omnipotent beings. This does not signify a loss of spirituality in the wealthy world, but it may reflect the failure of established, organized religion to respond to changing needs and values. People moving from Material to Experiential phases are becoming increasingly interested in personal spiritual fulfillment. Rather than being processed through traditional rituals, people want individualized spiritual practices suited to their daily lives. According to Alan Wolfe, a sociologist at Boston University, the importance of self and individuality is behind the spirituality boom in late-stage Material and Experiential populations where people are looking at how faith and spirituality can help make them more effective, more fulfilled individuals.[28]

People in wealthy countries are increasingly turning to new outlets for spiritual rejuvenation amid the science-oriented, technology-dominated modern world. There are growing numbers of people exercising in ways that combine both spiritual and physical elements into an experience of religion. Recent surveys found that 25% of Americans regularly practice yoga, meditation, or other stress-reducing exercise,[29] and 55% consider nature to be "spiritual" or "sacred."

BUDDHISM: CO-OPTED BY THE WEALTHY WORLD?

While Buddhism has a short history in the West, it is a religious and philosophical tradition that stretches back over 2,500 years. Today, Buddhism has about 500 million adherents in the world, with the majority residing in East Asia. Buddhism is roughly based on the idea that people need to be "woken up" from a deep slumber that prohibits them from seeing and knowing what life really is. A Buddha (one who has woken up) teaches out of compassion for this suffering of beings and for the benefit and welfare of all beings.

The implications for a post-modern world are obvious: an individualized and personalized spiritual system that can coexist with other faiths. The Western incarnation of Buddhism seems to revolve around doing good and trying to better the world through personal responsibility and action. Modern Westerners are attracted to the faith's lack of rigid organization and strict rituals, although the restrictions on women Buddhist priests are somewhat surprising. There is no overarching church order that dictates when and how you practice. Meditation has also caught on as a way to connect with a larger spiritual sense.

Buddhism has found a popular outlet in Experiential parts of the U.S. where Americans, over the past 30 some years, have become increasingly attracted to non-Western religions. As a result, Buddhism has filtered into mainstream popular culture. It certainly has gotten strong popular endorsements from a string of American celebrities who claim to be practicing Buddhists. Some use their practice to promote issues of global concern: Richard Gere started the Tibet House and punk-rap band the Beastie Boys has been instrumental in the Tibetan Freedom Concerts. Perhaps it is its non-dogmatic nature, rationality, spiritual guidance, and opportunity for individual reflection and transformation that have made it so attractive. Indeed, these qualities instantly place Buddhism in the sights of post-modern experientialists who are seeking a more individual, holistic approach to life and perhaps spirituality.

While church attendance and the reported importance of "God" in life have declined, the *Human Values Survey* has shown that the importance of a different kind of spirituality actually rose in many industrialized nations. When asked "How often, if at all, do you think about the meaning and purpose of life?" there were marked increases in most industrial nations.[30] To prove the point, a Gallup poll released at the end of 1999 found that 7 out of 10 Americans believed that a person could be religious without going to church.[31] Another Gallup poll found that the percentage of Americans who said they felt a need "to experience spiritual growth" grew from 58% in 1994 to 78% in 1999.[32]

The rise of spirituality is not confined to the private realm; it has even extended to the workplace. Boeing and Xerox for example, are among the growing number of Fortune 500 companies that have hired consultants to cultivate the spiritual energies of their employees,[33] and some companies—like Shell Oil, for example—provide free yoga instruction and other meditation-oriented classes to their workers.[34] In wealthy societies with competition for highly skilled labor, companies are recognizing that employees may be interested in more than stock options and higher wages. To attract and retain these employees, many companies are actually using spiritual "perks" as part of a total compensation package.

Additionally, Experiential trenders are feeling more freedom to combine aspects from different religious traditions, as well as pop culture, into a spiritual system customized for their own needs, says Berkeley professor Wade Clark Roof, author of *Spiritual Marketplace*. In the book, which explores the effects of the baby boomers on American religious tradition, Roof notes that the biggest change in religion in recent years is the emphasis on individualized "spirituality": "It's the new lingua franca. It's the experiential nature aspect of religion, something deeply felt. Each person seems to have his or her own, and that has an incredibly wide appeal." While Wade does not suggest this is "The Great Awakening," he notes that to "dismiss it as New Age psychobabble is a mistake."[35]

One of the more provocative theories regarding the new variations of religion and wealth is Rodney Stark's concept of "religious economy." Stark argues that individuals buy into a religion like any other consumer good. In a "free-market religious economy"—particularly wealthier Material and Experiential economies that promote religious plurality and tolerance—there is a ready supply of choice: "The more competition there is, the higher the level of consumption. This would explain the often remarked paradox that the United States is one of the most religious countries in the world but also one of the strongest enforcers of a separation between Church and State."[36]

For a free marketeer, such a theory has great appeal. This analysis does not diminish the seriousness with which people choose their spiritual path, but it helps illuminate how so many variations of Christianity, for example, can flourish like so many styles of tennis shoes or movie genres. It fits neatly with Fukuyama, Maslow, and Inglehart's common ideas about rising individuality with wealth. Indeed, it is an intriguing notion that explains the rise of diverse new religious movements like Scientology, among others, and the general spirituality boom in wealthier countries.

JUDAISM AND THE MODERN WORLD

Judaism is the oldest of the world's major monotheistic religions. It's also the smallest, with only about 18 million followers around the world. Most Jews live in either the U.S. or Israel, with the remaining spread largely across industrialized countries. More than 90% of the Jewish population lives a Material or Experiential life.

The longevity of Judaism may very well be due to its remarkable flexibility, pragmatism, and adaptability. Judaism focuses on life *in the here and now*. As such, adherents concentrate on their current choices rather than on esoteric concepts of heaven and hell or a clearly defined afterlife. In many ways, Judaism's focus on personal responsibility, individualism, and life in the present, rather than the afterlife, made it particularly receptive to the changing social climate brought on by industrialization.[37]

Many branches of Judaism are also quite flexible regarding ritual and overt religious practice. In fact, many people regard themselves as being Jewish without taking part in many religious practices, or even accepting the core beliefs of Judaism, because they identify themselves with the Jewish people and follow the general customs of secular Jewish life. A recent study reports that even among people who identify Judaism as their religion, 42% profess a secular outlook and 14% say that they don't believe in God.

Much of the Jewish population has also been remarkably urban-centered and has participated and benefited from the wealth creation process of the modern era. High rates of intermarriage and assimilation may also play a part in the cosmopolitan tolerance for things foreign and different.

Like all modern religions, Judaism has its inner conflicts as tradition butts heads with modernity. There are various sects of Judaism; some are more conservative than others. Extremely Orthodox Jews, for example, question the legitimacy of various Reform movements. These differences have led to sometime violent clashes, namely in Israel over the ultimate shape of the Jewish state. Moreover, there is a boiling crisis in Israel over whether the country will remain a "Jewish" state or a secular democracy in the wake of the growing Palestinian population. It will be interesting to see how this ancient theology adapts under such modern tribulations, the latest in a long history of conflicts and challenges.

RELIGIOUS CONFLICT IN THE WEALTHIER WORLD

Despite the rise in individualized spirituality and the shift toward greater secularization in much of the world, there are areas of the world that retain a tight connection to strict, traditional religious structures, sometimes to the point of extremism. Threatened by the global erosion of traditional lifestyles, these extremists can be moved to radical, violent action.[38]

This is even more obvious now in the wake of the September 11th attacks on the World Trade Center and the Pentagon. The intersection of traditional religious and modern secular lifestyles will undoubtedly continue to cause conflict in the coming decades. Samuel Huntington suggests that major future clashes will be along cultural and religious lines.[39] Huntington postulates that there are nine civilizations—the West, Sinic, Japanese, Orthodox, Muslim, Buddhist, Hindu, Latin, and African—and that some will collide as economic integration brings people and ideas into more frequent contact. These conflicts, he argues, will not be diffused through economic commonalties, but will persist and cause increasing fragmentation. Similar thoughts are echoed by Zbigniew Brzezinski, former U.S. National Security Adviser, who sees "religious extremism" as an important component to international relations in this new century.[40]

Jenkins actually sees an impending showdown between Christianity and Islam in the near future as both are making huge gains in the world's fast-growing, Biological populations. He believes that there are not only cross-border tensions between these two religions, but maybe even more *within* a country's borders. Jenkins cites looming conflicts in large populations like Nigeria, Indonesia, and the Philippines, where Christian–Muslim anxieties run high.[41]

Within the U.S., there has been a persistent battle over religious issues, including violent anti-abortion movements and a campaign to allow prayer in public schools.[42] Some extremist religious groups deny the authority of any outside governmental entity, such as the Branch Davidians, whose armed resistance resulted in the 1996 Waco tragedy. In Asia, Japan has dealt with the well-publicized AUM Shinrikyo movement, which launched the sarin gas attacks in 1995 that killed eight and injured others.

REVOLUTIONS OR EVOLUTIONS?

Regardless of all the wealth and progress over the last century, religion has not disappeared. In fact, the wealthier world has seen religion and spirituality proliferate, as one writer notes, "in both intensity and variety. New religions are springing up everywhere. Old ones are mutating with Darwinian restlessness."[43] Everywhere—in the Biological, Material, and Experiential worlds—religion and spirituality seem far from static, and this dynamism has the potential to cause great conflict.

Will the world spiral out of control through religious collisions? Probably not. It is true that industrialization and secularization have drastically diminished the rigid religious standards of agrarian days. However, this very phenomenon has left open possibilities for new values and traditions, with greater tolerance for ethnic and cultural differences and individual choice. As British sociologist Colin Campbell has written, "Ironically enough it could be that the very processes of secularization which have been responsible for the 'cutting back' of the established forms of religion have actually allowed 'hardier varieties' to flourish."[44]

6
Wealth and Education:

Reading, Writing, and Riches

As knowledge spreads, wealth spreads.
President Rutherford B. Hayes (1822–1893)

Education costs money, but so does ignorance.[1]
Sir Claus Moser (1990)

The capacities to conceive of and implement new ideas drive all spheres of human progress, and cultivating these capacities is the goal of education. How populations are educated, therefore, will determine a country's economic potential and trajectory. This correlation between education and prosperity has made schooling a priority in most Biological, Material, and Experiential populations. Over the past century, more people—in both absolute numbers and percentages of populations—have received better, more sophisticated education. Soaring primary and secondary school rates, widespread literacy, and more advanced degrees underscore this triumph. The net results: a far more knowledgeable, cosmopolitan, and inclusive world than the one into which our grandparents were born.

As you can see from Figure 6–1, formal and higher education are fairly modern constructs. University and general public education have accelerated only in the last 200 years, which has coincided with a corresponding spike in global output. Without advances in education, much of the wealth creation in the last century—particularly in the technology component—would have never coalesced.

105

Figure 6-1   Wealth and education trends, 2000BCE–2000CE.

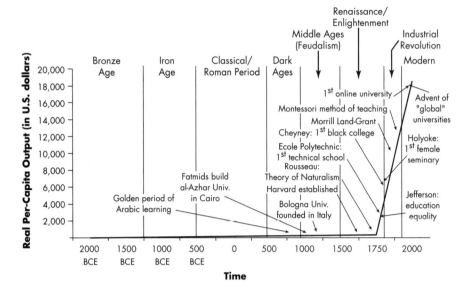

Data suggests that better educated populations are richer and healthier; live longer; and tend to participate more economically, politically, and socially in their communities. Education correlates with virtually all measures in the UN's HDI (see Table 6–1). Countries with the highest tertiary enrollment rates—Canada, U.S., Australia, Finland, Norway, and recently South Korea—are all among the wealthiest. On the flip side, the least literate countries are among the world's poorest: Niger, Sierra Leone, Burkina Faso, Afghanistan, Benin, Ethiopia, Mali, Haiti, and Bangladesh.[2] Little or no education can doom large populations to a cycle of poverty.

Given these numbers, it is of little surprise that people around the world are calling for better educational opportunities. During the 2000 World Education Forum in Dakar, 180 countries pledged to provide universal, quality primary education within 15 years.[3] The implicit understanding is that education is an essential precursor to wealth creation: Studies have suggested that the investment return on primary education is a remarkable 27% per annum.[4]

Recent history is sprinkled with examples of countries that combined the right blend of education policies to gain a foothold in the global economy. This process was illuminated by the East Asian success stories beginning in the 1970s. Central to their growth formula was a strong state commitment to cultivating human capital through schooling. In fewer than 15 years, South Korea, Taiwan, Singapore, and Hong Kong achieved universal primary schooling and earmarked substantial funding (both public and private) for universities. They sought well-qualified teachers and paid them competitive salaries to ensure quality. Moreover, they developed technical knowledge through ongoing training, vocational programs, and research institutes for scientists and engineers.[5] The educational strategies of these countries successfully fueled economic growth, helping them industrialize in less than 30 years, more than twice as rapidly as most Western nations. See Figure 6–2 for south Korea's enrollment rates.

Hand in hand with economic development is more access to better education—a truly cyclical process.

Many developing nations have strived to emulate the East Asian model, but mass education is not a simple proposition for even wealthy countries. Obviously, the poorest countries—where education is needed most—have the greatest difficulties implementing it. In traditional Biological societies with low output levels, education takes a backseat to survival needs such as food and shelter. As Table 6–1 shows, all measures of educational attainment (and virtually

Table 6-1   Wealth, Education, and Many Human Development Factors Are Linked, as Shown by the UN's Human Development Index (HDI) (2001)

	Adult Literacy (%)	Combined First-, Second-, and Third-Level Gross Enrollment (%)	Real GDP per Capita (PPP$)	Life Expectancy at Birth	Education Index	GDP Index	HDI
U.S.	99	96	24,680	76.1	0.98	0.99	0.94
Japan	99	78	20,660	79.6	0.92	0.98	0.93
Sweden	99	80	17,900	78.3	0.93	0.98	0.93
Mexico	89	65	7,010	71	0.81	0.96	0.845
Thailand	93.6	54	6,350	69.2	0.81	0.95	0.832
Turkey	81.1	62	4,210	66.7	0.75	0.69	0.711
Indonesia	82.9	61	3,270	63	0.76	0.53	0.641
Kenya	75.7	56	1,400	55.5	0.69	0.22	0.473
Cambodia	35	30	1,250	51.9	0.33	0.19	0.325
Mozambique	37.9	25	640	46.4	0.34	0.09	0.261
Afghanistan	29.8	18	800	43	0.26	0.12	0.229

Figure 6-2   Education and wealth: South Korean enrollment rates versus economic growth, 1966–1995.[6]

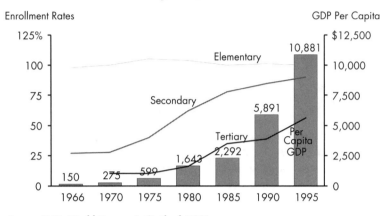

Source: IMF, World Economic Outlook 2001

every other measure of progress) for Biological countries are significantly lower than those in Material countries.

Even for societies in the Material and Experiential-trending stages of development with near-universal primary and secondary enrollment and high college-level attendance, there is still room for growth and improvement. For ongoing wealth creation, populations need to continually refine their skills and boost productivity. With growing competition from new Material workforces in Asia and other parts of the world, high-income countries must constantly move forward to stay on the cusp of new technologies and innovations. Because of successful educational reform, many former "body" countries are now growing "heads." In Taiwan, for example, the population has moved effectively from low-skill assembly into more value-added services and technology. At the same time, in China, former agricultural workers are learning how to assemble computers and college-educated Chinese are writing sophisticated software. At each level of economic development, new knowledge is essential to climbing the rungs. Everywhere, education is a race with no finish line.

Because of successful educational reform, many former "body" countries are now growing "heads."

Education and economic development spin another virtuous cycle: As people gain more economic independence and free time due to learning, their ability to cultivate more education grows. The democratization of schooling has been one of the most important

Table 6-2   Education for Advanced Economies, 1820–1992 (Years of Education per Person Aged 16–64 [Average for Both Sexes])[7]

	U.S.	France	Germany	Netherlands	UK	Japan
1820	1.75	n.a.	n.a.	n.a.	2.00	1.50
1870	3.92	n.a.	n.a.	n.a.	4.44	1.50
1913	7.86	6.99	8.37	6.42	8.82	5.36
1950	11.27	9.58	10.40	8.12	10.60	9.11
1973	14.58	11.69	11.55	10.27	11.66	12.09
1992	18.04	15.96	12.17	13.34	14.09	14.87

developments of the modern wealth creation era. As Table 6–2 illustrates, in the early 1800s, only the super-rich in the wealthiest countries had the time and money to learn to read and write; Americans averaged fewer than two years of formal education in 1820, and fewer than four by 1880.[8] But, the emergence of new economic, social, and political ideas in the Industrial Age spurred mass education. Like industrialization itself, this process started in the West, but has since spread to developing countries around the world.

FIRST STEPS

Low schooling levels and illiterate populations consign many Biological societies to the periphery of the global economy, and hinder domestic social progress as well. Literacy, for example, improves all aspects of society, not just the economy in isolation. In addition to combating disease and improving health and hygiene, education creates a progressive mindset and culture. As Grondona noted, it functions as an important social leveler, nurtures inquisitiveness and creativity, and fosters greater self-expression and satisfaction. Universal primary school enrollment, therefore, must be a fundamental goal of Biological societies seeking to end the cycle of economic and social stagnation.

It bears noting that in many Biological societies, women have little or no access to education. In India, for example, there is a 16.6% difference between the school enrollment of girls and boys aged 6–14. Closing the gender gap in education is crucial because, aside from the obvious advantages to the women themselves, female education has been tied to improving domestic health, particularly reproductive health and child welfare through knowledge about immunizations and nutrition. Education for women may also increase condom use, a necessity for the containment of AIDS. Greater female schooling also correlates with lower fertility rates and lower infant mortality, which accelerate industrialization and wealth creation. A child in Africa, for example, born to an uneducated mother, has a 20% chance of dying before the age of five; this risk drops to 12% for a child with an educated mother.[9] Moreover, schooled women have a greater ability to enter the formal workforce and contribute to the economy as well as participate in the political and social life of their community.

EDUCATION AND ECONOMIC DYNAMISM

Education—the cultivation of human capital—is perhaps the one investment that developing countries may need to stress above all. Take a look at the world's most populous nations, China and India. In some aspects, they have a lot in common. Both boast ancient civilizations, spicy cuisines, nuclear missiles, diverse populations of over one billion people, and possibly limitless economic potential. They also share many problems: mass poverty, growing urban/rural divides, oppressive bureaucracies, and widespread corruption.

But economically speaking, China has surged ahead. In the late 1980s, India and China had roughly the same GDP per capita. Today, China's GDP per capita is twice that of India's. China's stock market, too, is perceived as more attractive than India's. The market cap of China Mobile, the country's most valuable company, equals 45% of the total value of the Indian stock market. Due to its large market capitalization, China is on most global fund managers' radar screens, with India lagging in this respect. At least part of this difference can be attributed to education: China boasts an 81% literacy rate versus India's 54%, and higher enrollment rates. China's more educated workforce has provided for greater economic dynamism as workers have been able to rapidly fill jobs ranging from low-skill manufacturing to high-skill computer programming. While India's software expertise is well-known, China is not far behind. In 2001, Indian software sales totaled $6 billion versus China's $850 million. However, for 2002, Chinese software will top $1.9 billion and will continue to grow briskly. Based on some optimistic estimates from the Gartner Group, by 2006, the Chinese should catch up to the Indian software sector, and both are projected to sell a remarkable $27 billion each.[10]

From 1977–1997, the number of Chinese enrolling in higher education grew from approximately 500,000 to more than 3 million.[11] In 2001, Chinese universities granted 465,000 science and engineering degrees, comparable to what U.S. universities are producing. By 2004, China may be the world's second largest microchip producer. The country is also making strides in the biotech industry, with Chinese research teams being among the first to decode the rice genome.[12]

Foreign companies are clamoring to enter China, not only to gain access to the huge pool of relatively skilled cheap labor, but also to market to the growing middle class of consumers. China has been able to attract large amounts of foreign direct investment, possibly 15–20 times what India has attracted.

Of course, a host of other government policies, geography, and cultural factors have undoubtedly also contributed to these different development paths. But it is important to note that China's broader educated population has adapted much faster to the 21st Century's economic realities.

The persistence of child labor in many Biological countries is another obstacle to achieving universal education. Many families in poor countries need children to work rather than go to school—this is a harsh reality. Apart from the brutal effects on the children themselves, child labor fosters a vicious poverty cycle by condemning a population to low-skill work due to lack of education. In countries with large pools of cheap, unskilled labor, technological advances are delayed: A seemingly endless supply of low-wage workers does not encourage industry to undertake the expense of technological upgrades. When children are employed, fertility rates remain high, and populations swell, making universal education even more costly. To break this cycle, governments with large Biological populations must promote universal education from an early age. In one study, it was found that countries with greater policy emphasis on education and stricter child labor laws were able to reduce fertility rates, industrialize quicker, and develop better long-term income equality.[13]

Another continuing problem for many developing countries is the conflict between traditional local customs and modern education. To engage in the world economy, certain skills and social values are imperative. When government resources for public schooling are unavailable, however, fundamentalist groups often offer the only accessible education. For example, for centuries, the Maddrassas (Koranic) schools in Muslim societies have filled educational voids left by governments, but have failed to impart the practical knowledge and skills critical for social and economic success. They have also excluded women from the process entirely. There may be as many as 6,000–10,000 Islamic

> A continuing problem for many developing countries is the conflict between traditional local customs and modern education.

Madrassas around the world, with an estimated 600,000 students in Pakistan, 1.5 million in India, 3 million in Bangladesh, and many more throughout the Middle East.[14] Some Muslim countries are trying to modernize, but the process has not always been smooth. In Egypt, for example, there is a consensus that liberal education is a vital vehicle for national development, but there is no agreement about its form: The general population favors traditional Islamic-based programs, while Western-educated policy-makers want a more modern approach. After a 1992 fundamentalist challenge to the state, the government has tried to use public education to expose children to more globalized, secular culture with the hopes of creating a more economically competitive population.[15]

QUANTIFIABLE PROGRESS

Despite the confounding odds against poorer countries, there have been striking gains over the last two decades. Primary school enrollment rates in the lowest income countries, for example, increased 13 percentage points from 1980–1997. Global progress has also been made with respect to women's education, literacy, and school enrollment statistics (see Figure 6–3).

Figure 6-3   Female literacy rates, 1970–2000: growing in the poorest regions of the world.[16]

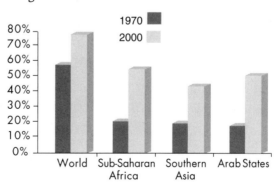

This learning progress is paying off. The World Bank estimates that every year of schooling has increased wages (for men and women both) by a worldwide average of almost 10%.[17] Studies from Cote d'Ivoire and Peru show that people with higher degrees garner higher wages, not only because of the knowledge they acquired at school, but also because having *gone* to school at all shows commitment and a work ethic.[18] In Thailand, the major economic transformation of the latter 20th Century coincided with an equally massive education boom: Between 1965 and 1995, real per-capita income quadrupled while primary and secondary enrollments rose (secondary rates more than tripled), the gender gap narrowed, and public spending on education rose to over 4% of GNP. This growth in education was both cause and effect of the Thai economy's shift from agriculture to manufacturing. According to the World Bank, in 1963, one-third of the economy was agricultural; by 1997 it was less than 10%, while manufacturing doubled from 14–28% of GNP.

But serious effort—both public and private—is required to build and foster domestic education. Unfortunately, even if countries have extra money and resources, politicians may not always choose to spend them on schooling, since education is a long-term process with benefits accruing largely in the future. It is far easier to spend money on large-gestured, public projects—like building dams or roads—with immediate results. This is a problem even in the wealthier countries such as the U.S., where long-term educational investments may not pay off during short political terms.

Although global schooling rates are rising, the knowledge gap that separates the super-rich from the ultra-poor is also widening: While Americans are attending postgraduate training programs in record numbers, children in Benin barely complete primary school. Concerned with potential global instability rooted in this educational gap, many international organizations and countries have been increasingly committed to the cause of universal education regardless of national boundaries. A growing number of international groups are working to this end, including non-governmental organizations (NGOs), private-sector groups, multilateral institutions, governments, and individuals. In Haiti, for example, virtually all education is provided through NGOs and religious organizations. In Ghana, the December 31 Women's Movement, also partially funded by NGOs, has been instrumental in promoting education for the very young because the government lacks the financial means to do so.[19]

Many countries realize that a well-educated population is essential for engagement with the global economy and for attracting investment and foreign capital. It is a lesson that has helped many nations progress to the Material phase. Data from the World Bank and the World Education Forum suggest that governments in developing countries are placing a higher priority on primary education than in the 1980s. Public spending on primary education in relation to GNP increased in almost all parts of the world between 1990 and 1998 (the exceptions are central and western Africa and central Asia).[20]

Brazil, for example, increased its primary school retention rates in the 1990s through its government's multi-pronged approach.[21] The Ministry of Education redistributed fiscal resources to the most impoverished and underserved areas, and established a yearly per-pupil spending floor to bridge some of the gaps in education around the country. The Ministry also set national standards and curriculum with greater emphasis on teacher training. Moreover, in a bold move, the state actually provided cash—approximately $40 per month per child—for families who would otherwise need to pull children out of school to work. Brazil's success has been impressive: In less than 10 years, primary school completion rates have risen from 50–75%.[22]

In many Material countries, where per-capita output exceeds $5,000 per year, primary enrollment rates are at or near 100%. With this sort of human capital, economies are able to shift easier from agriculture to greater industry and service orientations. People are able to adapt and reallocate resources based on economic opportunity, since workers with more education tend to be more flexible and take more risks.[23] As a result, education helps promote new industries and businesses, and can create the environment and willingness to innovate and change, the essential foundation of the economic and social dynamism needed to promote wealth.

As progress is made at the primary and secondary school levels, many countries are looking toward higher education and specialization. As illustrated in Figure 6–4, in some middle-income countries, the average years in school have risen from less than 5 in 1950 to more than 10 in 2000. More schooling means greater skills and higher earning potential, which boost the ability to plan for the future and create a culture of economic optimism. That is, with more education, people can begin to see a path to advancing themselves and their families socio-economically. Education begins to erode the "peasant culture," replacing it with the foresight and tools to improve life.

Figure 6-4   Average years in school for adults aged 16–64[24] (select
countries, 1950–1992).

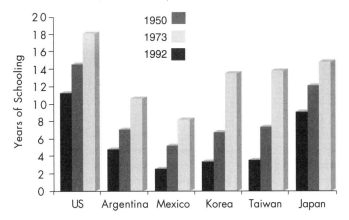

It should be no surprise that the greatest gains in education—
made notably in East Asia—generated the largest economic and
human development gains.

In East Asia (especially Taiwan, South Korea, Singapore, and
Hong Kong), for example, students are capitalizing on two generations of educational progress by improving their technological skills.
Fifty years ago, these "body" countries cut and sewed for a living.
One generation later, they progressed to assembling electronics,
computers, and microchips, relying on "head" countries for
research, development, and product innovation. Through education,
these countries today have grown their own "heads": They have
active research and development themselves, and now create and
refine high-tech products. East Asian tertiary enrollment rates in

Figure 6-5   Recent percentage of college enrollment in technical
fields.[25]

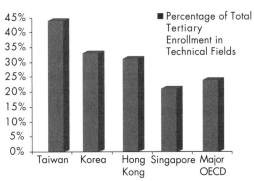

technical fields today (e.g., mathematics, computer science, and engineering) are surprisingly ahead of those in the OECD, as shown in Figure 6–5.

EDUCATION, DEMOCRACY, AND GOVERNANCE

Just as wealth and education are symbiotic, so too are education and governance. A well-educated population is an important component of stable regimes and strong civil society, and at the same time, government policy and involvement are critical in building and maintaining a modern education system.

Governments have not always dominated the education landscape: For much of human history, education was taken care of in the home with little or no formal schooling. But today, governments are generally the largest single source of funds for schools and they are the largest education providers. Public sources account for well over half of education spending in developing countries. Most governments generally spend 10–20% of their budgets on education (3–7% of GNP). This includes regulation and curriculum guidelines, standards for accrediting institutions, monitoring school and teacher performance, and issuing guidelines about standards and reform.

Education is thought by most political scientists to be an important prerequisite for stable democracy: Countries with higher primary schooling and smaller gender gaps in education tend to enjoy greater democracy while autocrats reign in places with low levels of education. Algeria, Sierra Leone, Liberia, Nigeria, and Sudan all rank at the bottom for educational indicators and all have undemocratic regimes in power. There are important exceptions such as Cuba; but on the whole, the lack of an educated population allows dictators to stay in power. Education and literacy are crucial in helping citizens develop the skills to participate in, or demand, a democratic government.

BEYOND THE BASICS

The acknowledged value of education is reflected in the higher wages enjoyed by more educated populations. The wage premium associated with tertiary education nearly tripled in the U.S. and UK between 1980 and 1996 and doubled in Canada.[26] Populations are now chasing these higher wages more than ever before. In late-stage Material countries, where primary and secondary enrollment rates are virtually complete, tertiary-level education continues to expand. In the OECD, the proportion of adults with college degrees has almost doubled over the past 25 years and now exceeds 41%. In the U.S., jobs that require tertiary education are now increasing faster that those that do not.[27] The U.S. Department of Education estimates that total college enrollment will grow from approximately 12.5 million students in 1987 to 17.7 million by 2011.[28]

Similar trends can be found in other late-stage Material countries. In the EU, for example, higher education enrollment grew from 5.6 million students in the 1975/76 school year to more than 12.2 million by the 1996/97 period.[29] In Japan, from 1960–2000, tertiary enrollment grew from approximately 600, 000 to nearly 4 million.[30]

In wealthier countries, education is also becoming increasingly *transnational* in scope as globalization becomes more and more pervasive. Part of this has been fueled by ever-cheapening transportation and communication. In high school, programs like American Field Services send more than 10,000 students and teachers abroad for educational experiences.[31] Most U.S. four-year colleges now offer semesters-abroad programs or accept transfer credits from accredited sponsor schools. According to one survey, perhaps 100,000 American college or graduate students study and/or work in foreign countries.[32] Some Material families, often from nations with large Biological populations, are sending their children abroad to receive education not easily found at home, primarily to English-speaking countries like Canada, the U.S., Australia, and Britain. Governments often support this effort with scholarships. In 2001, the U.S. hosted more than 514,000 foreign college students, comprising 4% of the overall student enrollment.[33]

With healthy life expectancy increasing by some 30 years in the last three generations, education in late-stage Material populations is being seen more and more as a lifelong process. One common strategy is to begin formal education earlier, a movement that has accelerated in recent decades. Approximately 64% of 3- and 4-year-olds in America, for example, went to preschool in 2000 as opposed to 5% in 1964.[34] Not all of these children attended private preschools. Head Start, a federally funded program geared to increase American children's school readiness with comprehensive child development programs beginning from prenatal stages to age 5, was established in 1965 to help economically disadvantaged children. The program actually goes beyond pure education and tries to support health (sometimes paying for dental, medical, mental health, and nutrition costs) and strengthen parental support for young children.[35] According to the National Institute for Early Education Research (NIEER), the program now has nearly four decades of experience and studies have found lasting improvements in a variety of areas from grade repetition, to special education, to high school graduation rates.[36] The U.S. has actually lagged behind much of Europe in early education. In 1991, France already had nearly 100% of their 3- and 4-year-olds in preschool, and more than 35% of their 2-year-olds, compared to 49%, 39%, and less than 5% for similar-aged American children at that time.[37]

At the other end of the age spectrum, many adults are returning to college and graduate school, driven by the higher value placed on education in the modern service economy. Most universities around the world now offer continuing education programs for those trying to keep up in their respective fields. People also enroll in extension courses and evening workshops, either to acquire new skills or just to follow up on an interest or hobby. Even older citizens are seeking to expand their education through enrollment in so-called "Elderhostels." Senior citizens can choose from over 10,000 institutions that host seniors and teach diverse subjects ranging from traditional liberal arts and sciences, to skills-oriented classes like computing, to highly specialized hobbies and interests such as gemology, cooking, and even astronaut training. In 2001, more than 250,000 seniors enrolled in Elderhostel programs in over 100 countries.[38]

ONLINE COURSES— TECHNOLOGY AND EDUCATION

Technology has had a profound impact on education. Twenty-five years ago, computers were rare sights on American college campuses. Today, they're everywhere, with many colleges requiring students to purchase a computer before they enroll. Laptops are increasingly common. In many Material countries, computers are even ubiquitous in most primary and secondary schools.

There is little doubt that technology can facilitate the democratization of education. Thanks to the development of online courses, enrollments at the tertiary level are increasing. Although off-site learning is nothing new, with British universities offering such degrees even in the 19th Century, the Internet has brought "correspondence courses" to an entirely different level. By one estimate, over one million Americans are currently enrolled in for-credit online courses, including urban and rural students, working single mothers, and busy executives. There are courses offered by an ever-widening range of institutions, from junior colleges to elite universities such as Stanford.[39]

A World Bank report on tertiary education estimates that in 2000, there were over 3,000 specialized institutions dedicated to online training in the U.S. alone. They have also been emulated around the world. The Mexican Virtual University of Monterey offers some 15 masters degrees using teleconferencing and the Internet to reach 50,000 students around Latin America. There are also 15 virtual universities in South Korea that service almost 15,000 students.[40] UNISA in South Africa has offered distance learning since 1946 and now has more than 25,000 students.

Virtual education breaks down the spatial barriers that can limit educational opportunity. This is particularly important in impoverished countries where education is not readily available, or where qualified faculty have fled. For example, the African Virtual University was established to train professionals in Africa to share high-quality teachers and materials with underserved communities in sub-Saharan Africa. In many cases, the virtual classroom gives them a chance to provide much needed training in healthcare, business management, science, technology, and other professional skills essential to economic development in the region.

AMERICA AT THE EDUCATIONAL CROSSROADS

Growing global economic competition and the acknowledgement that education drives further prosperity have inspired wealthier countries to critically examine the content and delivery of public education. In smaller homogenous countries, such as those in northern Europe, the common use of national standards, funding, and curriculum are relatively manageable and amenable to frequent reform. However, in countries where educational standards are localized, maintaining national competitiveness through public education poses greater challenges. This is particularly evident in the U.S., where local property tax-based funding for public schools has created disparate educational experiences across its population. The learning gap between students in wealthy suburbs and poorer urban centers has long been at crisis levels.

Many American public schools, particularly those in resource-stressed urban areas, have deteriorated amid overcrowding, funding battles, entrenched school boards, and lack of accountability. Parents dissatisfied with their local institutions have spearheaded a movement of "charter schools," public schools that are authorized and funded by the state but are designed and operated by professional educators, parents, community leaders, and educational entrepreneurs. Charter schools must meet the terms of their own public mandates, as well as all state requirements. If they do not, unlike traditional public schools, they are immediately closed. Less than a decade after the first charter school opened its doors, there are now more than 2,700 in the U.S.[41] Some charter programs have been shown to successfully educate children underserved by traditional public schools, and they are providing more instructional time and innovative curricula in a cost-effective manner.[42]

Charter schools try to promote three principles in public education: autonomous curriculum and management, accountability, and school choice. In terms of autonomy, charter schools fuse community inputs and produce programs from a clean-slate perspective. While accountable to educational standards, they are free to experiment without bureaucratic red tape. The charter school experience is also driven by individual choice; both teachers and students choose a charter school based on what it offers, with a critical consumer mindset. In the traditional American public school system, a student's geography determines which school he or she attends and therefore the quality of the education received. By contrast, the charter school movement seeks to offer students and teachers an array of options to be evaluated.

Choice is also the essence of the school "voucher" debate in America. Under such programs, students receive vouchers that may be used to pay for a variety of public or private schools in their home areas. Parents get to evaluate and select the school that best fits their child's needs. In 2002, a landmark Supreme Court decision held that Cleveland, Ohio's school choice program was constitutional, which may pave the way for other states to push forward with voucher-based programs.[43] In a 1999 Manhattan Institute study, 66% of voucher parents were "very satisfied" with their school's academic quality versus less than 30% of traditional public school parents.[44]

U.S. educational change is also seen in the alliance of the private sector with the public in reforming education. Businesses in particular are offering more support. Companies such as Microsoft and Apple are sponsoring school-based learning activities that teach basic computer skills to families. In one academic year, for example, Microsoft organized Family Technology Night in 30 cities, providing free one-hour computer seminars.[45] Many charter schools have been founded by wealthy entrepreneurs with an avid interest in improving the nation's educational system, and some are managed by private operators like Victory Schools of New York City.

Even in school systems that are performing adequately, many U.S. parents opt to augment public school education at their own expense. Based on much of the same reasoning behind Head Start, private pre-kindergarten programs and nursery schools have flourished over the last two decades. Parents are also bolstering public school educations with a myriad of extracurricular activities, from private music and art classes, to highly organized sports leagues, to private academic tutoring and academic test preparation. All of these efforts are made to give children a competitive edge that the average U.S. public school may not provide. One would expect this trend to expand globally, as parents try to help their children best prepare for the future, regardless of their geography.

Because U.S. public schools are largely financed locally with property tax receipts, families with sufficient resources have always been able to "choose" a public school by choosing where to live. A glance at suburban real-estate listings reveals that school districts are a major factor in American home sales. Well-funded, high-performing school districts command higher home prices, which in turn further expand the property tax revenue base. With higher per-capita spending, these wealthier school systems tend to have smaller classes, better facilities, more enriched curricula, and greater parent participation.

There are also a growing group of U.S. parents who bypass public schools entirely by enrolling their children in independently managed private schools. In the 1999/2000 academic year, these schools accounted for 24% of all U.S. schools and approximately 10% of its students.[46] According to the U.S. Department of Education, the primary reason parents choose to educate children privately is a function of size: On average, independent schools have smaller enrollments, smaller average class size, and lower student/teacher ratios than public schools.[47] Moreover, such choices often reflect parents' ideological values, whether they are academic, religious,[48] or interest-based (music, sports, etc.). Many private secondary schools also have superior college placement rates. Of all the students entering a recent Harvard freshman class, 35+% were from private secondary institutions, although such schools only educate 14% of the nation's high school students.

Regardless of the specific educational complaint, Americans unsurprisingly believe the remedy lies in choice. The charter school movement, voucher programs, and private alternatives all represent an Experiential desire for greater control over educational destiny. Americans are so market-driven that they believe—rightly or wrongly—that with choice for parents, students, and teachers, competition among schools will allow weak institutions to fail and better ones to rise to the top. It should not be surprising that U.S. citizens favor democratic, market-driven solutions for school problems, as they try to apply such principles to many other aspects of American life.

KNOWLEDGE = MONEY

We have seen that a country's most valuable resource is not natural but human. Japan and a half dozen Asian tigers are recent examples of how human capital can promote economic development in a relatively short span of time. But, Asia is not the only place where education has made a difference. Many of the former Soviet Union countries—particularly those with extremely high literacy, secondary, and tertiary school enrollment rates—were able to transition quickly into market-oriented democracies in the 1990s largely because they possessed huge, but previously stifled, human capital. Even a cursory look at the research leads us to conclude that poverty and prosperity are linked to education. While huge gaps still exist, they are being closed more and more every year.

We have also seen that in late-stage Material and Experiential-trending societies, education is now a lifelong process. In these countries, human capital is often being cultivated at the pre-natal stage, nurtured via preschools through college, and increasingly through graduate school. Enrichment education is also pursued as part of our individual self-actualization journeys, not just as a pathway to a job.

As the global landscape of learning evolves, so does our collective prosperity. For most of the 20th Century, a handful of Western countries sped ahead of the rest economically due largely to more and better education. However, the improving education of developing country populations may begin to level the playing field sooner rather than later.

7
Wealth and Family:

From Survival Unit to Psychic Sustenance

The family is the association established by nature for the supply of man's everyday wants.

Aristotle (384BCE–322BCE)

The family has long been considered the bedrock of society. It may still be so, but the traditional definition of "family" is being challenged in the 21st Century. The domestic images depicted in the 1950s sitcom *Father Knows Best*, popular just a few decades ago, seem quaint today, and the family on *The Waltons* seems like ancient history. Families have not only grown smaller with prosperity, but also their composition, function, and *raison d'etre* have changed radically. As people progress through the Biological, Material, and Experiential stages, what they need, desire, and demand from family shifts, evolving from an economic necessity to a personal one. This chapter explores the dynamic nature of modern families, and shows that while economically advancing societies don't *need* families in the same way their ancestors did, they certainly value and indulge them like never before. With growing wealth, people have begun to see families as extensions of themselves—often as the ultimate form of self-actualization.

THE WAY WE WERE

What, historically, has been the purpose of family? Beyond perpetuation of the species, the answer is simple: money. The "family unit" has always been a convenient social structure for organizing and supporting economic activity. The traditional family as understood in the West today—a mom, a dad, and two or three kids—is merely a vestige of the agrarian economic structure of the Biological phase. As recently as one century ago, nearly all of the world's population depended on family farming for economic survival, and billions in the developing world still do today.

As Figure 7–1 notes, family life and the roles of women and children have shifted dramatically only in the last century. Family size largely declines with wealth creation, as societies enjoy greater control over their lives through greater economic and political rights, as well as emancipation from time-consuming chores and involuntary pregnancy via technology. Children, too, have evolved from farmhands to protected populations in modern life.

Both industrialization and wealth creation dramatically influence the form and purpose of families. The move from fields to factories and offices can produce massive social and economic dislocations, fundamentally redefining the meaning of home life. Moreover, with prosperity, a number of factors combine to

Figure 7-1   Family trends and GDP, 2000BCE–2000CE.

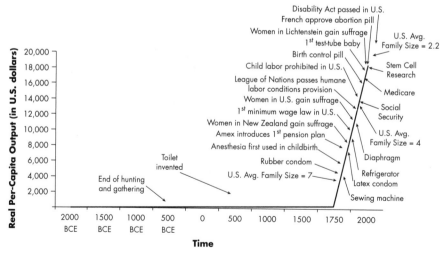

revamp the gender roles that characterize the agrarian family, triggered largely by women's gradual economic, political, and social enfranchisement.

In traditional agrarian societies of the past and present, the family is, first and foremost, a unit of economic production. These agrarian families also perform functions assumed by state and social institutions in more advanced economies: education of children, eldercare, transmission of functional and occupational skills, and religious instruction. Biological societies stress tradition, inherited status, and community needs, supported by absolute religious standards and rigid roles for men, women, and children.[1] These roles were evident in pre-industrial America, where 95% of the population farmed, and still can be found today in many regions of the Biological world, including Latin America, the Middle East, Africa, and Asia.

In many agrarian societies, women were (and still are) essentially caretakers, with rights granted only through their husbands.

These social and economic realities of farming are the basis for most familial relationships in Biological cultures. In this context, marriage is, in many ways, a business transaction with property and possessions trading hands—more like a corporate merger than a personal union of choice. In the 17th and early 18th Centuries, this concept was codified in the West: Laws of the time gave parents the power to "dispose" of their children in marriage, and it was expected that parents would take an active role overseeing their child's choice of a spouse.[2] Similar structures can be seen today in traditional societies, where parents arrange marriages for their children based on economic, social, and community convenience. Individual choice in marriage, for both men and women, based on a concept of romantic love, is a relatively newly accepted social norm in the West and still is by no means universal.

The agrarian family structure places particular hardships on women. While they are thankfully a thing of the past in post-Biological societies, these burdens remain the reality in many parts of the world. One of the most significant obstacles to women's progress is early motherhood. Whereas many Material women have the choice to defer or forego marriage, and have personal control over the number of children they wish to have, women in Biological cultures often don't have these options. In many developing countries, at least 20% of women—in some countries half—give birth to their first child before age 18. The religious, parental, and societal expectation is that women will marry young, produce a child as soon thereafter as possible, and continue bearing children for as long they can.[3]

The agrarian way of life also gives "childhood" a different meaning in many Biological societies than it holds today in wealthier countries. Of course, most parents love their children and want the best for them regardless of economic status. But children in poorer agrarian households are, by necessity, considered "little adults," and are expected to perform grown-up duties as soon as they are able, sometimes as early as age 10.[4] The nature of agriculture requires a large number of these inexpensive farmhands, which, in conjunction with high rates of infant and child mortality, disease, malnutrition, and daily hazards, encouraged large families until the early 20th Century in the West and in many countries today.

There is a direct link between fertility rates and economic growth; lower rates seem to go hand-in-hand with greater economic achievement. In 1790, the average size of a U.S. household was 5.8 people. In 1890, it was 4.9, 3.3 in 1960, and 2.6 by 1993. As noted in Figure 7–2, wealth rose sharply as family size decreased.[5] This trend is now global, with many countries shifting toward smaller nuclear families. Even in countries where the fertility rate is high, women indicate they would like to have fewer children, but do not have the financial means or cultural freedom to access the medical technology they need (i.e., contraception or abortion). In Kenya, for example, the gap between desired and actual fertility is two children.

Figure 7–2   Rising wealth, shrinking families in the U.S.[6]

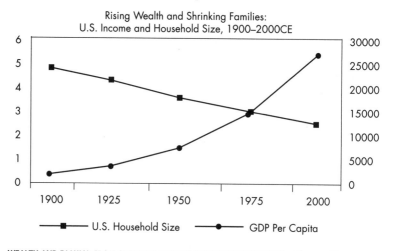

Rising Wealth and Shrinking Families:
U.S. Income and Household Size, 1900–2000CE

—■— U.S. Household Size   —●— GDP Per Capita

Yet fertility has already fallen in Kenya, from a high of more than 8 children per woman in the 1970s to under 4.5 children in the second half of the 1990s.[7]

A 2000 UN global study on women noted that smaller families are also linked to more favorable conditions for children's education and nutrition, better health for all family members, and improved opportunities for women to expand their role in society.[8] It makes economic sense: With fewer children, there are more resources available per child (see Figure 7–3). By decreasing the number of dependents, parents can provide more for the mouths they do have to feed. It is a virtuous cycle of family planning: Smaller families promote greater economic opportunity per capita, and greater opportunity encourages education and social investment, which lead to smaller families. The very process of industrialization, *de facto*, promotes smaller families: People move to cities and have less space and less need for children to help in the fields.

As agrarian life has waned around the world since the 1970s, fertility rates have declined globally as well. Not surprisingly, regions that reduced their fertility rates were among the most economically dynamic. East Asia, for example, slowed its rate from more than 5% to less than 2% (comparable to U.S., Japan, and West Europe rates) in 32 years—the world's fastest reduction— while its economy grew the fastest. In historical perspective, it took Great Britain almost 100 years, beginning in the 19th Century, to lower its fertility rate by this amount.[9]

Figure 7–3   Wealth and family size globally, year 2000.

Smallest Families			Largest Families		
Country	GDP/ Capita	Household Size	Country	GDP	Household Size
Luxembourg	$45,100	2.9	Congo	$110	6.0
Switzerland	$39,980	2.5	Burundi	$140	5.8
Norway	$34,310	2.3	Sierra Leone	$140	5.7
Denmark	$33,040	2.3	Guinea-Bissau	$160	5.3
Japan	$32,350	3.0	Niger	$200	5.9
U.S.	$29,240	2.7	Malawi	$210	5.9
Iceland	$27,830	2.3	Mozambique	$210	5.6
Germany	$26,570	2.3	Tanzania	$220	5.4
Sweden	$25,580	2.2	Rwanda	$230	5.8
Belgium	$25,380	2.4	Sudan	$290	6.0

Figure 7-4   Fertility rates, 1970-1992.

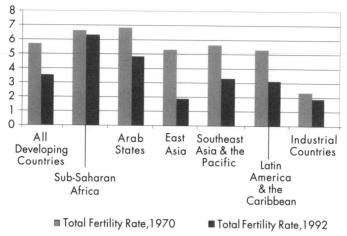

■ Total Fertility Rate, 1970   ■ Total Fertility Rate, 1992

Source: World Bank

Unfortunately, the reverse cycle is often apparent in Biological societies where poor access to healthcare and family planning and the low social status of women continue to drive high rates of population growth and large family sizes. This is particularly evident in sub-Saharan Africa, the Middle East, and parts of South Asia. As Figure 7–4 illustrates, the poorest countries continue to have the highest fertility rates, almost 7% on average versus less than 2% in industrialized countries.[10]

URBANIZATION AND MIGRATION

Family life has also been affected by shifting dwelling patterns. At the beginning of the 20th Century, only 10% of the world's population lived in cities and towns; today, half do.[11] The urbanization that enveloped the world with industrialization has pushed people from farm to factory, encouraged by industrial jobs and higher incomes and better access to services and education. Figure 7–5 illustrates this trend.

This movement has had a profound impact on the extended family. Whereas Biological home life includes extended relationships and overlapping kinship systems, the urban, Material family tends to be separated geographically from relatives. In rural areas of sub-Saharan Africa, for example, urbanization has led to long distances between young people and their parents and grandparents, who

Figure 7-5   Total urban and rural populations, 1550–2030[12] (est).

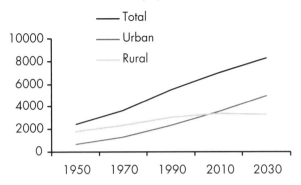

previously played a special role in traditional education and socialization. In the Middle East, traditional extended families are gradually withering; in Egypt, for example, only 16% of all households support extended families versus more than half in the mid-20th Century.[13] Urbanization has also had an impact on the nuclear family. Urban society requires greater autonomy and responsibility from each of its members: greater autonomy, because family proximity is no longer a permanent feature that helps solve problems that arise; greater responsibility, because family stability demands more resolve amid the frictions and aggravations of urban life.

Urbanization has been most pronounced in the U.S. and western Europe. In 1800, only 5% of the U.S. population lived in urban areas. A result of economic opportunity, this number rose to 50% by 1920. Today, in both the U.S. and western Europe, the urban population stands at 70%.[14] The move to urban areas is now accelerating in developing countries as well. In 1950, only 17.8% of their populations was considered urban. The Population Council estimates that by 2030, this number will approach 60%.[15] This process is occurring most rapidly in Material countries, where economic opportunity is pulling people toward cities. For example, Mexico's urban population grew from nearly half in 1960 to almost 80% in 2000 and Turkey's rose from 30–75% during the same period.[16]

THE FEMALE FACTOR

Most of the family's change in form and function—not just size—is inextricably tied to women's evolving roles in society. In many agrarian places today, women are limited to domestic roles, with rights granted only through their husbands. This is similar to conditions in the West in the 18th Century. Back then, after a woman married, she was no longer allowed to own property, even if she had inherited it or brought it to the marriage. If a woman worked outside the home, all of her earnings belonged to her husband. Under English Common Law, a married woman did not possess rights of her own, because her rights were "covered" by those of her husband. The idea of "coverture"—that a man and woman are one person—was supported by the religious and philosophical ideas of the time. Socially, single women were ranked far below those who were married. Since women's activities were essentially restricted to childrearing, church-going, and homemaking, a single woman had little, if any, social life. Additionally, supporting unmarried daughters placed an extra burden on parents, who could ill-afford an additional mouth to feed. Marriage, then, became a woman's key means of survival as well as her only means of social interaction.[17] Women were also barred from most forms of civil participation (from voting, to sitting on juries, to suing), were forbidden to speak publicly outside of church, and had few educational opportunities (the first college to admit women in the U.S. was Oberlin College in 1834, some 200 years after Harvard College opened its doors to men).[18] These repressive social and domestic structures are still tolerated in many developing countries. Even if limitations on women's rights are not legally codified as they were in the pre-industrial West, cultural and religious strictures remain powerful.

However, industrialization, prosperity, and the decline of religious authority have created greater opportunities for women in societies that have progressed out of the Biological stage. After centuries of social and economic subordination, women in the industrialized world have been gaining access to education, employment, and leadership opportunities. Many are postponing, or even rejecting entirely, the traditional roles of wife and mother, opting to pursue other goals instead.

The progress of women's rights in the West can be linked to one key factor: wealth. It is greater prosperity that has encouraged better and more accessible education opportunities, undoubtedly vital to women's economic enfranchisement. With women's newfound ability to support themselves, the whole nature of why they marry and procreate takes on a new meaning with far-reaching social reverberations.

Since 1980, women's economic activity rates, measured by formal employment, have increased almost everywhere except in sub-Saharan Africa, the transition economies of eastern Europe and central Asia, and Oceania. The largest increase occurred in South America, where female economic activity rates rose from 26 to 45% between 1980 and 1997. At the same time, women's education (both primary and secondary levels) rose to 85%. The lowest rates were found in northern Africa and western Asia, where less than one-third of women were economically active[19] and less than 50% were enrolled in primary and secondary education. It must be noted that measures of women's economic activity generally do not include "domestic" or "household" activity. Indeed, the UN has estimated that women work, on average, more hours per week than men in most parts of the world, but are rarely compensated for this work. In Kenya, for example, while almost 80% of men's work is income-earning, only 41% of women's work is income-earning.[20]

One major historic obstacle to women's participation in the formal workforce has been strong cultural and practical restrictions on those with babies or young children working outside the home. In wealthier societies, as women are more integrated into the labor pool, these hurdles are shrinking. A November 2001 report from the U.S. Commerce Department's Census Bureau shows major changes in maternity leave and employment patterns for new American mothers from 1960–1985. According to the study, women's work schedules are less likely to be interrupted by the birth of their first child, and women today are making longer term commitments to working than in the 1960s.[21] The number of U.S. women working during pregnancy before their first birth increased by 23% between 1961–65 and from 44–67% in the 1991–95 period. Also, whereas only 14% of mothers returned to work by the sixth month after the birth of their first child between 1961–65, 52% of mothers had returned to work by that point from 1991–95.[22] The increased labor force participation of pregnant women and new mothers has resulted in a change in public policy and workplace regulations in the U.S. In 1991–95, 43% of women received paid leave before or after their first child's birth, while only 16% did in 1961–65. While the U.S. is still behind many developed nations in regard to its maternity/paternity leave and childcare policies, the presence of new mothers in the workforce is effecting serious policy adjustments.[23]

FROM WAR TO WORK: WOMEN AND THE AMERICAN ECONOMY

According to the U.S. Bureau of Labor Statistics, in 1940, only 25.8% of women participated in the labor force. By 1999, nearly three of every five women of working age were in the labor force.[24]

The nature and social acceptability of women's work changed drastically during World War II. Until then, women were largely relegated to "feminine" jobs of a domestic or secretarial nature. But as the availability of working-age men fell during World War II, women were needed to fill essential roles in the war production assembly lines. The first wave of female laborers was drawn from women already working, but gradually the call went out for young girls and high school graduates. By 1943, the U.S. government was targeting ads to housewives, a hitherto unapproachable group. "The real situation is that unless industry draws 2.8 million more women away from household or school duties in 1943 ...production quotas will have to be revised down," said an article in *Business Week*.[25] Between 1940 and 1945, the number of American women in the workforce increased by 50%.

Not all Americans were pleased with this development; many protested the breakup of the household. "Women who maintain jobs outside of the home..." wrote *Catholic World* in 1943, "weaken family life, endanger their own marital happiness, rob themselves of a man's protective capabilities, and by consequence decrease the number of children."[26] But the work was billed as "temporary," until the fighting boys could come home.

What is significant, however, is that many of these women *continued* to work outside the home. By 1940, about one in four women were in the workforce; by 1950 it was more than one-third; by 1960, this number rose to 37.7%; and as of 1999, it was 60%.[27] This movement had profound effects not only on women's place in American society, but also on the family. With two-income households and greater economic freedom, families were able to consume more and girls were given different role models. And the process has been accelerated in the move from factory to office. The rise of the service sector has provided even more spaces for women to participate in the economic and political offices of the country. This participation, in turn, has had an immeasurable impact on the way women are perceived in society, not only in the U.S., but all around the world.

More women are also staying in the workforce during their reproductive years. In the 1970s, economic activity rates peaked for women in their early 20s in the West as well as in less-developed countries. Now, according to regional data for 1990, labor force participation rates globally are high for women in their 20s, rise through their 30s, and only decline after age 50. This trend is both cause and effect of smaller family size and increased employment opportunities.[28]

BUILDING AN EQUITY CULTURE IN WOMEN

While the tradition of women staying home and tending to families is strong, women can add tremendous human capital to the wealth creation process, as we've seen in the West. Sadly, women's poverty typically results in the physical and social underdevelopment of their children. One successful movement to counteract this cycle in developing countries is "microcredit." This program, which provides small loans to help women start businesses and help their families, is building the human capital necessary for future wealth creation. At the same time, women themselves benefit from the higher social status they achieve within the home when they are able to generate income, thus satisfying many personal needs and building greater human capital for the future.

In many emerging countries of Asia, Africa, and Latin America, more than half the population is often self-employed. By borrowing relatively small amounts of money (between $25 and $100) at reasonable rates (versus very high rates offered by traditional moneylenders), small micro-enterprises are born. While sometimes such programs offer only capital, the better ones combine financing with training, networking, and peer support. Surprisingly, while these programs sound risky, microcredit repayment records are strikingly high, often higher than those of conventional borrowers. Part of the success is attributed to the peer support and pressure used in many microcredit models, whereby borrowers police each other's success and help ensure that group members repay their loans.[29]

Microcredit Summit offers this example of how such a program works: *"La Maman Mole Motuke lived in a wrecked car in a suburb of Kinshasa, Zaire with her four children. If she could find something to eat, she would feed two of her children; the next time she found something to eat, her other two children would eat. When organizers from a microcredit lending institution interviewed her, she said that she knew how to make chikwangue (manioc paste), and she only needed a few dollars to start production. After six months of training in marketing and production techniques, Maman Motuke got her first loan of $100 U.S., and bought production materials. Today, Maman Motuke and her family no longer live in a broken-down car; they rent a house with two bedrooms and a living room. Her four children go to school consistently, eat regularly, and dress well. She currently is saving to buy some land in a suburb farther outside of the city and hopes to build a house."*[30]

Not only is there greater occupational opportunity available to women in more advanced economies, but women are also starting to be valued more as employees. The discrepancy between women's and men's earnings in the manufacturing sector narrowed between 1990 and 1997 in 26 out of 36 countries surveyed by the UN.[31] Indeed, according to a Gallup poll on gender and society (see Figure 7–6), the majority of people in the countries polled believed that the lives of women were getting better (though men were still better off).[32]

Figure 7–6   Gallup poll: Have the lives of women gotten better or worse?[33]

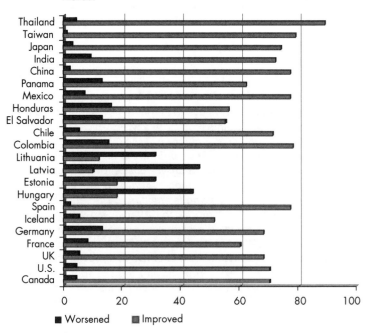

WEALTH AND MARRIAGE

Marriage, for most women engaged in the wealth process, has evolved from a survival necessity into a matter of choice: Love and a relationship are now considered higher needs, which is a shift from the focus on procreation and security. In fact, many women are choosing not to marry at all. According to the 1998 U.S. census, 40% of adult women (18 and over) are single, versus 30% in 1968. The percentage age of unmarried women in the U.S. ages 25–29 and 30–34 tripled between 1970 and 1998,[34] and the majority of one-person households in wealthy countries is now made up of women.[35]

Women in industrial nations are also postponing marriage until much later in life, wanting, it seems, to pursue careers before having a family. People are opting to "find themselves," to explore all of the options open to them, before settling into a binding relationship. Twenty-somethings, regardless of gender, in all advanced nations, have the economic ability to support themselves outside of the convention of marriage. Since 1980, the marriage age has risen everywhere. The greatest increase is in the wealthiest countries, with an average increase of 3–4 years for both men and women. There has also been an increase in southern Africa (3 years for women and 2 for men). In northern and eastern Africa, the marriage age of women has increased by a year. Not surprisingly, the youngest ages for marriage are in the poorest regions of southern Asia and sub-Saharan Africa, averaging 20 and 21 years, respectively, and reflecting the Biological, agrarian lifestyle that still dominates those regions.[36]

As people become more concerned with their individual needs in Material and Experiential societies, there has been a major increase in divorce rates. The number of divorced or separated women aged 45–59 increased, on average, from 5% in 1980 to 9% in the 1990s in Europe, and from 9–14% in the developed countries outside of Europe. Even in Latin American and the Caribbean, the number of divorced women aged 45–59 increased from 7–10%. Countries like Belgium, Luxembourg, the Nordic countries, Switzerland, and the UK have divorce rates of 40 out of 100 marriages (about 51 in Sweden and the U.S.).[37] As traditional roles have changed, people are not constrained by social or religious conformity and are free to pursue their individual fulfillment within or outside of marriage.

THE NEW FAMILY

Wealth creation has not only affected the composition of the family, but also our perceptions of gender, sex, divorce, religion, and abortion, to name a few subjects. Once strictly defined, "family" in the wealthier world is a more flexible term, with many people hard-pressed to define it at all. In Material and Experiential strata, family now encompasses single-parent households, working mothers, same-sex relationships, and lifelong non-traditional unions.

There are significant statistics that reflect the increasing number of couples in the high-income world who cohabit without marrying.[38] In six European countries, more than half of women aged 20–24 with partners live in unmarried unions; in Sweden, it is more than 75%. There has also been an increase in consensual unions in lower income countries. For example, in Botswana, the increase is thought to be due, at least in part, to the shift from a rural to a more modern cash economy.[39]

Moving even further from the traditional family, in wealthier societies, same-sex couples are tying the knot. The Netherlands was the first nation to eliminate marriage as an institution limited to a man and a woman. Any pairing of humans can now qualify for a marriage license. The new law also grants divorce and adoption rights to atypical couples.[40] While the Netherlands—a country with very Experiential values—is definitely on the vanguard of homosexual rights, similar movements are gaining attention and validity in most developed nations. In Germany—another Experiential-trending country—an August 2001 law took effect allowing gays and lesbians who register their relationship the same inheritance rights as heterosexual couples. They can also now share a surname and bring foreign partners to join them in Germany.[41] In the U.S., although no state allows same-sex marriage, more states are granting same-sex couples many of the privileges of marriage.[42] For example, in Massachusetts, a law was recently passed that extends many "domestic partner" benefits to all state employees, whether the "partner" is of the same or opposite sex.[43] Of course, these trends are still not the norm. In many parts of the world—particularly in Biological and Material states—homosexuality is still condemned, if not outlawed, and in some extreme cases, individuals can be imprisoned for expressing their sexuality.

> **Stripped of its economic efficacy, marriage has become a voluntary (and sometimes temporary) social institution.**

ART REFLECTING LIFE: TV'S CHANGING FAMILY MIRROR

If TV programming can be considered a reflection of our lifestyles, then some interesting changes have been occurring in the institution of the family. In the middle of the 20th Century, popular TV shows, such as *Father Knows Best* and *Leave it to Beaver*, glorified the archetypal family: the traditional two-parent household, rigid gender roles, and all. All the kids were relatively obedient and respected their elders. Compare these households to *The Osbornes* or *The Sopranos* and you'll begin to see a different perspective on family life two generations later.

Look at divorce. Sure, there were single-parent households on late 1960s and early 1970s TV shows such as *The Courtship of Eddie's Father*, *Family Affair*, and even *The Partridge Family*; but they were typically widow/widower stories. However, things started to change just about then. Programs like *Julia*, *The Mary Tyler Moore Show*, *Rhoda*, and *One Day at a Time* reflected working woman households and divorced homes. In the 1980s *Kate and Allie*, two divorced moms raising their children together in Manhattan, started to push the envelope of what was considered a family. *My Two Dads*, a show about a young girl being raised by two men, her mother unsure of which was the biological father, challenged family taboos even further.

The most critically acclaimed and watched TV shows of the past decade have been programs like *Sex and the City*, *Seinfeld*, *Ellen*, and *Friends*, shows that truly offer a different perspective on life, love, and family in the modern world versus 1950s TV. In these programs, most characters are not married, many live with roommates, some are openly gay, and there are few children. Where there are kids, they are sometimes part of alternative family structures. On *Friends*, for example, the character Ross has fathered two children: a boy, who lives with his mother (Ross' ex-wife) and her lesbian companion, and a girl who lives with his one-time girlfriend, Rachel.

Alternative lifestyles and non-traditional gender preference are becoming quite common on TV. Take Will, in the sitcom *Will & Grace*, an attractive gay man looking for Mr. Right; or the dysfunctional household of *Six Feet Under*, an odd family with a mix of gay and hetero children; or Showtime's *Queer as Folk* (the first show completely about gay relationships); and NBC's short-lived *Bob and Rose*, about a gay man who's fallen for a straight woman. Imagine any of this on 1950s American TV. While these TV shows are anecdotal, they do offer evidence of a shift in the notion of the family in the Material and Experiential worlds.

The *Human Values Survey* suggests that, in the advanced nations of western Europe, North America, and East Asia, the form and function of families continues to evolve.[44] The survey shows that from 1981–1990, views toward divorce became more lenient in 18 out of 20 societies, including the U.S., Canada, Mexico, Britain, West Germany, France, Italy, Spain, Netherlands, Belgium, Ireland, North Ireland, Norway, Sweden, Finland, Iceland, Japan, and Argentina. The only hardening was found in Hungary and South Africa, two countries that were experiencing political and economic crises throughout the 1980s.[45] This change is very telling. Marriage, the traditional foundation of the family, is no longer a sacred, unbreakable union. Stripped of its economic efficacy, marriage has become a voluntary (and sometimes temporary) social institution.

Similarly, 19 out of 20 societies became more permissive toward abortion: U.S., Canada, Mexico, Britain, West Germany, France, Italy, Spain, Netherlands, Belgium, Ireland, North Ireland, Norway, Sweden, Finland, Iceland, Hungary, and Argentina. South Africa was the only exception.[46] Like the changing attitudes toward divorce, the greater tolerance of abortion makes a strong statement about beliefs concerning family; procreation is no longer the primary purpose of a union.

SEX, NOT PROCREATION

Sex is no longer just about making babies. It is now looked on as a pleasure, a necessity, a right, and even a commodity. Not only is the "why" of sex changing, but also the "who," "what," "where," "how," and "when." In large part, this is due to changing attitudes regarding sexual standards: Gone is the traditional condemnation of out-of-wedlock intercourse as sin. Many people around the world are now taught that sex is good, healthy, and should be enjoyed and prudently managed.

Liberating sex from pregnancy should not be underestimated as a catalyst for this attitudinal shift. Single, working women, a rarity in agrarian societies, are very common in Material and Experiential strata societies. A woman's ability to pick and choose lovers based on voluntary affection or pure lust—and not economic necessity—has reshaped life beyond *Sex and the City*. This changing social norm has far-reaching consequences for traditional views on marriage and has helped end some barbaric customs such as female circumcision.[47] Wealth clearly has fostered greater self-determination over sexual practice.

Technology, specifically in contraception, has been a huge factor in redefining sexual attitudes. Contraceptive use has increased in most developed and developing nations since 1980. In most advanced countries, typically 70% of married women use some form of birth control, and in China and Thailand, for example, contraception is used by over three-fourths of both married and single women.[48] Perhaps this development is a symbiotic result of the wealth, technology, and gender enfranchisement process over the 20th Century. Compare the economic advancements of the last century with the following contraceptive timeline:

1912: Advent of the modern birth control movement

1914: Margaret Sanger arrested for distributing birth control materials

1916: 1st birth control clinic is opened and closed by Brooklyn police after only 10 days

1925: First U.S. diaphragms manufactured

1928: Timing of ovulation is established

1937: American Medical Association (AMA) endorses birth control; North Carolina adds it in public health programs

1942: Planned Parenthood is formed

1955: First national fertility survey

1960: Food and Drug Administration (FDA) approves the pill; intra-uterine devices (IUDs) are approved.

1965: In Griswold vs. Connecticut, the Supreme Court strikes down laws banning married people from using contraceptives

1972: Medicaid for family planning

1973: Roe versus Wade legalizes abortion

1990s: FDA approves Norplant, the female condom, and the morning-after pill

---

CHILDREN AND THE YOUTH BULGE

With wealth creation in full motion, children in the Material world, and even many in progressive Biological societies, are no longer expected to "earn their keep" by working early in their lives. Instead, they are nurtured throughout ever-lengthening childhoods. They begin formal schooling earlier and generally continue, supported by their parents, until their late teen years, and often into their early 20s in Experiential-trending populations. Controlled fertility has allowed wealthier societies to invest more per capita in

Figure 7-7   Global population composition by age, 2000.[49]

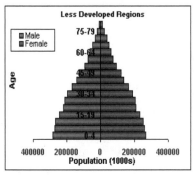

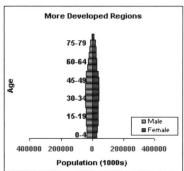

child development than ever before, seeding greater human capital for continued prosperity. To enforce this changing attitude toward children's status, laws banning many forms of child labor and exploitation have been implemented in the last century, making children some of the most protected members of Material and Experiential-trending societies.[50]

Even in the Biological world, children can no longer "be seen and not heard"; their sheer numbers dictate attention. The UN estimates that in 2000, there were 1.1 billion people between the ages of 15 and 24, representing an unprecedented 18% of the global population. Eight out of 10 members of this age group live in the developing world. Figure 7–7 illustrates global population composition by age.

The size of this young population is the result of high fertility rates during the 1960s and 1970s, combined with declining mortality rates of children under five, particularly among infants. According to the UN, in the four decades from 1960 to 2000, infant mortality in the developing world fell from 141 to 63 deaths per 1,000 births.

Not only are there large youth pockets in Biological nations, but they represent a very large proportion of their respective populations. In both Asia and Latin America, nearly one-third of the populations are under age 15. Africa, with 43% of the population, or 338 million young people under the age of 15, continues to be the youngest region. Globally, by 2010, there will be 2.7 billion people between the ages of 10 and 34. Despite the drop in fertility that has occurred in many countries since 1970, the large numbers of children born to the preceding "high-fertility generation" ensure that the "youth bulge" will continue for several decades. This creates an extraordinary demand for social services, such as health and education, as well as for jobs in the developing world.

THE GRAYING FAMILY

Compared to the robust population trends in Biological and early-Material countries, the wealthier industrialized nations present a striking contrast. People under the age of 15 average approximately 18% of late-stage Material and Experiential-trending populations, which is less than half of most developing countries. The U.S., with 21% under age 15, actually has one of the higher proportions of young people among advanced economies. The lowest proportion is 15%, found in Japan, Spain, and Greece.[51]

This "graying" process, where a society's average age increases with lower fertility and longer life expectancy, raises new challenges with regard to senior citizens. For example, the extended agrarian family often includes grandparents who live under the same roof with grandchildren. Indeed, in some traditional societies such as India and China, sons have often borne the traditional responsibility of taking care not only of their parents, but also of their wives' parents. In this respect, sons have served as "social security," or an "individual retirement account," for parents and in-laws, one reason that male children are highly desirable in these societies.[52] This system works well within the Biological demographic structure, with a relatively higher number of young people taking care of parents with shorter life expectancies.

However, for Material societies, where people are now living, on average, 20–30 years longer than those in Biological-dominant places, long-term eldercare has emerged as a serious social concern. Adding to the pressure is the physical mobility that comes with prosperity; children and parents are often separated now by great distances. To meet these concerns, in wealthier Material and Experiential-trending countries, a variety of public and private pension schemes have developed to allow workers to save and live independently for relatively long periods after retirement.

Furthermore, many private-sector alternatives for eldercare have emerged: full-time nursing homes, assisted living facilities, and in-home care services, among others. The options are many, but they are also costly. In the U.S., for example, public and private spending for long-term senior care services (including nursing homes) was estimated at more than $127 billion in 1998, and may top $340 billion by 2040.[53] While sons and daughters may not be required to board older parents and in-laws as in the past, familial obligations still exist. American adult children still provide "informal" caregiving (such as supporting parents with food, transportation, and other assistance), which totals nearly $200 billion in value each year.[54]

Wealth and longevity have converged to form the so-called "Sandwich Generation," middle-aged parents who are caught in the bind of caring for children (many now in school until their 20s) as well as parents (many now surviving into their 80s). There has also been an emergence of four-generation "Club Sandwiches," with those in their 50s or 60s feeling responsible for aging parents, adult children, and grandchildren, or those in their 30s and 40s caring for young children, aging parents, and grandparents.[55]

In the past, taking care of parents with physical ailments was common. Now, while health and longevity have improved, the cognitive problems that accompany old age are becoming more prevalent. In 1998, the percentage of older Americans with moderate to severe memory impairment (including Alzheimer's disease and other forms of dementia) ranged from approximately 4% among persons aged 65–69 to about 36% of those 85 or older.[56] Why is this statistic important? Because in the U.S., Japan, and parts of Europe, individuals 85 years and older are among the fastest growing population segments. In the U.S. alone, there were 4 million people aged 85+ in 2000, and this is expected to rise to 18 million by 2050.[57] Over the next two generations, therefore, there may be some 6+ million Americans with severe or moderate memory impairment.

As wealth has brought extended life, it has also brought the burdens of greater longevity. Government debates over pension and health policies have already begun, and the stress, both financial and emotional, that meeting the needs of the elderly places on families is evident. The Material and Experiential-trending world is only in the early stages of this trend, but dealing with a rapidly aging population will be a critical challenge in the coming decades.

THE FUTURE OF THE FAMILY

The family may have been the most revered social institution to be transformed by the wealth creation process. In Material and Experiential societies, home, or "private," life and work and "public" life are no longer integrated. Mothers work outside the home, leaving the care of children to schools, day-care centers, or nannies. Many retirees no longer have to depend exclusively on their children after their working years are finished; they use their own

WEALTH AND FAMILY: FROM SURVIVAL UNIT TO PSYCHIC SUSTENANCE Chapter 7

accumulated savings to live alone, with hired assistance or in elder-care institutions. Industrialization, urbanization, secularization, and women's entry into the formal economy have combined to profoundly reshape the concepts of intimacy and family, as well as the roles of women and men, mothers and fathers, grandparents and children. Widespread wealth has allowed for more mutually agreeable, voluntary unions. Individualism, promoted by prosperity, has allowed men and women to make *their own* choices about intimate relationships, whether based on love, money, convenience, or lust; whether they are sanctified by a church or recognized by the state; whether they are long-term or short-term, many or few. Families are no longer formed solely for economic usefulness; having children is a personal choice for most, not a societal or religious imperative. Children are born to married couples, gay couples, single women and anonymous sperm donors, or surrogate mothers; they are adopted, sometimes from around the globe; they are created by the modern miracles of fertility drugs, in-vitro fertilization, and egg donation. In a very real sense, people now look toward the family they choose to create as their core reason for living, part of their self-actualization. Families in the wealthy world are the products of conscious choice. They are expressions of deep, heartfelt hopes and desires.

These dramatic changes in values and lifestyles have only been made possible through the economic and social transformations that have occurred during the last century, a relative blink in history. Many may bemoan these changes as a loss of tradition. But it is clear that wealth and freedom are connected, and the exercise of this freedom has created a more flexible, inclusive definition of "family" in the modern world. As long as the wealth process continues, we should continue to see greater variety in the form, function, and purpose of family. These are the "family values" of the wealthier world.

8
Wealth and Leisure:

The Merging of Consumption, Culture, and Lifestyle

The superfluous is very necessary.

Voltaire (1694–1778)

*To be able to fill leisure intelligently is the
last product of civilization.*

Arnold Toynbee (1889–1975)

Has the nature of everyday life been radically changed by wealth creation? Absolutely, and it's happening everywhere at this very moment. This chapter explores the symbiotic nexus among leisure time, consumption, lifestyle, globalization, and culture. Over the last century, civilization has evolved away from a *production*-focused agrarian existence to a greater emphasis on the *consumption* of goods and services. In this respect, a 22nd Century archeologist rummaging through our collective refuse might dub our eras "The Consumer Age": more people around the world are buying things and having experiences that, until recently, were reserved for the super-rich.

More money encourages people to want more things. As democratic politics and free-market reforms have spread over the last century or so, more individual lifestyle choices have been offered amid a marketplace overflowing

The ultimate prerequisites for mass consumption are surplus time and money.

with goods and services that go well beyond filling basic physiological needs. Globalization—produced by wealth creation—has promoted a mass consumer culture based on surplus *time* and *money*. These consumption and lifestyle patterns bring both the benefits of greater wealth and the frantic concerns over loss of local culture and identity.

THE DEMOCRATIZATION OF PROSPERITY

How have we evolved from creatures of production to those of consumption? In the West, consumer culture started in the early 1900s as the Industrial Revolution was well underway. New technologies and economic efficiencies were dramatically altering life and work, freeing up people to pursue non-agricultural endeavors. In addition, the percentage of income spent on biological necessities fell precipitously over the 20th Century. These factors would provoke some of the greatest lifestyle shifts ever witnessed in history.

Around the beginning of the 20th Century, free time emerged— 10 minutes, an hour, an entire day—in which people could finally do something besides physically toil and rest. The great result was leisure—once the domain of only the wealthiest families—for the rising lower and middle classes. Suddenly, millions of people had extra time to consider non-survival needs and desires, and higher wages to indulge them. In 1870, the average American worker labored 3,069 hours per year, six 10-hour days per week. By 1950, these hours had fallen to 2,075.[1] Today, it is closer to 1,730 in the U.S.[2] This change has been repeated around the world. In 1960, the average Japanese worker toiled 2,432 hours a year during a 6-day work week. By 1988, growing prosperity helped drop this to 2,111, and by 2000, it was down to 1,878 hours.[3] Free time provides people the luxury of *choice* and the *ability* to consume.

More time and money provide people the luxury of choice and the ability to freely consume.

Leisure's growth is linked not only to a reduced work week, but also to a longer lifespan and a smaller percentage of life spent in the workforce as compared to our ancestors. American life expectancy was approximately 30 years less in 1900 than in 2000. As a result, expectations of when and how long one needs to work have been completely altered.

In modern economies, formal work starts later in life and ends earlier. Instead of laboring on the farm, many now spend much of the first 18 years of life in school, with occasional part-time or

Figure 8-1 Soaring free time, or how the average American worker spends wakeful hours, 1870–1990.[4]

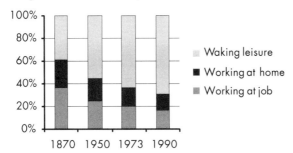

summer work. Moreover, with greater demand for education in wealthier societies, employment is increasingly postponed until after college (usually about age 22), or perhaps even after graduate or professional school (well into the 20s).

From 1880 to 1990, the average American's lifelong spare time increased from 48,300 hours to 246,000 hours.

Americans typically retire at age 62, with approximately 20 years left for full-time leisure.

Nobel prize-winning economist Robert William Fogel has actually quantified these lifestyle gains in time. He divides "lifetime discretionary hours" into "earnwork" and "volwork"; where "earnwork" is the time spent earning a living and "volwork" is voluntary activity (which may or may not earn money). In his estimates, the average lifetime discretionary hours for Americans will have grown from 225,900 hours in 1880 to 321,900 by 2040 (meaning they will live almost 100,000 hours longer!). Simultaneously, "earnwork" hours will actually *decline*, from 182,100 in 1880 to a projected 75,900 by 2040.[5] As Figure 8–1 notes, while only 40% of an American's life was at leisure in 1870, by 1990 it had grown to approximately 70%. In total, from 1880–1990, the average American's cumulative lifetime leisure time grew more than five-fold, from 48,300 hours to a remarkable 246,000 hours, or 22 years!

Professor Gary Cross describes the significant distinction between "free" time and "work" time, with more people thinking of free time as "fun."[6] This democratization of leisure or fun—now spreading globally—has created new products and industries needed to fill this extra time.

Figure 8-2   Wealth and leisure trends, 2000BCE–2000CE.

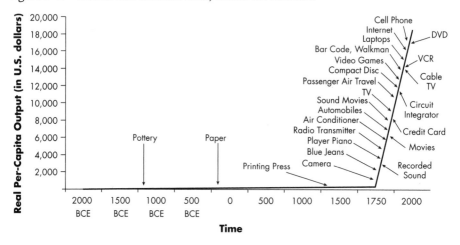

As people have moved from farms to factories, more excess time and money have resulted in redefining Material and Experiential lifestyles in the modern world. Figure 8–2 notes how technologically, leisure products, experiences, and wealth have all grown symbiotically in the last century or so.

FUELING THE LEISURE LIFESTYLE: GREATER PURCHASING POWER

At the same time that leisure time increased, free markets were expanding and strong price deflation trends began, as Delong described in his 1895 Montgomery Ward catalog example. Wages began to increase with industrialization, giving people more purchasing power while workdays shortened. As noted, many products—now in mass production—became cheaper and more affordable for the average laborer. While prices are typically high when goods are initially introduced to a market, through economies of scale, they fall quickly as demand rises. In the early 1900s, this process was underway as people for the first time had real discretionary money to spend on what are called "nonessentials," or treats. Whereas a soda cost a nickel and took about 20 minutes of labor in 1900, by 1910, the same soda (still costing 5 cents) took just 15 minutes (see Table 8–1). By 1920, the labor time had dropped to 5 minutes, and today it's down to less than 90 seconds!

The results of these developments—longer lives, less work, and cheaper goods—were reflected in historic shifts in spending patterns

Table 8-1   Cost of Selected Snack Items, 1900-97:
Nominal Price and Minutes of Labor[7]

	1900	1920	1940	1964	1984	1997
Coca Cola	5¢	5¢	5¢	16¢	28¢	33¢
Minutes	19.9	5.5	4.6	3.8	1.8	1.5
Hershey Bar	5¢	5¢	5¢	5¢	30¢	45¢
Minutes	19.9	5.5	4.6	1.2	2.0	2.0
Wrigley's Gum	5¢	5¢	5¢	5¢	18¢	25¢
Minutes	19.9	5.5	4.6	1.2	1.2	1.1

for Americans and other wealthy countries during the 20th Century. The percentage of American income going to basic needs (including shelter, clothing, and food) decreased from 75% of total household expenditures at the turn of the century to less than 40%.[8] Where does this extra money go? To nonessentials, including movie tickets, TVs, CD players, vacations, designer sunglasses, a health club membership, or an extra car; in short, to fill a variety of Material and Experiential needs (see Figure 8-3).

This process is now spreading globally as more places and people are being incorporated into the international economy. For parts of the developing world, such as Mali, the majority of household money continues to go to fill basic Biological needs. However, many countries have managed to move above this level and are now consuming nonessential goods in greater numbers. Pockets in Asia, Africa, and Latin America are moving from agriculture into manufacturing, freeing up both time and money. Granted, in some cases,

Figure 8-3   From Biological to Material households: how Americans spend, 1901 and 1995.

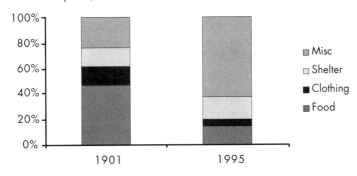

it might only translate into a few extra hours and dollars a week, but with virtually *any* extra income, people consume more. Whether it is an extra bottle of milk, a vaccination, a newspaper, a flour grinder, a refrigerator, or an automobile, as wealth is created, a new consumer segment is born.

As people earn more (and have more time), what they value is reflected in what they consume. In a Biological society, physiological needs rule: A man toils in a field to produce wheat for bread and other basic survival items. As industrialization takes root, however, he'll begin to earn more from a factory job. Suddenly, with some extra purchasing power, he might simply want to eat more bread (particularly if he has been undernourished). He may start buying his bread at the store rather than making it at home (also saving time and creating leisure), particularly if mass-producing bakeries bring down the cost of bread.

As this man accumulates more money and free time, his wants will change, and he will focus on quality needs. When his desire for bread is satisfied, he will use his extra income to purchase different things. After all, there is only so much bread a man can eat. So maybe he'll buy butter for the bread. Perhaps he will desire a *choice* of bread to buy: enriched white, nine-grain, rye, or pumpernickel. Or perhaps he'll want special breads, maybe fresh baked croissants, bagels, or muffins. As he grows wealthier, and is no longer concerned with basic food, perhaps he'll adopt a low-carbohydrate diet and realize he no longer wants bread at all, but instead low-sugar, high-protein bars. This is wealth and the beginning of consumer culture: the extra time and money that provides people with a choice of what to consume, and thus, the consumption cycle spins.

In pre-industrial Biological societies, people have few options. They work to simply survive. But as people move along the economic continuum and get to approximately $2,000 per capita per year, what they consume changes. Now, along with food on the table, they can buy a bicycle to go to work versus walking, creating more free time. Moreover, as wages grow another $40 per week—or an additional $2,000 per year—they can buy a telephone, a radio, and maybe a TV, all of which increase their contact with the larger world.

As per-capita annual income ratchets up to the $2,000–4,000 range, demand for durables, or "white goods" like washing machines and refrigerators, increases. At $5,000 and higher, entertainment (CDs, movies, electronics) and banking—along with other financial services—become important because there is money to save. At Material income levels between $10,000–30,000, demand for automobiles and higher quality goods accelerates. Above that, demand for Experiential goods and services—voluntary healthcare and wellness, travel, and many other luxuries—increases. An analysis of changing consumption patterns reinforces the observations made by Fukuyama about "recognition" needs and by Maslow about personal value and self-worth. Fukuyama argues that economically and politically, open systems are most conducive to achieving recognition by allowing people to freely participate in meaningful social and economic work. A corollary to this process is greater wealth and greater consumption.

ENTERTAINMENT: AN ESSENTIAL NEED?

With more time and money to enjoy than ever before, how people entertain themselves has become an important element in modern life. As I researched the confluence of needs, values, lifestyle, and economics, I stumbled into the following thought-provoking quote:

"Entertainment has become a necessity.

The statement seems unsupportable: Can entertainment be necessary in the sense that food, clothing, and shelter are necessary?

Certainly, people are spending more of their time and money on entertainment than ever before, demanding it in more kinds and greater volume; certainly it is vital, integral—but necessary?

Perhaps, though, the problem is not with the word "necessary," but with the word "entertainment." As recently as 20 years ago, "entertainment"—diversion, amusement—would have served adequately to describe the vast majority of movies, TV, radio, popular print, and recorded sound. But today, the word seems inadequate, outdistanced by events. The role of these media is now something far more various and crucial than the pleasurable passing of time. In their mechanical operations—the projection of photographic images onto a screen to simulate movement; the magnetic reproduction of sound frequencies; the transmission by broadcast waves of sounds and images—the media are essentially the same. Yet in their personal and social usefulness, they are utterly changed.

What happened?

The pace of world industrialization that has steadily accelerated since the 19th Century is widely believed to have effected a severe change to individual identity: An increasingly efficient and standardized world jeopardizes personal freedom, importance, and opportunity, with a consequent sensation of the disenfranchisement of self....Having allowed technology to create the problem, man has begin using technology to redress it. With the exponentially increased availability of all forms of communication, the media of "entertainment" have pressed into service the individual with models of experience, opportunities for self-recognition, and the ingredients to identify. Never has mass "entertainment" been as necessary to the lives of as many individuals as it is today."

Indeed, entertainment has become a staple for Material and Experiential lifestyles, and is even growing important to the Biological world. What is truly amazing about the above statement is how prophetic it would be; it was written in 1977, well before technologies like cable TV, personal computing, satellite transmission, and the Internet became ubiquitous. It was made by the company that eventually would evolve into AOLTime-Warner, which in many ways symbolizes the merging of media today by combining dozens of leading online, print, movies, recorded music, and other entertainment products and services under one roof.[9]

THE GLOBAL BAZAAR

Consumption, exemplified by the U.S., is now a universal trend. Whether it's Chinese families buying their first refrigerator, Bolivians opening their first can of Pepsi, or Poles watching music videos, lifestyle convergence has been vastly accelerated in the past few decades as technology has broken down international barriers. The rise of the consumption leisure lifestyle has been pushed along by the drive for open trade and financial markets, which more governments have recognized (or have been forced to recognize) as required for growth and progress. During the 20th Century, international trade and capital flows exploded. Fueled by decreasing transportation and communication costs, this resulted in more international interaction and contact than ever before. It made the once luxurious, exotic, and nonindigenous—like pineapples, mahogany, or coffee—common household items in wealthy countries. It also exposed more foreign ideas and cultures to more people than ever before.

International borders have been dissolved through economic agreements such as NAFTA and the EU. NAFTA aggregated a market with more than 350 million people generating $6 trillion in economic activity.[10] The EU has created a free trade zone of 15 different countries. Flights among Italy, France, Germany, Belgium, Netherlands, Luxembourg, Portugal, Spain, Denmark, Sweden, and

Finland have been considered domestic since October 1997.[11] The breakdown of borders reinforces the breakdown of cultural barriers. These processes are reinforcing one another in a virtuous cycle, creating more communication between countries, more consumption, and more wealth than ever before.

Fewer borders to economic and cultural exchange create more consumers. The democratization and commodification of culture mean that goods and ideas are exchanged at a rapid pace between countries—flows that go both ways. Not only are American goods popular overseas, but goods from other countries stream into U.S. and European markets as well. The U.S., for example, runs massive trade deficits, importing cars, clothes, toys, and other products from dozens of countries around the world.

What the world is witnessing in this new millennium is a realm of ideas that is growing in acceptance as a way to live. This includes representative, democratic governments that allow people to express their ideas and desires regardless of their income and a free-market economic framework that allows for comparative advantage, technology, and mass production to help reduce labor and costs for goods and services. Free from religious traditions and ideological constraints, such a common "culture" of civil, voluntary production and consumption, and protected, enforceable private property rights has been formed in the last few decades, and shows no signs of reversing. Fukuyama agrees, noting that the wealth creation process helps satisfy "an ever-expanding set of human desires. This process guarantees an increasing homogenization of all human societies, regardless of their history or culture. All countries undergoing economic modernization must increasingly resemble one another; they must unify nationally on the basis of a centralized state, urbanize, and replace traditional forms of social organization like tribe, sect, and family with economically rational ones based on function and efficiency."[12]

SHRINKING WORLD, MELDING CULTURES

In 1962, Marshall McLuhan noted prophetically: "The new electronic interdependence recreates the world in the image of a global village." In many ways, our ability to relay information, ideas, and goods globally makes the world seem even smaller than a village. Lifestyles and cultures are far more interlinked than ever before due to greater import/export flows, tourism, immigration, urbanization, and universal media access. The new speed at which information is transferred permits rapid, unprecedented cultural exchanges.

Think of transportation in the mid-19th Century, a time when more than 95% of the world's populations lived in rural settings. The fastest way to get somewhere then was by horse. Now it is by jet. The Steam Age brought about the first tourists, with ships making the first Dover–Calais run in 1821; by 1840, an estimated 100,000 people were traveling that route. That same year, the Britannia—a steamship—made the trans-Atlantic crossing in 14 days.

The earliest coast-to-coast airplane flights took two days (10 stops, including one overnight). This 36-hour trip cost $200 in 1930, more than 250 hours of American work. Through economies of scale, air travel costs have plummeted: In the summer of 2002, one could find $200 round-trip tickets from New York to California (for about 14 hours of labor). And more and more people are flying. In 1999, the total number of passengers traveling by plane was 610,628,716, up from 455,263,066 in 1989.[13] Moreover, think about how much ground we cover everyday, simply going to work: The average American covers at least 24 miles per day in motorized transport, and similar commutes are logged by hundreds of millions of working people each day around the world.

On the global level, tourism has grown into an enormous industry. According to the World Tourism Organization, cross-border tourist traffic will climb from approximately 625 million a year in 2000 to 1.6 billion in 2020. By then, travelers will be spending over $2 trillion U.S. on tourism versus $445 billion U.S. today. Moreover, travel is increasingly directed to different regions. While France is currently the top international destination, China is projected to surpass it by 2020.[14]

The cost of transporting goods, voice, and data, too, have helped shrink the world. Overseas freight rates have plunged more than 80% in the last 80 years, while telephone rates have plummeted as well. A three-minute transatlantic call has dropped more than 90% since 1950, even more so when inflation is taken into account. And in terms of long-distance service domestically, most phone companies offer 5-cents-per-minute service coast-to-coast in America.

At the personal level, human global interaction is getting cheaper by the moment. Email allows all types of messages, documents, music, and even film to be transmitted instantaneously for very modest costs. Satellite and cable TV, already ubiquitous in the U.S., are gaining penetration outside: Now, 40% of all TV households globally have dozens of channels beamed into their living rooms.

As a testament to the cross-fertilizing nature of consumption, the international trade of cultural goods has grown exponentially over the last two decades, and not just from the U.S. to the rest of the world. Between 1980 and 1998, annual world trade of printed matter, literature, music, visual arts, cinema, photography, radio, TV, games, and sporting goods surged from $95 billion U.S. to nearly $400 billion U.S.[15]

GLOBAL PROSPERITY, CONSUMPTION, AND CONVERGENCE

Perhaps the greatest benefit of the wealth creation process has been the democratization of prosperity for billions beyond subsistence. The phenomenon of driving down production costs has created near-universal access to what were considered luxuries throughout history. While the production side of wealth creation has been well-documented, what about consumption? Do humans have an insatiable appetite for goods?

The general debate over the motivation behind material accumulation and consumption—some say, excessive consumption—was probably first raised by Thomas Veblen in his famous study of late 19th Century England. "Since the consumption of more expensive goods is an evidence of wealth," he wrote in his often-quoted 1899 piece "Conspicuous Consumption," "[buying certain goods] becomes honorific; and conversely, the failure to consume in due quantity and quality becomes a mark of inferiority and demerit."[16] Author Harold Perkin echoes Veblen's observation: "If consumer demand, then, was key to the Industrial Revolution, *social emulation* was the key to consumer demand."[17]

This social emulation theory provides some insights regarding the Biological, Material, and Experiential needs framework. Think of it this way: Once, the only people who could afford to drink real champagne from France were royals and aristocrats. Because of this historic fact, drinking champagne offered a public indication of higher economic and social status. Naturally, to satisfy Maslow's esteem and status needs, many people aspired to drink champagne as to say, "Yes, I've made it. I drink champagne, too, just like the wealthy. Therefore, I should be recognized and treated accordingly."

Due to wealth creation processes, many people (and not just in France, but all around the world) can actually afford real champagne today. Now there are plenty of inexpensive, fine-tasting sparkling wines available for a few dollars a bottle—essentially the same bubbly stuff—but they are not from France's Champagne region. Many people can emulate champagne drinking with less expensive sparkling wines from California, Spain, or other countries. Modern free markets have brought the costs down immensely, and yet, these emblems of success still motivate consumers. Perceived status associated with consumption is rooted in human needs for acceptance, esteem, and status. These human needs are why the global economy is so stratified today.

What was once considered "high" culture—particularly literature, music, and the visual arts—has been democratized and blended into the Material life of leisure. Books, theater, dance, music, and many other art forms—once the sole domain of the wealthy—are completely accessible in mass-produced, reproduced forms. Few will get to see the real *Mona Lisa* in France (although more and more do every year) or have Dutch Masters hanging in their living rooms, but most will see some on TV or decent reproductions in books and magazines. Not everyone can enjoy a live performance of La Traviata in an Italian opera house, or hear Bruce Springsteen sing live at the Meadowlands, but most can have relatively easy access to these experiences on TV or with recorded music and DVDs. Not everyone can afford a Rolls Royce, but a basic automobile—one that provides the same transportation utility as a Rolls—is certainly within reach for many. In 1950, there were only 50 million cars in the world. By 2000, that number had grown to 600 million, and it is estimated to grow to 1.2 billion by 2025.[18] So now "culture," or a leisure lifestyle, comes to us neatly delivered and easily accessible; it has been commodified. Dwight Macdonald wrote in 1953: "Mass culture is very, very democratic: it absolutely refuses to discriminate against, or between, anything or anybody."[19] If you can afford it, you have earned your recognition.

FROM BIOLOGICAL TO MATERIAL

To truly appreciate the reach of global consumption, keep in mind what it was like when consumption was simply about survival. In Biologically oriented societies, there is little time or resources available for leisure. People quite literally work to live. In 18th Century Europe and the American colonies, the average person worked every day except Sunday, which was spent at church, according to the strict traditional religious norms of the community. Leisure activities may have included quilting bees for women, socializing at the pub for men, or church outings for families, but not much more.

This is not a condition left wholly in the past. Today in Mali, one of the poorest regions of the world, one family reported that they each spend 112 hours per week working. This translates into 16 hours per day, leaving only 8 hours for sleeping and any other activities. They reported wishing for an irrigation system, a motorcycle, and an enclosed garden, all possessions that would aid in survival, and make life a bit easier. [20]

As people get wealthier, their needs change: The wishes of that family in Mali may soon grow beyond the enclosed garden and motorcycle and include a car, perhaps a garage, and the ability to go on vacation. Indeed, this has been the trend of the world over the past century. Obviously, the cultural changes of today are vastly different from what they were even 50 years ago. In centuries past, children could look forward to a life similar to that of their parents and grandparents; social and physical mobility had yet to be discovered. Families grew up in small towns and villages and pretty much stayed in the same place their entire lives. Foreign influences and goods were rarities; the sight of a foreign person even more so.

However, the evolution of Biological societies to Material brings wholesale changes in lifestyle. One of the largest trends is urbanization, as people begin to move from farms to factories and offices. In doing so, extended families are left behind. According to the UN, in 1950, only an estimated 17.8% of less developed populations lived in urban centers. By 1975, this figure swelled to 26.8%, growing to nearly 40% by 2000, and it may approach 60% by 2030.[21] While this process might have taken three to five generations in the West, it might now occur in less than a decade or two in many developing countries—a true lifestyle shock.

As labor migrates to factories, and free time is created in dense urban cities, one can see how cosmopolitan and consumer culture take root: shopping at specialized stores and supermarkets (versus traditional open-air markets), the growing importance of convenience services (laundry, restaurants, etc.), as well as the increased consumption of entertainment (movies, TV, music, etc.). This lifestyle shift creates greater personal interaction with a wider variety of people and tastes than in the older agrarian world. A lifestyle of discount shopping, ATM banking, entertainment, cellular phones, and fast food can easily evolve during this manufacturing/urbanization phase. As a result, what once in agrarian villages may have been considered a luxury, exotic, in bad taste, or even taboo can be seen as mainstream, fashionable, or cool in the new urban setting. This trend is global. In China, there are 95.6 TVs per 100 households, 89.8 in Mexico, 89 in Azerbaijan, and 65 in Algeria.[22] Blockbuster has opened 2,000 outlets in 26 countries outside the U.S. Tower Records has 70 stores in 15 countries. International sales of software and entertainment products outsold any other U.S. industry, rising to $60 billion by 2000. Stores like IKEA, Wal-Mart, and Costco are now in countries like Mexico, and cell phone density usage in some Asian countries is much higher than in the U.S.

The demand for this cosmopolitan life of leisure and freedom—what Ben Barber has called the "culture of fun"—should not be underestimated. In Romania, the biggest tourist attraction is Southfork ranch, a billion-dollar replica of the one on the 1980s hit TV series *Dallas*.[23] Author James Twitchell notes: "One of the most startling aspects of seeing the refugees streaming in from Kosovo was the number of adolescents dressed in Adidas, Nike, and Tommy Hilfiger clothing."[24] Even in Afghanistan, one of the most politically and economically isolated countries under the Taliban, large numbers of people still managed to see smuggled copies of the Academy Award-winning film *Titanic*.[25] Teenagers all around the world—regardless of their address—dream about flashy convertibles, MP3 players, stylish clothes and hairdos, and pocket money for discretionary treats.

This purported U.S. or Western-style consumption in developing countries—which is arguably a universal phenomenon, experienced first but not exclusively in the West—also reflects the desire of poorer countries to say, "Yes, we're modernizing, too. We're making it like the rich First World." When traveling to developing countries, it's not unusual to see historic monuments crumbling next to modern shopping complexes. Locals sometimes value going to a mall and stopping for Kentucky Fried Chicken more so than a stroll through a historic neighborhood and eating at a traditional restaurant. Indeed, walk through one of the several newer shopping centers like Plaza Obelisco in Guatemala City, and you will find it vibrant, clean, and full of window-shoppers peering at the latest Calvin Klein or Polo outfits, somewhat resembling suburban mall life in a place like Paramus, New Jersey. While wealthy countries might lament the passing of quaint Third-World life—and the growth of "crass" consumerism—many people in the Biological-to-Material phase view visible consumption as an indication of true progress: more spare time and money to freely spend than ever before.

LOOKING FOR MEANING: FROM MATERIAL TO EXPERIENTIAL CONSUMPTION

As more discretionary time and money are earned, social and self-actualizing needs begin to show up more in consumption patterns. The most visible changes are the growing "quality" demands (as defined by Pilzer), moving from utility needs to luxury desires. Our possessions begin to define who we are and what we want to be. This is particularly true in the advanced industrial countries of western Europe and North America, where per-capita income well exceeds $20,000. This stratum is nearing the top of Maslow's pyramid. With Material needs satisfied, people are seeking more Experiential fulfillment. People toil not merely for survival, but to play and self-actualize.

Modern Materialistic and Experiential consumption and entertainment are remarkably individualistic. In his *Bowling Alone: The Collapse and Revival of American Community*, Harvard professor Robert Putnam notes that between 1980 and 1993, the total number of bowlers in America increased by 10% (to more than 80 million), while league bowling decreased by 40%. While bowling statistics may seem insignificant, the example underscores Putnam's main argument: that modern life is very individualistic (in his view, to a flaw), people have their own needs, and they want to sate them on their own timetable with little compromise.[26]

After two generations of unprecedented wealth surges and mass urbanization in which rural populations dropped from 60% to less than 30%, America began a trend toward suburbanization, which was echoed abroad. In 1950, the share of metropolitan area residents who lived in central cities was 57%, but by 1990, this had fallen to 37%. Similar patterns emerged in Europe, whereby cities expanded geographically in Amsterdam, Copenhagen, Frankfurt, Hamburg, Paris, and Vienna, but populations living in city centers decreased or only grew marginally. The preference for a suburban lifestyle is a function of widening affluence and the rapidly expanding middle and upper-middle classes since 1950. With wealth comes greater demand for bigger houses, gardens, and the ability to afford cars and commuting. American houses today are some 50% larger than in 1950, with more bedrooms and bathrooms, while household size has decreased by 30%.[27]

This dwelling trend, however, is being taken to a higher Experiential level, at least in the U.S. In their much-cited book, *Fortess America: Gated Communities in America*, Blakely and Snyder estimate that nearly 9 million Americans live in 20,000 gated and walled communities, up dramatically from the 1960s.[28] Moreover, the Community Association Institute estimates that in 2002, there were some 47 million Americans belonging to 231,000 community associations; in 1965, there were only 500 of these private neighborhood organizations. The Blakely and Snyder study notes that gated communities are often clusters of people who value similar things: prestige, an active lifestyle (golf, tennis, etc.), security, control, even a search for "community." However, the key commonality is their Experiential, "privatized" sense of what they want in terms of police protection, street maintenance, recreation, and entertainment, which public services do not provide. These trends reflect a greater desire for control over our most basic lifestyle issues: where to live, how much space we desire, and who our neighbors might be.

WHY BUY?

Alchemic quality demands go beyond simply living in a better house and a better neighborhood. In the U.S. and other advanced industrial countries, there has been a major trend toward individualized, high-end specialty goods in virtually every sector, from designer clothes to sport utility vehicles (SUVs). Marketing, of course, has a lot to do with this: selling the lifestyle images that focus groups say they want to emulate and be part of. There are athletic shoes for every type of activity and style sensibility; the amount of money Americans spend on sneakers rivals the GNP of many small nations.

In this world of almost infinite choice, brands play an important role, catering directly to human social and esteem needs. Consumers ultimately decide which products help them define themselves. Consumption critics often argue that our obsession with brands actually limits choice by making us willing victims of marketers.[29] However, Veblen's social emulation and conspicuous consumption theory probably doesn't fully capture the role of leisure in the modern world. The motivation to consume is, and always has been, more complex than anti-consumerists believe. Some of the more interesting modern analyses of human consumption have shown

WEALTH AND LEISURE: THE MERGING OF CONSUMPTION, CULTURE, AND LIFESTYLE Chapter 8

that our material world functions in many ways to produce meaning for individuals. As Cross notes: "Modern people, and especially Americans, communicate to others and to themselves through their goods. The consumer society has not necessarily produced passive people alienated from their true selves, as regularly assumed by traditional critics."[30]

The French author and social commentator Pierre Bourdieu has argued that consumption goes beyond basic social emulation theory.[31] Instead, he argues that consumption is far more driven by the human need to *differentiate*, whereby individuals strive to actually distinguish themselves from others through materialism, which is the exact opposite position anti-consumerists often take. Jo Dahn argues similarly: "[W]ithin the domestic sphere there exists what might be thought of as a 'landscape' of objects," which she calls an "Objectscape." Dahn believes that the worlds we create—our houses, offices, and the material things we possess—offer "both psychic and practical functions, and forms part of the multi-layered environment that each individual inhabits. The assembling of the Objectscape, and behaviors with regard to it, continues throughout life...[and] can be 'read,' providing insight as to (for instance) character, or fiscal status." Dahn notes that "gifts and inherited objects, for example, are both capable of evoking close personal ties... for within the Objectscape there will be many items that stand witness to that network of other people with whom each individual seeks to interact, and whose understanding and approval is an important factor in the process of individual and social self-definition."[32]

Indeed, as goods and services have become commodified, the global marketplace has simultaneously grown more specialized. People want *certain* goods that reflect their own particular personality. We live in a 21st Century world of infinitely segmented product lines, with prices ranging as widely as individual tastes and aesthetics. Wal-Mart offers blue jeans for less than $12, while Levis sells $20 basic jeans and $110 specialty denim pants. There are $300 basic refrigerators by Kenmore and $10,000 high-tech SubZero refrigeration systems disguised by beautiful cabinetry. DaimlerChrysler manufactures subcompact cars for around $10,000, as well as $400,000 customized Maybach limousines, and dozens of vehicles in between to suit a variety of personal needs, styles, and personalities. People like to distinguish themselves by how unique and independent their needs are. As many are consuming more, they are also trying to consume more individually.

THE NEW MARKET EQUATION:
FORM + FUNCTION = FANTASY

In advanced capitalist economies where a consumptive middle-class lifestyle has been the norm for a couple of generations, the evolving nature and importance of style and product design is worth keeping an eye on. While the slogan "You are what you buy" may seem overly simplistic, it does, indeed, represent a mindset of human needs in many wealthier countries. Veblen first wrote about "conspicuous consumption" more than 100 years ago, and the world's burgeoning middle class demands products whose form and function promote the fantasy, or experience, they desire.

For example, let's take a look at cars. In essence, they all have a similar purpose: to transport small groups of people and their belongings. Most cars hold more or less the same number of people (convertibles and minivans being the exceptions), so what motivates people to buy certain ones versus others is often less about function than style and image. My favorite example is Volkswagen's (VW's) cute-as-a-bug new Beetle, introduced in 1999. Mechanically, the car was virtually the same as VW's Golf line, and not that different from a dozen small cars on the market. Yet, the new Bug was different. It was one of the most visible products that tapped into a demographic psyche—the fun, free-wheeling 1960s association of freedom, youth, and simplicity. The new Beetle said: Sure, people need cars, but they also need some exhilaration, fun, and meaning in what they drive. The car, in essence, becomes a personal statement of the owner. It is no shock that some of the hottest cars in recent years—the Beetle, Chrysler's Prowler and PT Cruiser, BMW's revived Mini Cooper, GM's Hummer H2, and the rejuvenated convertible market (beginning with Mazda's Miata in the late 1980s, followed by BMW's Z3, Porsche Boxster, and Ford's retro Thunderbird)—represent the desire to satisfy psychic, Experiential needs high up in Maslow's pyramid. In this vein, the recent trend toward SUVs represents a similar vibe: the need for a staid, boxy station wagon, but the desire not to be caught dead in one. While most SUVs have 4-wheel drive, few really ever take advantage of the off-road capabilities.[33] And take note: For many buyers of these in-demand cars, price is generally not a concern, and profit margins tend to be much greater versus their commodified brethren. According to R.L. Polk, the number of U.S. households that bought a third or fourth car jumped more than 30% in recent years, and typically such a car would fall in this "road candy" category.

It goes beyond cars. Take Apple products like iMac computers or the iPod MP3 player. In essence, their functions are fairly ordinary and can be purchased more cheaply in clunkier packages in less attractive colors. But, Apple iMacs and iBooks look *cooler* than their competitors, and Apple users *feel* cooler than those who use the clunky-looking products. Certainly, some of the competition has caught on and begun to integrate design more readily into their products.

In the kitchen—much to the delight of the Viking and SubZero companies, as well as competitors who have wised up—we have hundreds of stainless-steel appliances to make us feel like professional chefs. We use spices, pans, and cutlery that Bobby Flay or Martha Stewart wield in their kitchens, making us feel more confident and content in our everyday culinary duties.

The desire for style, status, and meaning, indeed, becomes blurred with brands, products, and designs. And these desires are not limited simply to super-wealthy Experiential economies. Even in developing countries in Asia, Latin America, or the former Soviet Union, the desires to drink Pepsi, wear Dockers, watch *The Sopranos*, or drive a Harley Davidson or a Dodge Ram pick-up are intrinsically bound with a desire to feel cool and confident, and promote a specific desired public image.

Successful companies invest substantial effort and resources into harnessing such "placebo effects" in product design. As Carnegie Mellon professors and authors Jonathan Cagan and Craig M. Vogel note in their book *Creating Breakthrough Products*: "We are not just talking about products that are competitive, but products that redefine their markets and often transcend their original program goals to create new markets." Indeed, manufacturers of everything from underwear to washing machines must consider design and image issues on par with—or even paramount to—functionality and performance.

In some cases, selling Experiential fantasies, literally, has become big business. Always wanted to travel on the Orient Express or trek on an African safari? No problem, luxury travel companies like Abercrombie & Kent will be happy to map your itinerary out. Ever fantasized about playing professional baseball or another sport? There are no less than two dozen fantasy sports camps that, for about $4,000/week, will allow you to play with some of your childhood sports heroes in professional stadiums. There are thousands of schools and weekend classes that will teach you how to cook like Emeril, drive a racecar like Jeff Gordon, dance like a Joffrey ballerina, climb Kilamanjaro, write like Hemingway—you name it. And even if you can't really perform like your hero, you *feel* like one, even if only for a short while.

BEYOND THE MATERIAL WORLD

The question that wealthier Material and Experiential people (or what Americans call "middle" and "upper-middle" class) have been asking themselves is: Are we done yet? And the answer, in many cases, is yes. In the post-Material world, people are striving for greater experience and meaning in their lives. Economic and material achievements are no longer the top priorities; rather, they have been displaced by an increasing emphasis on "quality of life" or "wellness." Many over-consumers have realized that the costs of pursuing excessive wealth may outweigh the benefits in some cases: Some people are working long hours in jobs they despise, spending more money than they make, and gobbling up the earth's resources at a dizzying rate. They want more free time and less stress, and may be willing to accept less money in the bargain. After all, wealth is supposed to be about freedom, and many people feel chained to the production consumption treadmill. In a recent poll, 69% of Americans said they would like to "slow down and live a more relaxed life," versus 19% who said they would like a "more exciting, faster-paced life."[34]

In an essay on simple living, Duane Elgin identifies some of the main components of the concept: investing time and energy in civic and community programs; spending quality time with family and friends; developing a holistic sense of self, including physical activity; fulfilling emotional and spiritual needs; connecting with the earth and recycling; lowering the patterns of personal consumption; and pursuing a livelihood that reflects these goals and contributes to the world. Many of these components reflect an Experiential mindset.[35]

Fukuyama also sees this trend: "It is perhaps no accident that in the most [Experiential] part of the U.S., California, one finds the most obsessive pursuit of high-risk leisure activities that have no purpose but to shake the participant out of the comfort of bourgeois existence: rock climbing, hang gliding, skydiving, marathon running, Ironman and Ironwoman races, and so forth. For where traditional forms of struggle like war are not possible, and where widespread material prosperity makes economic struggle unnecessary, [Experiential] individuals begin to search for other kinds of *contentless* activities that can win them recognition."[36]

This is not to suggest that all Experiential-trenders are moving away from consumption and production. Inglehart says these people "do not place a negative value on economic and physical security—they value it positively, like everyone else; but unlike [Materialists], they give even higher priority to self-expression and quality of life."[37] Experientials may seek more individual and thoughtful consumption. They may want products that are sensitive to the environment, or customized items that reflect their own particular aesthetic rather than the latest and greatest mass-marketed materials—further adding to the mushrooming marketplace of specialty products.

EXPERIENTIAL BUSINESS

Creating goods and services that consumers value is central to any capitalistic system. But what do Materials and Experiential trenders value these days? A peek into an average American's refrigerator, cupboards, clothes closets, or garage will probably reveal hundreds of branded products, some fancy, some fairly plain. Sure, some pay extra for things like "organic certified" food, tennis shirts with polo players, and sneakers with swooshes. Everyone has his or her own values and tastes. But, would an average American or European pay the same price for things that were equivalent in quality to branded goods, but were actually produced in a socially responsible, ecologically sustainable way? Would he or she buy goods that helped the less fortunate climb aboard the global wealth creation process?

In the Experiential-trending world, the answer is increasingly "yes." Take Newman's Own salad dressing. In 1982, actor Paul Newman agreed to brand products (originally just salad dressing, but now the line includes popcorn, lemonade, salsa, pretzels, and pasta sauce) with his well-known face and donate profits to educational and charitable organizations. Since its inception, Newman's Own has spread globally to Experiential markets in Australia, Iceland, England, Germany, France, Israel, and Japan. Thousands of charities have received over $125 million in donations from these sales. For roughly the same price of any premium salad dressing, you can buy Newman's Own and send some money to a worthy charity.

The "Fair Trade" movement takes the social-mindedness of Newman's Own a notch higher. While acknowledging the realities of free trade, Fair Trade is a philosophy of paying workers a "living wage," enough for decent living conditions within a country. Moreover, Fair Trade producers are required to engage in practices that promote environmental sustainability and safe working conditions. Instead of buying products because of style, marketing blitzes, or status, customers who patronize Fair Trade do it because they feel better about the way the product is made. In this respect, a Fair Trade logo isn't really that different from a polo player on a tennis shirt—a brand with which one can identify for personal satisfaction. Fair Trade is simply a badge of social responsibility, not financial status.

After requests from many customers, Starbucks has committed to brewing Fair Trade coffee once a month, along with selling Fair Trade bulk beans in every store. Depressed prices in recent years have resulted in coffee middlemen pressing global farmers to lower wages and employ children in the fields. To counter this, Starbucks has guaranteed to pay Fair Trade cooperatives approximately $1.25 per pound for beans (versus current market prices of 50–70 cents). By joining forces with Starbucks and other corporations, farmers are now able to guarantee sustainable prices at a rate at which they can operate. Starbucks makes the extra cost back by charging a buck or two more per pound for Fair Trade coffee.

There are dozens of successful Experiential branding ventures, such as the mid-1980s "dolphin safe" campaign to promote better fishing practices using the "Flipper" logo on canned tuna. Recently, 400 companies, including Home Depot and Staples, agreed to sell wood and paper made from "sustainably-managed timber," another Fair Trade-like movement that promotes better logging practices. Worldwide, Fair Trade sales total only $400 million each year for a mere 0.01% of global commerce—small, but the trend could easily grow. As wealth increases and consumers increasingly exercise their Experiential values through their consumption, tremendous social and ecological progress could be made globally. Imagine entire lines of clothing, foods, or even electronics carrying Fair Trade-type logos. Or imagine how major MNCs could potentially use such social-minded logos, like Starbucks has, to attract a wider audience. The net result would be greater wealth creation around the world.

These Experiential values are also mainstreaming into the financial world. The term "socially responsible investing (SRI)" came into vogue in the 1980s, reflecting certain environmental, labor, and human rights that needed to be incorporated in business. In April of 2000, TIAA–CREF—one of the largest pension funds in the world—launched a socially responsible fund that screened out alcohol, tobacco, weapons, and nuclear energy, as well as companies that fail to practice sound environmental policies and the like.[38] In another SRI advance, the influential California Pension Employee Retirement System (CalPERS)—with over $170 billion in assets—announced in June 2000 that it would start allocating capital for SRI as part of its overall investment strategy.[39] According to one report, CalPERS is "throwing its weight behind new goals: creating jobs, rejuvenating inner cities, providing affordable housing, and putting pressure on developing countries to give citizens basic freedoms."[40] In Europe, nine new SRI stock indices emerged in 2001, along with resolutions passed in Belgium, France, Germany, and Sweden requiring public pension funds to disclose how SRI is accounted for in investment decisions.[41] As of late 2002, there were approximately 75 actively managed SRI funds in the world.[42] Four of them had more than $1 billion under management and were rated as 5-star funds by Morningstar. Most important for wealth creationists, 58% have actually outperformed the S&P 500 since inception.[43]

Who said social responsibility has to mean charity?

WESTERNIZATION OR CROSS-FERTILIZATION?

Although critics charge that Western countries are foisting junk food and shlock entertainment on consumers in the developing world, the reality reflects far more of a cultural exchange than one might expect. Anti-globalists often forget that places like America are vast melting pots of cultural trends and tastes. Immigration to the U.S. over the last 100 years has dramatically altered what constitutes American "culture." The U.S. is forever borrowing from abroad, whether it's food (think about pizza, sushi, Chinese take-out, and Taco Bell), fashion (stores filled with European names like Dior, Versace, Prada, and Armani), or entertainment (*Harry Potter, Pokemon*, John Woo films, and reality-TV shows like *Big Brother* and *Survivor*). Most of America's professional sports leagues are filled with world-class, international-born players. While European immigrants in the early 20th Century brought many continental tastes to the U.S., one would expect growing Latin and Asian influences over the coming generation to reflect the greater immigration trends and influences from these regions.

In the evolution from a Biological to a Material society, similar patterns emerge. Most societies have strands of traditional sensibilities woven into their modern, more cosmopolitan lifestyles. In India, for example, with the younger generation, "anything American—from DKNY and Nike to Pizza Hut and McDonald's—is often considered 'cool.'"[44] But the youth retain their Indian roots in terms of traditional values regarding sex and marriage, for example.

Particularly in the realm of culture and entertainment, remember that the West has experienced three to four generations of mass wealth and leisure, and has created enormous industries around this lifestyle. Entertainment is where many wealthy countries' comparative advantages *currently* lie, but this is changing. Entertainment industries are sprouting in developing countries, such as the Bollywood film sector in India (which annually produces some 800 films, considerably more than U.S. production).

Increasingly, there is a broad, international, cultural exchange in entertainment. For example, take one of America's great multinational operators, Music Television, or MTV. MTV Networks (which also includes VH-1, Nickelodeon, CMT, and BET, among other channels) reaches an estimated 1 billion people in more than 160 countries, and more than 80% of its audience actually lives outside the U.S.

MTV's great success—creating possibly the most ubiquitous global brand after Coca Cola—is not due to a "push" strategy of playing only U.S.-produced content and showcasing the latest Brittany Spears video. Instead, MTV has developed a policy of broadcasting at least 70% local content into Asia, Africa, Latin America, and eastern Europe; indeed, most global MTV viewers don't think of MTV as American. The company does not own a record company, leaving itself conflict-free regarding what music it broadcasts. While there were occasional political snafus in MTV's early global expansion, MTV Networks' president Bill Roedy has noted that governments around the world have generally welcomed MTV into their entertainment/media communities: "We've had very little resistance once we explain that we're not in the business of exporting American culture."[45]

MTV's success and global acceptance are derived from seeking out local talent such as Spanish-speaking sensation Shakira in Colombia (a multiple Grammy winner in the U.S.) and Alejandro Sanz from Spain and Juanes; Russian performers like t.A.T.u and Alsou; Scandinavian groups like Royksopp, Bofunk MC, and the Hives; and Asian stars like Japan's Hikaru Utada and China's Jay Chou, Na Ying, Jolin Tsai, and Adrian Sami. In addition to broadcasting local music, MTV has cultivated specific local programming which is as varied as *Rockgol* in Brazil (where Brazilian musicians and music execs play soccer), *Twelve Angry Viewers* in Russia (a talk show), *MTV Kitchen* (where musicians cook) in Italy, and *Conexion*, a live show from Mexico broadcast throughout Latin America.[46] According to one MTV international strategist, the focus on local content is "the only globalization strategy that truly builds value in the long run. MTV wants to cater to the lifestyle of 2–3 billion people globally in the 10–35 age bracket. This is the demographic of high personal consumption on music, clothing, and food. Our job is to help promote and deliver what local consumers want in dozens of local markets, not to tell them what's worth buying or watching."

MTV is also focusing on interactive technologies to help drive localized programming. *Total Request Live (TRL)*, whereby listeners call in and choose their favorite videos, is incredibly popular all around the world (perhaps echoing Fukuyama's universal desire for recognition). The company's Asia group has also launched something called LiLi (Mandarin for "pretty"), a computer-generated, anime-styled female VJ that viewers can interact with on a real-time basis. LiLi functions in five Asian languages, interviewing local musicians and chit-chatting about popular culture.[47] Finally, as a testament to how much local programming is being produced, MTV now hosts 11 regional *MTV Video Music Award* shows around the world annually.

THE MODERN CONSUMER: ALL-POWERFUL OR POWERLESS?

Since Veblen's writing in the late 19th Century, there has been an endless debate over why people consume. In the wealthier new millennium, the discussion now focuses on whether people are consuming *too* much and for what reasons. This became even more hotly contested in 1990s America, a decade that started supposedly with less conspicuous consumption than the "greed-is-good" 1980s. However, combining technology advances with greater purchasing power and income—and easy credit—many Americans went on a spending binge for a second or third car, new computers, vacations, and designer everything. Is there something inherently wrong with this?

Some argue that all this consumption has not made us happier. There are social theorists who blame corporate culture for exerting mind control, making us buy what we don't really want or need. Banks lend us money easily, addicting us to credit cards. The media reinforces consumptive messages by shamelessly bombarding us with lifestyle images that can never be achieved by average people. Such anxieties keep us awake at night, only to be met by Orwellian infomercials on cable TV hawking products and services to better cope with such anxiety.

There's some truth to the message that too much consumption is bad for us, just like eating too much is unhealthy. Yes, many people spend more than they make and rack up unnecessary debt. Yes, most of us worry too much about what others think of us. But the apparently "empty" existence of the modern consumer may be more full than many critics think.

Today's consumer might be considered more powerful than ever. Just 50 or 100 years ago, we were forced to buy whatever stores wanted to sell us, at much higher relative prices to our labor. Competition was nonexistent. Today we have access to infinitely more goods—in wider ranges of quality—with dramatically lower prices. Mass retailers have seen the purchasing power of consumers ratchet up quickly while prices drop and margins fall even faster. The Internet has only accelerated this trend.

Instead of being overwhelmed, think of it this way: Your ability and options for purchasing goods and services have never been greater. A dizzying trip to a modern supermarket confirms this, with 50-foot aisles of assorted breads, hundreds of sodas and drink choices, etc. The average grocery store carries approximately 30,000 different items today versus 800 in 1950.[48]

Are we all being held hostage to the global consumption machine? The answer lies with each individual consumer. Whatever pressures there are to drink Snapple, lease a new BMW or join a country club, the process is, in the end, voluntary. We all have the right to buy what we want, and our greatest right may be to *not buy at all*. The growing simplicity and downscaling movements in the U.S. and other wealthy countries represent the Experiential trend toward a "higher" quality of life—less stress, less stuff, fewer entanglements, fewer headaches. The hectic, consumptive life of keeping up with the Joneses is a matter of personal choice.

Instead of feeling helpless, people should feel empowered by the ability to control what they consume. Don't forget that the U.S. government actually subsidizes *philanthropic* consumption, providing tax deductions for money voluntarily going to nonprofit organizations. In many respects, people who want to work for a better world—versus shopping—can support a variety of charitable causes and actually be subsidized to do so. Our free-market system has driven down the costs of living dramatically, and we should feel good about that monumental accomplishment. That process is spreading globally. 21st Century Materialists and Experientialists have more options than ever before: The choices between more designer clothes or more charity, less work, and less consumption are a triumph of prosperity, not an indictment of it.

CLASHES OR COMMON GROUND?

Wealth has produced free time and disposable income, and that combination has led to a consumer-driven, leisure culture in Material and Experiential-trending societies. Globalization has intensified these trends, but it has not resulted in a homogenization of culture; to the contrary, choices available to the consumer are almost infinite. The transforming impact of consumerism is not just material in nature; it is at the heart of the modern human's need for self-esteem and recognition. In Experiential segments of society, the marketplace extends even further, to choices that are philosophical and self-defining in nature.

But not everyone around the world finds these developments good news. Time and time again, this process of globalization has promoted strong, knee-jerk reactions against the perceived threat of forced assimilation. In Canada and parts of New England, local communities are fighting to keep out the giant Wal-Mart retail chain for fear it will replace traditional, small-town stores. In France, there was staunch cultural opposition to the construction of EuroDisney, tagged "a cultural Chenobyl" by one local Paris newspaper. Both France and South Korea (among others) have quotas on the number of American films that can be screened. In the developing world, protesters have occasionally stormed Pizza Huts and Burger Kings in violent protests of Americanization.

There are people who find these trends so threatening that they are willing to die to stop them. This clash of cultures, or "Jihad versus McWorld," as Barber called it in 1995, clearly has ramifications for the rest of the world. The advent of mass, instantaneous communications has brought the Biological world increasingly into conflict with more Material and Experiential places. As September 11 demonstrated to most Americans, privileged Materialists and Experientials can no longer sit back and enjoy Big Macs, Levis, and PowerADE without contemplating what such consumption and lifestyles mean for the world, particularly those not yet engaged in the wealth creation process.

But rather than marking the demise of local culture and tradition, cultural cross-fertilization and consumer trends may actually provide the mechanisms for all cultures to thrive. There are billions of children now growing up around the world with a common lifestyle: one of increased leisure, entertainment, individual choice, and fun. As Cross mentions, "Consumerism—the understanding of self in society through goods—has provided on balance a more dynamic and popular, while less destructive, ideology of public life than most political belief systems in the 20th Century."[49] For most of history, the ability to see and experience any foreign lifestyle was an impossibility; today, we can partake of global culture while still maintaining local traditions. The progression of our days may be similar: millions wake, eat, go to school or an office, relax to TV, movies, music, books, magazines, or newspapers, wear clothes chosen for style, and communicate via cell phones or the Internet. But people have more choices than ever before; no one culture or set of traditions has a monopoly on our minds or wallets.

The progression into this wealthier world of leisure and choice is slow for many, but it is happening. Chinese in the 21st Century care far more about individual consumerism than Mao, and the Russians tossed away Marx and Lenin more than a decade ago. The leisure culture of today is a contemporary "Esperanto," a second language that allows people all over the globe to communicate, yet at the same time preserve their own languages and cultural identities.

9
Wealth and the Environment:

The Costs of Success

Everything has its price.

In 1798, the Reverend Thomas Malthus published his now-famous prediction that the growing human population would one day be unable to feed itself. While this prophecy has not yet come true, the wealth creation process has had profound impacts on the earth: Consumption, production, and people all deplete resources and create waste. Today, we have vastly more consumption, more production, and more people than ever before, and growth shows no signs of slowing.

But, are turbo-capitalism and environmentalism implacable enemies? Are the two ideals, one economic and the other social, mutually exclusive? Not necessarily. Values toward the environment shift with prosperity, and wealthier Material and Experiential trenders are among the most vocal in protection of the natural world. Saving the environment ultimately means reshaping consumer and commercial patterns, changes that have significant economic costs attached to them. This chapter will explore how the Biological, Material, and Experiential worlds are grappling with prosperity's impact on the world's resources and the contentious global debate over how to manage environmental degradation.

THE HANGOVER OF PROGRESS?

Human impact on the environment is a function of three main factors: population size, per-capita consumption of resources, and technologies—not surprisingly, all are part of the wealth creation story.[1] Since 1900, the world's population has tripled while the global economy has grown 20-fold, fossil fuel consumption 30-fold, and aggregate industrial activity 50-fold.[2] According to the World Wildlife Fund's (WWF) *Living Planet Report* (1998), between 1970 and 1995 more than 30% of the non-renewable resources that sustain life on the planet were lost. Every product comes from the earth and returns to it in one form or another. Forests are shrinking, fish stocks are declining, temperatures are warming, topsoil is eroding, and water is increasingly polluted or scarce. Indeed, our demands on the environment continue to expand as populations grow and consume more, raising serious questions concerning long-term survivability.

A SNAPSHOT OF ENVIRONMENTAL EGRADATION[3]

There are countless ways that human activity leaves marks on the natural environment. Fishing, farming, land use patterns, and the growing need for more material goods all lead quite directly to the problems discussed below. These problems, in turn, impact human life in very real ways. Health is compromised, as is nutrition and sustainable agriculture. In the long term, without proper management of our natural resources, an increasing proportion of people in the world may be consigned to lives of poverty and want. Here are eight areas of concern noted by the World Bank:

Global climate change—During the 20th Century, the earth's mean global temperature warmed steadily, and six of its warmest years occurred in the 1990s. It is believed that the large-scale human use of fossil fuels has increased the amount of heat-trapping carbon in the atmosphere by over 30% since the Industrial Revolution began. Global sea levels have been rising by approximately 2 centimeters each decade, but some fear they may rise by 95 centimeters by 2100, flooding certain low-lying coastal areas.

Stratospheric Ozone depletion—Ozone, which protects life from ultraviolet-B radiation, has been depleted at increasing rates since 1979. This leads to rising ground levels of UV rays with serious ramifications for human health.

Loss of bio-diversity—Since 1600, 484 recorded animal and 654 recorded plant species have become extinct. Human activity may cause a loss of biodiversity at 50–100 times the average rate of species loss. A quarter of the world's plants are threatened with extinction by 2010, and more than 38% of U.S. amphibians are endangered.

Deforestation and unsustainable forest use—Only 20% of the world's original forests remain in an unmanaged state. More than one-fifth of the world's tropical (and most diverse) forests have been cleared since 1960. Deforestation leads to desertification and rapid/unsustainable environmental change. Forests are also host to most of the world's species, and deforestation undermines these habitats.

Desertification and land degradation—Over one-fourth of the world's land surface is used for farming. Poor land management leads to desertification. By 2025, the World Bank estimates that the people adversely affected by this process could double to 1.8 billon.

Freshwater degradation—Today, one-third of the world's population is living with moderate or severe water stress. In 2025, this number may grow to two-thirds. 1.3 billion people lack access to adequate safe water, and 2 billion do not have access to adequate sanitation.

Marine environment and resource degradation—Many coastal waters have been contaminated around the world. Red tides have increased everywhere, and total marine fish production is leveling off as more than two-thirds of the world's fish stocks have been fished at or beyond what may be sustainable.

Persistent organic pollutants—These are chemicals that resist natural breakdown and persist in the environment. The average American has traces of some 500 different chemicals. By the time the Mississippi River reaches the Gulf of Mexico, it contains enough toxins to poison a lake the size of New Jersey.

The relationship between development and the environment has been described as an "environmental Kuznet curve," an inverted U-shaped curve.[4] Growing GNP increases environmental destruction *to a certain point*, and then it begins to decline. This means developing countries need to promote growth and consumption to improve the lives of their citizens, which in turn will lead to greater demand for environmental protection. Generally, subsistence economies in low stages of development have a minimal impact on their environment and on a country's resources. Think of nomadic or small farming population areas. As agriculture, industrialization, and resource extraction grow, waste generation, resource exhaustion, and pollution accelerate, as they have in China in recent decades, and as they did in the West during the 20th Century. However, higher levels of economic development and wealth creation (as in parts of the U.S. and western Europe today) also produce advanced technologies and information service industries that are more efficient and less resource-intensive. Additionally, a social demand for increased environmental quality leads to a leveling off or decline in environmental damage.[5] People demand better environmental protection because, in many ways, they can afford it.

The underlying reasons for environmental degradation go beyond the obvious increase in population and material wants. Poor public policies, inappropriate technologies, and the failure to take advantage of the latest, cleanest methods are also at fault. Often, it is not in the immediate, short-term economic interests of governments, companies, and consumers to use the cleanest means of production.

BIOLOGICAL-TO-MATERIAL ISSUES

Growing energy consumption may be linked to atmosphere changes. Expanding agriculture has diminished forests and led to desertification around the world. Industrial waste and poor sanitation have degraded world water supplies. While these issues are global in scope, for developing nations, environmental degradation poses a unique problem as it is intertwined with economic development and long-term national security. For these nations, the problems are immediate, such as contaminated water and polluted air. A 1997 World Bank study estimated that the cost of air and water pollution (due to lost productivity) in China during 1995 was equivalent to an astonishing 7% of the country's output.[6] Among the country's biggest issues are soil erosion, deforestation, land degradation, water shortages, and wetlands damage. Another study estimated the health costs of air pollution in Jakarta and Bangkok in the early 1990s at around 10% of these cities' income.[7] In 1996, 84% of Chileans thought their health had been affected by environmental problems, up 28 points from a 1992 study. Eighty percent of Peruvians also agreed.[8]

Not only are developing countries saddled with the consequences of their own environmental problems, but also the fallout from thriving industrial countries. Approximately 20% of the world—largely advanced Material countries—have accounted for approximately 50% of global carbon dioxide emissions since 1950. And while deforestation is concentrated in the developing world, over half of the wood and the world's paper is consumed by the world's wealthier 20%.[9] The conspicuous consumption of the rich has a lasting impact on the poor.

It is not terribly surprising that developing nations are wary of strict environmental rules proposed by international institutions and wealthy nations. Countries amid industrialization and growth are generally concerned with physical sustenance and safety, which are not Material or Experiential concerns. They do not necessarily have the luxury of embracing environmentalism. A 1998 U.S.IA poll in India found that only 7.6% of respondents indicated the environment as the first priority in government spending. This came behind population control (18.7%), job creation (10.4%), infrastructure projects (9.4%), and education (8.3%).[10]

EXPANDING WORLDWIDE CONSUMPTION

Countries migrating from the Biological to the Material stage leave their mark on the planet. Throughout the lifecycle of a good—from production to use and disposal—there are innumerable environmental impacts. Table 9–1 shows long-term trends in the private consumption of selected items in both the industrial

Table 9–1   Long-Term Trends in Private Consumption of Selected Items, by Region [11]

Item	Year	World	Industrial Countries	Developing Countries
Meat (mil. of tons)	1970	86	57	29
	1995	199	95	103
Cereals	1970	473	91	382
	1995	866	160	706
Total Energy (mil. of tons of oil equivalent)	1975	5,575	4,338	1,237
	1994	8,504	5,611	2,893
Electricity (bil. of kilowatt-hours)	1980	6,286	5,026	1,260
	1995	12,875	9,300	3,575
Petrol (mil. of tons)	1980	551	455	96
	1995	771	582	188
Cars (mi.)	1975	249	228	21
	1999E	600	465	135
Bicycles Produced (mil.)	1970	36		
	1995	109		
McDonald's Restaurants	1991	12,418	11,970	448
	1996	21,022	19,198	1,824

and developing world. Note that while wealthier countries are the largest consumers, developing countries are catching up through faster growth rates.

Today, many developing governments recognize the need for sustainable development but lack the means to provide these services to their populations. Poor countries may have a choice either to repeat the industrialization process of the wealthier world or to use technologies and public policy to pre-empt harmful environmental fallout. A 2000 World Bank report suggests that some are doing just that.[12] The report shows that, in some cases, countries are able to improve water and air quality *before* they hit a "middle income" level. For example, another World Bank study found that steel production in open economies is more likely to utilize the latest technologies, reducing pollution by 17% as compared to production in closed, statist economies.[13]

THE GREENING OF THE EXPERIENTIAL TRENDING WORLD

In the industrialized West, concerns over the environment have roots in the Material need and value shifts of the early 20th Century.[14] However, environmentalism, as it is now known, is a relatively recent cultural and political phenomenon. Not until the 1960s, when widespread activism began to challenge the status quo, did the conservation movement begin to have real social and political meaning. Rachel Carson's book *Silent Spring* (1962) about the effects of DDT on birds was among the first popular books underscoring the environmental impacts of modern life. In his 1963 essay "Environment: A New Focus of Public Policy?" Lynton Caldwell indicated a shift in American attitudes to the environment precipitated by more knowledge regarding human impact

Not until Material activism in the 1960s did conservation gain social and political traction.

on natural surroundings. It was at this time that "environmentalism" entered the lexicon as a replacement for "conservationism,"[15] and the focus shifted from resource and land management to pollution and waste management and their impact on individuals and local communities.

From the 1960s and 1970s rose recognizable groups devoted to the cause of environmental protection: The Sierra Club, Friends of the Earth, Greenpeace, the Natural Resources Defense Council, and the Environmental Defense Fund became highly visible and were instrumental in shaping the environmental legislative agenda at the U.S. state and federal levels. Increasing public awareness of environmental issues led to the passage of several important legislative milestones, including the Clean Air Act (1963) and the Wilderness Act (1964).

FROM LUNATIC FRINGE TO MAINSTREAM—
A SHORT HISTORY OF GREENPEACE

Perhaps some of the most memorable images of the early modern environmental movement are of the David-and-Goliath battles waged by Greenpeace: tiny vessels confronting large whaling ships or trying to enter nuclear test zones in protest. Indeed, the first Greenpeace mission in 1970 consisted of a rented boat and a trip to the site of a nuclear test at Amchitka, Alaska. The group's founders were frustrated by what they saw as the general inaction of mainstream environmentalists.[16]

When it was initially formed in 1970, Greenpeace was a radical, grassroots environmental organization with a deep desire to shake up the way people see and interact with the environment. While many of their missions failed in specific intent, the publicity and support they generated spawned a whole new form of environmental protest. According to the group's first president, Robert Hunter: "If crazy stunts were required in order to draw the focus of the cameras that led back to millions and millions of brains, then crazy stunts were what we would do."[17] Greenpeace became the leader in action-oriented environmentalism.

The organization slowly developed a wider, global following. And after the bombing of a Greenpeace vessel, the Rainbow Warrior, by French security agents in 1985, the organization swelled into one of the largest global environmental organizations, surpassing in membership many of the more mainstream groups. By 1990, Greenpeace had offices in more than 150 countries worldwide, as a testament to changing global sensibilities and values regarding the environment.

Today, Greenpeace is a more mainstream organization than radical environmental group, with international lobbying efforts. This transformation underscores the worldwide shift in environmental consciousness as individuals have become more aware of their impact on the natural world.

By the 1970s, environmentalism had developed a consistent following and an agenda that began to be accepted by the greater body politic. A Gallup poll from that period shows that concern about air and water pollution grew from 15% to 53% between 1965 and 1970. A growing individual concern and awareness of the natural environment became a focal point for larger scale activism, and the movement began to influence the business and political communities of North American and western European societies. Now the movement has been accepted as a cultural norm.

As societies continue to grow economically and achieve an undisputed level of financial security, their concerns shift from economic well-being to self-expression and quality of life. The *World Values Survey* has shown a high correlation between environmental concern and wealth.[18] Higher income countries are about twice as likely as middle-income countries to favor environmental protection and are 4–10 times as likely to be active members of environmental organizations.[19] Not surprisingly, the highest levels of support for environmental protection are in the Nordic countries and the Netherlands, which have some of the highest concentrations of Experiential populations in the world.

Since the early 1980s, environmentalism has become more pervasive in the West, as shown in Figure 9–1. In the U.S., for example, 74% of Americans polled in 1990 agreed with the following statement: Protecting the environment is so important that requirements and standards cannot be too high and continuing environmental improvements must be made regardless of cost. In 1981, just 45% agreed.[20] Not surprisingly, these preferences have had an impact on government policies and politics in general. Across Europe and

Figure 9-1   Percentage of people who say they are willing to pay higher prices to protect the environment, select industrial countries.

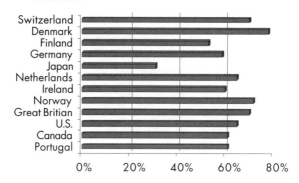

North America, political parties have, in some cases, altered their agendas to include this new environmental constituency. In other cases, new parties have been formed to compensate for the lack of conservation concerns in existing parties.

In West Germany, the early unresponsiveness of the Social Democrat Party to environmental concerns (mostly about nuclear energy) led to the formation of the Green Party. In 1983, the West German Green Party was able to surmount the 5% hurdle and enter parliament. In 1998, the Greens became an integral part of Chancellor Gerhard Schroder's coalition government, garnering three ministerial posts. Green parties also emerged in the Netherlands, Belgium, Austria, France, and Switzerland. In the 1997 election, France's various nascent Green groups won 6.8% of the vote.[21]

> **In Europe and North America, political parties have altered agendas to include the environmental constituency.**

The acceptance of Green parties across western Europe is a result of a growing sense of environmental peril. A 1999 Eurobarometer poll asked the following question: Some people are concerned about environmental protection and the fight against pollution. In your opinion, is it an immediate and urgent problem, more a problem for the future, or not really a problem? The majority of western Europeans responded that environmental protection is an "immediate and urgent" problem: 55% in Belgium, 70% in Denmark and Germany each, 91% in Greece, 73% in Spain, and 52% in France.[22]

While Green parties have not quite found the same political support in the U.S., the environmental agenda is increasingly affecting the tone in American politics. Environmentalism is now a major campaign issue, highlighted by the fact that Ralph Nader, Green Party candidate for the 2000 presidential election, won 3% of the vote nationally and as much as 10% in Alaska.

EMISSIONS TRADING: HOW THE MARKET CAN HELP THE ENVIRONMENT

Legislation that affects the environment is often caught between big business and environmental populism. It is a constant struggle for governments to find viable ways to address environmental degradation while ensuring continued economic success. Much legislation has involved command-and-control regulation by which the government dictates the level and form of environmental restrictions. These restrictions are often costly and inefficient.

Market-based instruments have been proposed as one possible way to deal with this environmental Catch-22. These mechanisms can, in the best-case scenario, provide environmental protection while simultaneously providing economic gain. A 1999 PriceWaterhouseCoopers survey found that market-based regulatory programs that enable air polluters to trade emissions allowances are valuable tools in regulating and curbing air pollution.[23]

Since the 1970s, a number of market-based emissions trading mechanisms have been introduced, especially in the U.S.: the Environmental Protection Agency (EPA) Emissions Trading Program, the national Acid Rain Program for sulfur dioxide trading, and the Regional Clean Air Incentives Market Program (RECLAIM) for nitrogen oxides and sulfur oxides trading in the Los Angeles air basin.

The Sulfur Dioxide Emissions Trading Program was created through amendments to the Clean Air Act passed in 1990. The switch to emissions trading is estimated to have saved around $1.25 billion during the first 5 years of trading. The system allows power companies to trade their right to emit sulfur dioxide. The government determines what the allowable emissions from each plant are, and then those plants that can clean up efficiently can sell their rights to others that are less successful at clean-up. Each year the government decreases the amount of allowable total emissions. These mechanisms provide a level of flexibility that rewards companies for devising creative ways to curb pollution.

Whether it's land, sea, or air degradation, pollution trading as a concept will most likely grow over time, mixing market practice and public policy to manage the mounting environmental stress in the coming decades.

Unlike in other areas of the economy where government interaction recedes as wealth grows, with environmental protection, policy actually plays a larger role. In the U.S., this has come in the form of legislation ranging from the Clean Air Act to the creation of the EPA and the protection of forestland. Spurred by popular support for environmental legislation, European governments continued to press for a global warming accord after the American rejection of the Kyoto agreement. In July 2001, 178 nations (without the U.S.) agreed on such an accord, which included mandatory greenhouse gas reductions for industrialized nations and funds to help developing countries adapt and build more efficient technologies to reduce pollution.

The outright rejection of this protocol caused environmental backlash against American President George W. Bush, both internationally and domestically. Bush's failure to address the environmental concerns of the nation led to a sharp rebuke from the electorate. A June 2001 poll demonstrated strong disapproval of the president's environmental policies. By nearly two to one, respondents said they preferred protecting the environment to producing more energy, and 57% indicated that, if needed, Americans should pay higher prices for energy to protect the environment. This poll revealed that one of the most pressing challenges facing a nation is the need to protect the environment that sustains life while safeguarding the economy that ensures ongoing wealth creation.[24]

Not surprisingly, the clash of environmentalism with traditional economic policy is most dramatic in Experiential parts of the world. As individuals begin to demand more environmental protection, the policies and practices of government and business that brought them prosperity are paradoxically challenged.

Environmentalists see the action of consumers and individuals as vital to the cause of conservation. The UN calls for "consumption for human development," that is, consumption that supports a healthy environment for all.[25] To some degree people are responding. A 1995 Gallup/Waste Management poll in the U.S. found that 95% of adults reported that they recycled some items. Forty-one states had comprehensive waste-management laws and 45 had waste-management goals.[26] In addition, earth-sustainable, organic food production is growing 20% per year.[27]

As Material and Experiential people turn toward a greater concern for the environment, they begin to exert their economic and political will in a manner that is difficult to ignore. Perhaps nowhere is the power of individuals more obvious than on their collective effect on the behavior of corporations. McDonald's—one of the world's most recognizable companies—was persuaded to modify its behavior under mounting pressure from consumers and environmental groups. The offense was the styrofoam clamshell packages that carried McDonald's hamburgers. Environmental organizations such as the Earth Action Network and the Citizens Clearinghouse for Hazardous Waste started a "send-back" campaign in which people mailed the packages back to McDonald's national headquarters. The campaign resulted in the replacement of clamshell packaging with recyclable cardboard boxes.[28]

MNCs, the great engines of global wealth creation, have also been some of the greatest global polluters. However, many have been forced to recognize, sometimes through legislation, that sustainable development must be incorporated into production and distribution processes. Restrictive environmental safeguards have been turned into seals of approval and marketing tools. Now MNCs are lining up to partner with environmental groups. Where Ford Motors once fought stiffer regulations on emissions and energy policies, it has recently announced its own plans to self-regulate and slash its emissions without a federal order. Starbucks coffee advertises an alliance with the World Resource Institute. ExxonMobil took out an ad in the *New York Times* to trumpet its energy-saving history, and British Petroleum redubbed itself "BP—Beyond Petroleum" in its recent ad campaigns. Sweden's forest products companies have been at the forefront of setting and adhering to environmental standards.[29] They are involved in "sustainability" certification practices that have also influenced other forest products companies worldwide. Both IKEA and Home Depot have committed to using wood that comes only from properly managed forests.[30]

Companies have learned how profitable pollution reduction and energy/resource conservation can be. Xerox reported doubling sales of reconditioned, used machines between 1992 and 1997.[31] Dow Chemicals actively promotes its global *Environment, Health & Safety Goals for the Year 2005*. These goals include increasing resource productivity by the reduction and better management of waste. The company plans to reduce energy use per pound of production by 20% and the amount of waste, including water, by 50%. After facing a number of protests in the early 1990s, the Coors Brewing Company embarked on a series of programs to institute an environmental management system. Coors now boasts that it has slashed its annual generation of hazardous waste by more than 90% since 1992.[32] About 10% of the plastics that IBM uses now come from recycled sources.[33]

Even the automobile industry, which has historically been one of the most environmentally harmful in the world, has begun to alter the way it views environmental degradation as well as its own role in the process. In the spring of 2001, Ford Motors, the world's number-two automaker, declared that it believed global warming was "real," after years of public skepticism.[34] The automaker also pledged to increase fuel efficiency in its SUVs though details are scarce. Toyota, after years of flat energy use, plans to decrease the energy needed to make a vehicle by 2005. The company has already started shutting off lights between shifts and more closely monitoring air-conditioning levels.[35] Virtually all the major car manufacturers have environmentally friendlier vehicles in the pipeline, including electric-powered, fuel cell, alternative fuels, and hybrid engines, among a variety of other reduced or zero emission technologies.[36]

The World Resources Institute (WRI) identifies the natural progression of steps that corporations go through as they make an environmental commitment. The process begins with basic compliance with regulations and then moves to reducing emissions beyond legal requirements. The final stage is resource efficiency and waste minimization.[37] Despite the high-profile programs outlined above, the WRI estimates that in the mid-1990s, less than 20% of North American and European companies could be described as proactive in their environmental agendas—the majority of firms fell in the compliance stage of the corporate cycle.[38] In 1999, according to a KPMG study on 1,100 companies, the number of firms with formalized impact reports on health, safety, and the environment grew to 24%,[39] up from 13% in 1993. According to the same study, the rate of environmental reporting has increased for companies in all countries except the U.S. Companies in Germany and Sweden topped this list.[40]

Capital has been flowing as environmentally friendly initiatives become more accepted cultural norms. The UN estimates that the market for environmental-protecting products alone is $500 billion.[41] Investment has been flooding into new energy technology funds, which in turn invest in companies on the cusp of micropower and renewables, important innovations toward making energy more efficient and clean. Merrill Lynch, JP Morgan, Britain's Impax Capital, and Switzerland's Sustainable Asset Management all have funds devoted to these new technologies.[42] There is a growing class of mutual funds like the Green Century Equity Fund and the New Alternatives Fund that are committed to investing in companies and industries oriented toward a clean environment.

All of these trends are representative of the gradual weaving of new values into the social fabric of a nation. Growing individual concern for the environment in the past few decades has been slowly infiltrating the social, political, and economic arenas of the industrialized world. Companies once only concerned about the short-term bottom line have been forced to consider the impact of their behavior on consumer perception.

Of course, the larger economy-wide shift from manufacturing to services as well as amazing technological innovations have also been important steps in combating environmental degradation and resource depletion. The growth of material resources has slowed in recent years and consumption patterns have turned toward less material-intensive goods and services. Energy efficiency has improved and per-capita use of many basic materials such as steel and timber has leveled off in the OECD. The UN calls this process "dematerialization."[43]

MORE DEVELOPMENT, MORE ENERGY, MORE PROFITS

Looking at the global wealth trajectory, one thing is clear: Energy demand will grow. Two billion more people will enter the global middle class soon, and they'll work in factories, buy air conditioners, drive cars, and fly aboard airplanes. A rule of thumb is that for every 1% increase in GNP, developing countries demand 2–3% more electricity. In the next 5 years, The World Bank forecasts that developing countries will need 45 million megawatts of new electrical-generating capacity. With countries like India and China growing at 4–8% per annum, environmentalists and governments see looming problems: Others see opportunities. Energy is a growth industry, and there are profits to be made. Wealthy countries should begin to develop greater alternative energy capacities to fossil fuels, not only for domestic needs, but also as technology exports.

Cleaner energies are no longer science fiction; technological advances have made renewable sources like wind, solar, and alternative fuels viable realities for the 21st Century. While none of these independently can wean the world completely off fossil fuels, they offer benefits that need to be seriously considered. First, alternative energy should be viewed by governments, particularly in advanced countries, as growth industries and should be stoked for job creation and technological progress. The European Wind Energy Association, for example, estimates that 15–19 jobs could be created for each megawatt of wind power capacity installed.[44] Wind electricity costs have dropped from 50 cents/kilowatt to under 5 cents since 1985 with a 300% increase in total U.S. capacity, making it now half the cost of nuclear power. Solar energy costs have dropped below $5/watt (from $200 in the 1950s), with countries like India and Mexico pledging to solarize more than 50,000 rural villages in the coming decades. With photovoltaic panels more than 20% efficient, costs should continue to decline. Some suggest that multilayer solar panels may hit 50% efficiency by 2010. The fuel cell trend in the automobile sector, too, will spawn a variety of new businesses as cars slowly adapt such technology, and possibly aircraft as well.

Alternative energies also promote greater political stability. Concentrations of petroleum in the Persian Gulf, for example, often pit otherwise friendly trading partners in potential foreign policy conflicts. Most Middle East foreign policies, in general, are driven by concerns about access to oil. Moreover, as noted in Chapter 3, few oil-exporting countries truly create wealthy domestic populations, with human capital development largely stifled by "petrocratic" regimes. In short, most people in the world could do with less reliance on these few oil and gas suppliers, even the citizens of the oil-exporting countries.

Even if First World governments begin to subsidize alternative energy use, don't sob for energy companies like ExxonMobil or BP: They won't go bankrupt anytime soon. Fossil fuel won't be abandoned, certainly in the short run. In fact, estimates are that developing countries will help push 2010 fossil fuel use up 35% from 1996 levels. Besides, these energy players are already active in alternatives. However, fossil fuel need not be a growth industry, and Material and Experiential consumers should incorporate energy alternatives into their lifestyles. It is estimated that wind, for example, could produce almost 20% of America's electricity needs with very little increase in utility bills.

Energy will be a major global issue of our future, one that can be shaped by market consumption and public policies. Governments in the EU, U.S., and Japan spend some $400 per citizen each year on farm subsidies. Imagine what such amounts could do for alternative fuel development and usage in terms of environmental preservation, profits for new industries, and reduced cross-border dependence on fossil fuels.

This is not to suggest that a greener world is a foregone conclusion. While there is a growing embrace of environmentalism in the industrial world, it is by no means universal, and most corporations grudgingly play ball. There is still much work to be done. Pollution and global warming are immediate concerns, as are waste and

There is growing international acknowledgement—regardless of wealth—that a more environmentally sustainable development model is needed.

renewable resource depletion. These are problems not only in the industrialized nations of North America and western Europe, but in the developing world where economic growth is arguably still the predominant concern of most citizens and governments. In such countries, there are moral and practical issues at hand. For example, should India or China—with nearly 40% of the world's population—be told how many cars its citizens can drive because of global greenhouse gas concerns? Indeed, this question goes to the heart of whether economic development and environmentalism are fundamentally antagonistic ideals.

One of the major impetuses for environmental action in developing and developed countries both has been the proliferation of NGOs devoted to conservation. While many of these groups originated in the developed world and have, at times, been considered insensitive to the struggles of developing countries, many are now gaining ground. The WWF, for example, has created a platform called "Indigenous Peoples and Conservation" to connect economic well-being with environmental protection. The program involves local communities in the management and conservation of their lands and wildlife.[45]

TREE HUGGERS MEET WALL STREET: HOW THE MARKET CAN ENCOURAGE CONSERVATION

How did a local Costa Rican NGO, Conservation International, and the Dutch and Swedish governments all help make Costa Rica an international eco-tourism center?

The answer: debt-for-nature swaps.

Debt-for-nature swaps emerged in the 1980s as an innovative response to the ills of both overwhelming debt burdens and environmental degradation in developing nations. Recognizing the link between economic and ecological crises, Thomas Lovejoy, Vice President for Science of the WWF, introduced debt-for-nature swaps in 1984.[46]

Through these swaps, environmental NGOs purchase debt on the secondary market after a debtor country agrees to redeem the debt for a slightly higher price to be paid in local currency. The difference between the secondary market price and the price paid by the debtor country is called the "conservation premium" and it is used to bolster environmental programs in the debtor country, while retiring debt.

From 1987 to 1994, $177.56 million was swapped in these transactions. Eventually, these swaps caught on and industrial countries began forgiving developing country debt in return for nature conservation. In 1989, Germany forgave $500 million in a debt-for-nature deal with Kenya.[47] Through the Enterprise for the Americas Initiative (EAI), the U.S. also became involved in debt-for-nature exchanges. By the mid-1990s, $134.1 million in local currency interest payments had been made to environmental projects from $1.6 billion in restructured debt through the EAI.

The debt-for-nature swaps in Costa Rica were quite effective in reducing the country's total commercial debt by approximately 5%.[48] Swap transfers managed to more than triple external aid for nature conservation by the end of the 1980s compared to before the swaps.[49] In addition, as tourism is the nation's third largest source of foreign exchange earnings, debt-for-nature swaps were used to channel funds into park creation and expansion, an area that normally would not get funding. The favorable experience of debt-for-nature swaps prompted the central bank to launch a new debt conversion program promoting sustainable development, thus institutionalizing the swaps.

COSTS AND CONFLICTS

Of all the major issues facing the world, environmentalism is one of the most contentious and hotly debated. While basic concerns about the planet's health are universal, where such concerns rank in priority varies in the Biological, Material, and Experiential-trending worlds. In poorer countries, where economic growth is brisk, environmentalism is taking a backseat to wealth creation, as it did in the West until the 1960s. Clearing forests, exporting metals and petroleum, depleting aquifers, and spewing pollution are all costs of such prosperity.

As wealth grows, concerns for environmental preservation increase in Material and Experiential populations, and are reflected in many ways: in the *Human Value Surveys*, in increased regulations of consumer and business practices, in growth of non-governmental watchdog groups, and through voluntary corporate action. However, when it comes down to it, there are still large gaps between expressed public sentiment and implementation through public policy or consumer behavior. One only has to look at American highways, which are crowded with gas-guzzling SUVs, cleverly classified as "light trucks," and thereby exempt from a variety of emission and fuel economy standards.

While there is a consensus on the environment being important, there has yet to be universal agreement on which global regulations to enact, what they will cost, who will pay for them, and which people need to alter lifestyles to help protect the planet. There is clearly still a long way to go in preserving the world's ecosystems. But the shift seen in more environmentally friendly business practices—such as increasing disclosure, voluntary individual action, and multilateral agreements—may be precursors to greater coordination to preserving our fragile environment.

The 20th Century has shown that prosperity has its price, and that largely this expense is borne partially by the environment. It seems inevitable that the process of wreckless wealth creation, particularly the industrial phase, could damage the planet unless new policies and technologies are employed. However, we have also seen that when the Experiential stage of wealth creation is reached, concern about environmental degradation becomes an important value, with Experientials' extra money available to absorb the costs. The hope is that governments will foster policies toward more effective resource management, and that businesses will adapt and invent technologies to meet the needs of this growing cultural demand. The wealth process and mass consumption may have created environmental problems, but perhaps the power of late-stage Material and Experiential populations will also help to solve them.

10
Wealth and the Future:

Mass Destruction, Stagnation, or Salvation?

The human race has had a long experience and a fine tradition in surviving adversity. But we now face a task for which we have little experience, the task of surviving prosperity.

Dr. Alan Gregg
20th Century Physician and
Humanitarian Activist

Yes, money has changed everything beyond the wildest forecasts of a century or two ago—almost unequivocally for the better. Most people enjoy longer, more healthful lives. More people are being educated for longer periods. Societies are more inclusive and democratic, and discrimination based on gender, religion, and sexual orientation has been reduced. Many people have more time to cultivate individual interests, and the human race has ever-increasing scientific and technological knowledge to propel it further in ways we can only imagine.

The three proven wealth catalysts—human capital, free-market economics, and finance—are now global trends that have led to converging needs, values, and lifestyles. Look at the U.S., Germany, and Japan: three countries at war some 60 years ago, with three different cultural inheritances, which have seemingly come together through successful economic cooperation. India and China, impoverished and economically written-off two generations ago, miraculously have improved their own wealth trajectories for more than one-third of the world's population with similar goals and formulae. The same stories are being written for many countries in Latin America, Asia, the Middle East, East Europe, and parts of Africa.

While HDI statistics should continue to narrow between poor and wealthy nations, and abject poverty should wither by the middle of the 21st Century, some countries and population subsets unfortunately will remain unengaged for the foreseeable future. Each day, there are still 30,000 children who die from preventable and treatable causes (including diarrhea and malnutrition).[1] Certain regions, such as sub-Saharan Africa and parts of the Middle East, for example, have not reduced high fertility rates much in recent decades compared to other regions, which will delay their demographic transition and wealth creation process. Then there are hundreds of millions who, although their countries are making statistical progress, may not live long enough to see substantial material or lifestyle gains. Moreover, while the broad bio-social trends are encouraging, there are dangers that could easily derail or even reverse the positive forces in motion, as we are reminded everyday in the newspapers, on radio, TV, and the Internet. Four of the greatest risks that can endanger future prosperity are nationalism, armed conflicts, environmental stress, and demographic imbalances.

RISK #1: NATIONALISM

Nobody said it was going to be easy. The process of economic liberalization and political opening comes in fits and starts, and sometimes painful changes wreak havoc on local areas. As modernization has coiled about the world, strong and vehement rejections of its meaning and message have erupted. Countries, governments, and population segments occasionally lash out at what they call "globalization," "liberalization," "Westernization," or "Americanization" in efforts to hold on to tradition and stand firm against perceived attacks on cultural identity. When traditional lifestyles are under attack, political rhetoric heats up in both rich and poor countries.

While protests emanate from both the right and left, a salient characteristic of the most vocal reactions has been nationalism: a fierce cry to pull inwards, to protect the country, to save traditional industry, and to expel foreigners and foreign ideas. In the face of increasing global interaction, local cultures are reawakening everywhere in the world, regardless of a country's income: in places like

India, consumers protest McDonald's restaurants for violating Hindu dietary laws, or in France, angry farmers uproot genetically engineered crops (saying they threaten domestic control over food production).

Protests and rhetoric should be expected. However, nationalistic policy-making is far more dangerous. In the 2002 primary elections in France, Jean-Marie Le Pen, from the extreme-right National Front Party, took second place with his unabashed xenophobia. Campaigning on a France-first platform, Le Pen shocked the world by garnering enough popular support to be one of two candidates in the final election. The French are not alone in this view: In Austria, Jurg Haider has made waves by lambasting immigrants, and the late Pim Fortuyn in the Netherlands frequently took potshots at foreigners. U.S. Presidential hopeful Pat Buchanan's recent book *The Death of the West* also highlights many nationalist views in the U.S. Around the developing world, too, leaders such as Hugo Chavez in Venezuela and Robert Mugabe in Zimbabwe have publicly attacked and resisted foreign influences.[2]

As more countries and populations blend into the global economy, competition grows intensely, an inherent feature of successful wealth creation. Some of the world's poorest countries and regions from the 1950s are now among its most vibrant economies. Nations formerly associated with fruits and cheap textiles now manufacture automobiles, capital goods, and high-tech products. In sectors once dominated by the U.S. and Europe just decades ago, former "backward" countries now compete and win in lower skilled sectors like clothing, steel, chemicals, and electronics, among others. This inevitability will continue as global productivity increases through widespread education and training.

Amid this increasingly competitive world, there are countries that will lose certain economic sector hegemony to others. This may spur nationalistic protectionism that is harmful to both wealthy and lesser developed countries. The world saw this when mass import substitution philosophies in the first half of the 20th Century stunted wealth in the former Soviet Union, China, and elsewhere. They produced uncompetitive, black-hole industries that sucked in human capital, destroyed comparative advantage and free-trade paradigms, and thwarted capital markets. The net result: lagging socio-economic progress compared to freer market economics.

Possibly the most harmful protectionism today relates to First World agricultural policy. According to James Wolfensohn, former head of the World Bank, farming subsidies in such countries now total approximately $350 billion, or 7 *times* the $50 billion that rich countries provide annually in foreign aid to the developing world.[3] As a standalone, such subsidies would rank as the world's 45th largest economy in 2001. In addition to boosting wealthy country food prices by 15–20%, such payments (going mostly to large agro-corporations, not nostalgic "family farms") ultimately undercut agricultural export efforts in developing countries. In essence, this allows wealthy nation farmers to sell goods overseas below their actual cost of production. In total, global trade policies may be excluding developing countries from $700 billion in commerce every year,[4] denying them not only needed foreign currency, but also commercial interaction to foster progressive culture.

Europe, for example, has operated under its Common Agricultural Program (CAP) since the 1950s. In the aftermath of World War II, CAP was geared to build food self-sufficiency and raise living standards for European farmers. While initially successful, by the mid-1970s, such policies led to overproduction and surpluses. For over 25 years, CAP has prompted periodic dumping of produce on world markets (which artificially depresses prices), adding further insult to developing country exporters. Today, less than 3% of Europeans toil in the fields for a living, and OECD reports such farmers receive 35% of their income from subsidies; in some places like Switzerland, farm subsidies total some 70% of farmer income.[5] The sad fact is that the average European cow receives approximately $2.20 each day in subsidies, more than what 2 billion people live on each day, and more than twice as much as the billion living in abject poverty.[6]

The U.S. is also an offender, subsidizing a range of agriculture from peanuts and sugar to cotton and grain—estimated at nearly $100 billion annually. American farmers receive 21% of their income as subsidies,[7] with an individual able to obtain approximately $280,000 per annum from several government programs for just being a farmer, for bad market conditions, for not making a profit, and for taking land out of production.[8]

Japan, too, protects agriculture and purportedly costs its consumers (largely urban) about $60 billion each year in extra food costs. Japanese taxpayers pay an additional $30 billion per annum in government subsidies to farmers. As in other industrialized nations, full-time farmers account for only 5% of Japan's workforce.[9] Japan's farm subsidies run as high as 69% according to one study,[10] with resulting rice prices, for example, 8–10 times higher than world averages. All of the subsidies accrue to a tiny but vocal industry dedicated to preserving the past at the expense of consumers and more competitive producers around the globe.

In global trade, the protectionist game goes well beyond agriculture. First, there are large headline moves, such as President Bush's unfortunate spring 2002 levies on steel imports, which were eventually scaled back because of global outrage and potential WTO violations. This was seen as a desperate lifeline to an ailing U.S. sector (one in decline for decades due to comparative *disadvantages*, with most steel operators in or near bankruptcy) to the detriment largely of foreign steel exporters. However, there are many smaller, less public First World tariffs that not only distort trade patterns, but also silently pickpocket their own citizens. For example, America imposes a "basic necessities tax" on its poor through duties levied on shoe and clothing imports, which amount to 47% of all tariffs collected.[11] Worse, there is a further regressive element to this structure: Shoes (of which 90% in America are imported) that cost less than $6.50 wholesale are subject to a 48% rate versus only 20% for shoes costing $12 or more.[12] In a similar context, expensive silk underwear carries only a 2.4% tariff versus polyester at 16.2%, and cheaper stainless-steel tableware incurs a 15.8% rate compared to 2.4% for silver tableware imports.[13] The net effects are that poorer Americans actually pay a higher consumption "tax" as a percentage of purchase prices for hundreds of everyday goods than what wealthier people pay for luxury items.

Developing countries, too, are caught in the protectionist web. According to the IMF, lower income countries, on average, slap 300–400% higher tariffs than wealthier countries on industrial imports, with agricultural imports being 18% higher.[14] According to UNCTAD, Thailand, for example, levies approximately 550 tariffs in excess of WTO-bound rates. Sectors including imported meat, dairy, processed fruits and vegetables, sugar, alcoholic beverages, tobacco, clothing, and motor vehicles all carry 50% tariffs.[15]

In total, developing countries actually may be hurting themselves more than industrial nations: In 1995, of $80 billion of tariffs paid, $57 billion went to other developing countries with protectionist policies and only $23 billion to high-income countries.[16] Moreover, whereas North-to-North hemisphere tariffs averaged 8/10 of 1% on industrial goods, comparable South-to-South rates were 15 times higher at 12%. While South-to-South trade grew from 21% to 39.5% from 1965 to 1995, and could rise to 50% by 2005, just imagine how much trade volume is being stifled by such ill-conceived protectionist policies.[17]

As modernization progresses around the globe, there will undoubtedly continue to be angry protests and violent outbursts. This is particularly true where people find that what is familiar is giving way to something new and uncertain. In the long run, protectionist policies shrouded in nationalism need to be resisted—not just tariff policies, but rigid labor and immigration laws, nationalization and re-regulation, capital controls, and regressive tax structures. Wealthy Material and Experiential-trending countries can't cling to the past in terms of old industries, class structures, and cultural homogeneities; history has proven that it is far more profitable to look forward and outward to create new industries and embrace new markets. In turn, poorer countries have generally grown richer through economic interaction with foreign countries, by refocusing fearful energies and policies into future-oriented, internationally engaged commercial activity. The late 20th Century march away from statist tendencies has improved the lives of billions of people. To bow to nationalism could halt, decelerate, and even reverse the progressive momentum and potential for lifting the remainder out of poverty.

RISK # 2: ARMED CONFLICTS

While Richard Rosecrance and others have suggested that the world is becoming less combative internationally, the last two decades show that war need not be conventional, or cross-border, to disrupt global trade, curb wealth, or even worse, destroy it. Countries amid military conflict cannot efficiently compete economically, cultivate human capital, or develop financial markets. More importantly, these flare-ups don't necessarily have to become world wars to derail progress. As of August 2002, there were 17 active armed internal conflicts, 27 nations hit by terrorist activity, and 37,000 UN peacekeeping troops from 90 countries deployed worldwide.[18]

Civil wars—many ethnically oriented, as Huntington has rightly noted—can inflict deep economic damage, and the percentage of countries experiencing such conflicts increased from the early 1960s from 7% to 13% by the late 1990s.[19] According to the Stockholm International Peace Research Institute, between 1990 and 2001, the world registered 57 different major armed conflicts in 45 different locations; all but 3 were internal.[20] Outside states contributed regular troops to one side or the other in 15 of the internal conflicts.[21]

Look at the former Yugoslavia, once an economically promising country. The nation's civil war, begun in 1992, wreaked havoc on 4.5 million people: Output contracted 79% from 1990 to 1995, and unemployment hit 90% immediately after the war (falling to only 45% by 1999). The human costs were also enormous: 200,000 people died, 27% of the population reported their homes destroyed, 2 million fled the country, and another 1 million were internally displaced.[22] In addition to losses locally, *Jane's Defense* reported that U.S. military costs totaled between $25 million and $65 million *per day* during the conflict.[23]

In the Middle East, the Israeli–Palestinian *Intifada* has cost both sides billions in lost commerce. After fighting broke out in 2001, Israel saw its economy contract while its unemployment rate spiked past 10%. Tourism—a major source of hard currency—shrank dramatically and defense spending in 2002 commanded 20% of Israel's economy. However, the Palestinians may have been hurt even more. In pre-*Intifada* 2000, Israel annually sold less than 0.25% of its GDP in goods to Palestine, while Palestinian exports to Israel accounted for 60% of all Palestinian sales. Much of this activity has halted since 2001.[24] There are other ongoing civil tensions (often ethnicity-driven) in many places, including 20% of sub-Saharan Africa, which is formally at war, and in Russia (with Chechnya) among others, all of which shave billions off output and arrest many of the world's already impoverished economies.

While cross-border conflicts may be less frequent, they still carry huge price tags. When Iraq invaded Kuwait in 1991, the resulting Gulf War cost coalition members an estimated $61 billion. In addition, some budget analysts estimate that each year, $50 billion (roughly one-sixth of all U.S. defense spending) has gone toward maintaining the Gulf deployment with a watchful eye over Iraqi President Saddam Hussein.[25] The recent 2003 invasion of Iraq by the U.S.-led coalition is expected to cost a minimum of $75 billion, plus untold amounts for the country's reconstruction.

Fortunately, in general, world military expenditures have been falling. During the Reagan Administration and at the height of the Cold War, both the U.S. and former Soviet Union (FSU) fueled a global military spending binge that tallied $1.36 trillion in 1987, or approximately 8% of world output according to the World Bank.

However, as the FSU dissolved and global tensions dissipated, by 2002, defense had dropped to less than $740 billion, or less than 2.5% of world output. To the extent that defense budgets grow with global tensions in the future, we could see the wealth process slow as economic resources are stockpiled into military capabilities or deployment.[26]

Of course, terrorism is another form of armed conflict that can devastate the wealth creation system. In addition to the tragic loss of lives, the economic costs of September 11, 2001 were immense. In lower Manhattan, approximately 30% of office space evaporated and many businesses were destroyed; nearly 200,000 jobs were lost or relocated out of New York City; physical asset damage tallied $14 billion for private businesses and $2.2 billion for state, local, and federal enterprises. Costs for the rescue and cleanup have been estimated at $11 billion, for a total direct charge of $27.2 billion.[27]

Then there are the extra defense expenses that came with September 11. According to Michael O'Hanlon of the Brooking Institution, in the first year after the attacks, the U.S. government spent an additional $70 billion on homeland security and defense, including costs to oust the Taliban and rebuild Afghanistan. O'Hanlon estimates the ongoing post-war expense of U.S. activity in Afghanistan between $1.5 billion and $2 billion per month.[28] Based on this experience, the Center on Budget and Policy Priorities has projected that American government spending on defense, homeland security, and "international issues" will be approximately $900 billion more from 2002 to 2011 than was estimated in January 2001.[29]

Additional losses associated with terrorism come in the form of business paralysis and uncertainty that hit economies and financial markets. September 11 hurt the insurance sector specifically, with claims estimated between $30 and $58 billion.[30] In the wake of the attacks, U.S. airline traffic plummeted and several operators subsequently filed for bankruptcy. Amid terrorism, few sectors are spared: In the first year after September 11, trillions were lost in stock market value around the globe. Such financial gloom has a way of depressing wealth culture: projections are lowered, business plans get scrapped, and investment flows decrease, essentially slowing the wealth creation process. Furthermore, terrorist attacks don't have to be as dramatic as those on September 11 to leave financial scars. The fall 2002 bombing of a nightclub in Bali by Islamic fundamentalists, which killed approximately 200 people, immediately sunk the Indonesian stock market by 10%, hurt the country's currency and tourism sector, and sent markets lower in Malaysia, Thailand, and the Philippines.[31]

Armed conflict—with all its associated costs—may indeed cloud our prosperous future. In addition to ongoing civil wars, and occasional cross-border invasions like the recent U.S.-led one in Iraq, there are potential cross-border powder kegs that could explode: in Kashmir, an area disputed by two nuclearized countries, India and Pakistan; between Taiwan and China (another nuclear power); in the Middle East, between Israel (also nuclearized) and several Arab factions (some of which claim to have weapons of mass destruction); and in the Korean peninsula, where North Korea has admitted to nuclear programs. These situations create uncertainty, which restricts the flow of capital and petrifies businesses, investments, and consumers. When tension turns into armed conflict, wealth and human life are destroyed irrevocably.

One can only imagine the losses, damage, and derailments by weapons of mass-destruction, a lingering, incalculable risk to the wealth creation story. Estimates range from 25 to 35 countries that are in the process of acquiring or developing some form of nuclear, biological, and chemical weapons or missile delivery system,[32] along with another 40 to 50 that may have access to missile material and technology to build nuclear weapons.[33] These risks—with fallout that could dwarf that of September 11—affect everyone's future world view and loom large in our consciousness.

RISK # 3: ENVIRONMENTAL STRESS

As noted earlier, there is mounting evidence to suggest that increased prosperity can contribute to environmental degradation. This can impede economic progress in many ways, including potential shortages and environmental changes that disrupt normal business operations and stricter regulations that add costs to all types of production, distribution, and consumption.

Specific concerns over growing greenhouse gas emissions, stressed natural resources, and climactic shifts have been discussed. Energy shortages, such as the oil shocks during the 1970s or even California's electricity squeeze in 2001, affect citizens and businesses with billions of dollars lost to work stoppages, extra expenses, or taxes. One can only estimate the scarcities and costs that may surface as 2–3 billion more people consume like middle-class Americans over the next 50 years.

While energy is a highly publicized trouble spot, water scarcity may become a bigger issue. Developing regions may be hardest hit, such as North Africa and the Middle East, which already face water scarcity problems today. According to the International Water Management Institute, by 2025, 1.8 billion people in more than 100 countries will live with water shortage issues, particularly large emerging markets such as India, China, and Pakistan. Water scarcity has far-reaching consequences: Without sufficient amounts, per-capita food production from irrigated agriculture may suffer. Countries may be forced to ration agricultural water for other pressing sanitation, industrial, and health-related purposes, leaving water-starved regions increasingly dependent on imported food.[34]

Weather change, too, can alter agricultural and aquacultural harvests, which may disrupt food supplies—as well as wildlife food chains—and stunt economic expansion. El Ninos, unexpected frosts, droughts, and flooding all have financial ramifications as expected land yields and fish catches may be less predictable than in the past, creating surpluses in some goods and shortages in others. Finally, simply poor environmental practices—such as chemical dumping or airborne pollution—may also lead to shortages and irreparable economic and ecological damage. For example, runoff from American farmland that spills into the Mississippi River Basin may have created the 8,000-square-mile "dead zone" in the Gulf of Mexico. Since the 1950s, fertilizer applications have increased seven-fold in the Mississippi basin, with the net effects including food chain alterations, loss of biodiversity, and high aquatic species mortality. And, the effect on fishing could be devastating if unchecked: The Gulf of Mexico produces almost 40% of the U.S.'s commercial fishing yield, including valuable shrimp and shellfish catches. There are many situations like this around the world, where unchecked pollution can cause immediate or future economic harm.

In the face of these environmental dangers, and the rising acceptance of pro-ecological values, a new host of regulations may be locally or globally enacted. Growing Green values in wealthy Material and Experiential populations may create wide-ranging domestic policy changes that raise expenses for both businesses and consumers. Higher costs in production and consumption could curb economic expansion, possibly through higher prices or additional taxes.

On the global level, the controversy over the Kyoto Protocol (which aims to lower greenhouse gas emissions to stem global warming) highlights the issues at stake. As of October 2002, 84 countries signed and 96 ratified or acceded to the proposal. The U.S. signed the Protocol on December 11, 1998, but has not ratified it.[35] The central tension is derived from that Kyoto's "per-capita" focus on emissions, which places a disproportionate burden on wealthy countries with high economic activity, and tends to favor lesser developed countries with large populations. While there is growing environmental support in the U.S., critics charge that Kyoto would do little to affect climate changes while imposing enormous costs, including higher taxes (perhaps 60 cents per gallon on gas, and a 50% rise in utility rates), as well as limits on car sizes and restrictions on when Americans could actually drive. The so-called "carbon tax" might also put nearly 5 million American workers in vulnerable industries at risk, some conservative groups report. In total, Kyoto could cost Americans $400 billion.[36] In addition to the economic fallout, President Bush also has been opposed to the Protocol, charging that it, *de facto*, exempts 80% of the world (including high-population countries such as China and India) from compliance.[37] Bush has been criticized for his environmental beliefs given his strong connection to the U.S. energy industry, his push for greater fossil fuel exploration in the Arctic Wildlife Refuge, and his refusal to attend the 2002 Earth Summit in Johannesburg. But his objections to Kyoto raise important issues about the relative responsibilities of Biological, Material, and Experiential-trending nations.

Kyoto's problems may portend growing environmental conflicts between countries around the world as globalization intensifies. Clearly, greater regulations are in the pipeline, with domestic and international pressures so strong that even President Bush released an alternative to Kyoto in February 2002. His proposal is based on reducing domestic greenhouse gas emissions relative to the size of the American economy (that is, how much it emits per unit of economic activity); the goal is to reduce emissions by 18% by 2012, versus Kyoto's per-capita concept.[38]

The arguments on both sides of the global warming debate or Kyoto's implementation costs are highly questionable. Nonetheless, they underscore a growing global reality: People are increasingly concerned about the stressed environment and the public may begin to spend more money, or consume differently, to address these anxieties. If wiser policies and better consumption practices are not enacted soon around the globe, predicted resource shortages may become realities and costly emergency regulations may be required. Environmental crises, like protectionism and armed conflict, have the potential to flatten the trajectory of our prosperity.

RISK #4: DEMOGRAPHIC IMBALANCES

As discussed earlier, there are sharply contrasting population trends in Biological, Material, and Experiential-trending countries: Developing nations are experiencing a youth bulge, while older, industrialized powers are aging rapidly. This divergence may present a variety of challenges to the wealth creation process.

In Biological places, the youth bulge offers economic opportunities but also contains potential landmines. In many of these countries, 50% of the populations are younger than 25 years old; in extreme cases, even younger. These nations are also among the poorest, the fastest urbanizing, and the least politically or institutionally developed, making them most susceptible to violence and instability, not exactly what's needed for prosperity to flourish. Some suggest that these age structures—which often include large subsets of unemployed, disenfranchised young men—might explain, for example, the growth of Islamic fundamentalism, pillaging bands of weapon-carrying warriors in sub-Saharan Africa, drug-trafficking armies emanating from Latin America and Southeast Asia, and large-scale youth protest movements such as those in Tehran and Manila. Large, young populations have also been shown to increase unregulated, unlawful immigration that can create long-lasting instability.[39]

While the Biological "youth bulge" demographics may hinder global progress, richer Material and Experiential population trends may paradoxically undermine success as well. Prosperity, while providing greater living standards and wellness, also results in lower birth rates and increasing longevity that could dampen long-term economic demand. In the wealthiest nations, less than 5% of the population was aged 65 or older in 2000, but this is expected to rise to 27% by 2050, with some estimates as high as 35% for Japan by then.

These demographic trends manifest themselves dramatically in labor markets. Between 2000 and 2010, several industrial nations—including Germany, Japan, Austria, Spain, Italy, Sweden, and Greece—will, for the first time in modern memory, register workforce contractions. In Japan, for example, the number of workers under 30 is projected to fall by 25% from 2000–2010. By the mid-2020s, overall populations in many of these countries may begin to shrink. Unless fertility rates begin to rise, or immigration and labor policies are modified, some worst-case projections suggest that West Europe and Japan could lose more than two-thirds of their total populations by the 22nd Century.[40]

In economies with stagnant or withering populations, the specter of lengthy "aging recessions" hang like dark storm clouds: vicious cycles of falling demand and deflation, collapsing asset values (including real estate), lower corporate profits, deteriorating household and bank balance sheets, weakening currencies, and soaring budget pressures. Paul Hewitt of the Center for Strategic Studies in Washington, D.C. notes that Japan may actually be the first country in such an aging recession.[41] Deteriorating Japanese property prices, in particular, have been instrumental in triggering the domino effect of a weakened banking sector, constrained credit, and bankruptcy.

The aging of wealthier populations also stresses public pension schemes that were conceived under different demographic circumstances, eras of robust population and consumption growth. For example, in the U.S., the Social Security system was originally organized when there were 8–9 workers per retired recipient. However, by 2000, that worker/recipient ratio dropped below 4:1, and by 2025, it could dip closer to 2:1. This problem is even worse in Japan and western Europe, where retirement benefits are already creating large budget holes, but may grow even worse in the coming decades without some immediate action.

Former U.S. Commerce Secretary Pete Peterson notes that immediate economic issues such as healthcare and retirement benefits for older populations may "crowd out" government spending on international affairs and defense. He also notes that shortages of appropriately aged military personnel will result in a greater reliance on military technology (in the wake of ever-shrinking families less willing to send children to war), but a potential unwillingness to fund such weaponry. This, in his opinion, plus a more conservative, risk-averse older population, may begin to shape future security arrangements like NATO or international participation in the UN. Peterson also believes that there are serious financial risks as global creditor/debtor roles reverse over time. For example, higher saving, faster growing countries may begin to exert greater influence as their money is used to finance wealthier countries' deficits. The international balance of power may certainly tilt, for example, if China becomes a large lender while the U.S., Germany, and Japan become large borrowers.[42]

In short, demographic imbalances may alter the wealth trajectory. Rapid population growth in Biological countries could produce instability from new political demands, intensified ethnic rivalries exacerbated by differential domestic growth, and youth bulges that overwhelm the capacities of weak governments. In wealthier countries, the aging trend needs to be addressed in terms of immigration, labor practices, healthcare, and pension liabilities. Without swift, carefully crafted reforms, the wealth creation process could be at risk.

FORWARD WEALTH
AND VALUE MOMENTUM

Although these four global risks may slow, halt, or even reverse global trends, there is hope that the overwhelming momentum of the last century will propel us all forward for the foreseeable future. Progressive human values have been and will continue to be nurtured by wealth, reinforcing the optimistic, forward-thinking world view needed to tackle existing and future problems and counter atavistic, static mindsets.

On the economic front, the wealth catalysts seem to be in full motion, with more people and countries progressing than ever before. The quantity of human capital cultivated since 1950 has produced the most literate, best educated population ever to live on the planet. Women and children are being schooled at rapid rates, building skills, competencies, and greater productivity that should benefit Biological, Material, and Experiential segments. In the coming two generations, developing country literacy should rise from 65% to almost 90%. Once literacy and secondary levels of schooling are widely achieved in current Biological and Material nations, one would assume that levels of higher education will increase, with college and graduate degrees being more prevalent in 50 years, perhaps like high school education today.

Continued innovation, technological application, and consumptive democratization should help improve health and provide advancement at every societal level. Global demographic transitions, rooted in lower fertility rates, may be complete by the mid-21st Century, flattening the world population at 10 billion, perhaps 2 billion less than projections in the 1980s. With less births, per-capita consumption should grow to statistics associated with wealthy countries today. While certain developing countries may suffer life expectancy setbacks due to HIV/AIDS, the overall trend should continue for most populations. Average life expectancy in these regions climbed from 64 years in 2000 to perhaps 78 years by 2050.Higher income countries may see lifespans increase another few years by 2050, to approximately 84, with many routinely living into their 90s.

As comparative advantage, free trade, and productivity accelerate globally, purchasing power should increase and deflate relative prices for all types of consumer products. We forget that democratized access to goods and services is at the heart of wealth: the ability to consume more at a cost of fewer resources. While the pressure and anxieties for wealthy countries to continue innovating may intensify with global competition, gains should still be registered through greater production cost reductions, less work time, and increased leisure. The global economy, estimated at nearly $40 trillion in 2000, should grow past $150 trillion by 2050, with per-capita average income doubling to almost $15,000.[43]

As more wealth grows, the size and composition of the global financial system should mushroom faster than global output. John Edmunds notes that financial assets expanded more than twice than global GNP from 1950–2000.[44] This could be accelerated, as De Soto suggests, if developing countries implement private property and securitization laws similar to those in richer states, whereby more efficient methods of saving and investing will reduce capital costs to fuel more wealth creation. At a growth rate of 1.5x global output, world financial marketization could grow more than 7-fold, or to a remarkable $75–80,000 per capita.[45]

With greater economic growth, more democratic trends should emerge in government. As wealth and personal empowerment builds so does the need for individual recognition in a country's political future. As more people are economically vested in Biological and Material states, traditional authoritarian power bases will erode and become increasingly replaced by rules of law and a political landscape diffused with more special-interest groups. Sovereignty certainly will be shaped by growing foreign influences—MNCs, cross-border investors, NGOs, the WTO, and other countries—as EU-style hookups and trade pacts rise into greater prominence. As financial assets grow, monetary policy may increasingly displace fiscal policies as government's primary progress tool.

The democratic trends in government will be mirrored in lifestyle choices, as families continue to shrink in size and redefine themselves globally. Foreign "culture" will feel less foreign as global media and trade help cross-fertilize lifestyles. Change will be a constant, and those who thrive in the future will understand this perpetual motion that is modernity. Flexibility in such an environment seems key: Occupational and intimate relationships will be more self-determined, as will religion and growing leisure, all shaped by individualistic pursuits of self-actualization.

The wealthiest countries are in a luxurious position to accelerate this human progress. By supplying effective financial assistance to struggling populations, incorporating foreign labor and markets in the global production chain, enfranchising new workers who will become tomorrow's consumers, and promoting greater human capital in home markets with better education, the wealthiest can promote a brighter, more secure future for poorer populations in less time. However, developing countries have some responsibility in this process: They must cultivate progressive values and accept new ways to live, govern, and manage their economies. While wealth philosophies may seem "foreign" or "Western" or "American," mass education, capitalism, and democracy know no physical or civilizational boundaries; they are broader, humanistic concepts that have been harnessed by virtually every race, religion, and country for progress.

The path to a wealthier future is arduous and filled with hardships, anxieties, tensions, and risks, just as the path to the prosperous present has been. Intelligence is often defined as the ability to learn and adapt. I am confident that the world has the collective intelligence to learn from the last 100 years—a bounty of information, technology, and experience unparalleled in history—and will adapt globally in this coming century. Already, Experiential values laced with greater social consciousness and responsibility are permeating governments and the marketplace. We know that wealth and progress mean more than rising GNP; they mean holistic wellness, free from privation on many fronts, as equitably spread as possible.

Endnotes

1. World Bank figures change regularly, but are publicly available at: *www.worldbank.org*

2. Fogel, Robert William. *The Fourth Great Awakening & the Future of Egalitarianism* (Chicago: University of Chicago Press, 2000), 143.

3. Throughout this book, a variety of statistics will be used to discuss country output and income, including Gross National Product (GNP) and Gross Domestic Product (GDP), depending on what was available. In situations where the statistics have been adjusted for purchasing power parity (PPP), it will be noted accordingly.

4. The two key reference books on Maslow's theories are his *Toward a Psychology of Being* (1968) and Motivation and Personality (1970). In addition, one might also investigate Clayton Alderfer's ERG Work Motivation Theory. Instead of five rungs, Alderfer offers three: Existence, or "E" needs, Relatedness, or "R" needs, and "G," or Growth needs. The low-level E needs correspond roughly with Maslow's bottom two rungs: food, water, shelter, and safety. Alderfer extrapolated this into work terms, noting that most E needs were satisfied by a traditional American job. It is interesting to note that Eastern yoga recognized a

similar progression of human needs thousands of years ago with its *chakra,* or energy centers, framework. By unleashing the *Kundalini* (potent life force) from the *Muladha,* or survival *chakra,* one can progress ultimately to *Sahasrana,* or "Super-State of Consciousness"—a realm similar to Maslow's self-actualization.

5. Information on Ghana is drawn from: United Nations, Development Program, *1998 Human Development Report* (New York: United Nations, 1998), Chapter 3; World Bank Group, "Ghana at a Glance" (October 2, 2001), online at: *www.worldbank.org/data/*; and CIA, *World Fact Book, 2001: Ghana,* online at: *www.cia.gov/cia/publications/factbook/index.html*

6. Indeed, I have often thought that a calculation of wealth might be something such as "spare cash/spare time." What I'm trying to do is capture the element of time to actually *enjoy* excess money saved.

7. Fogel, 266.

8. Pilzer, Paul Zane. *God Wants You to Be Rich* (New York: Fireside, 1995), 92–93.

9. Associated with Ernst Engel, the 19th Century German statistician who noted with rising incomes, the share of expenditures for food (and, by extension, other products) declines. Engel's Law does not suggest that the consumption of food products remains unchanged as income increases. It suggests that consumers increase their food expenditures (in percentage terms) less than their income increases.

10. Pilzer, 93.

11. All figures are from: *The Economist, Pocket World in Figures, 2001* (London: Profile Books, 2001), 200–201; and the World Bank Group, Department of Data and Statistics, online at: *www.worldbank.org/data/*

12. As author Virginia Postrel pointed out to me, Maslow's pyramid of needs probably does not work as linearly as Maslow himself suggested. Rather, several levels of needs may be gnawing at individuals at the same time, particularly in the higher Maslow rungs. And as September 11th proved, even the most highly evolved individuals can slip back and relinquish "higher" needs when security and life are threatened.

13. Inglehart, Ronald. *Modernization and Postmodernization* (Princeton: Princeton University Press, 1997), 29.

14. All figures are from: *The Economist, Pocket World in Figures, 2001* (London: Profile Books, 2001), 218–219; and the World Bank Group, Department of Data and Statistics, online at: *www.worldbank.org/data*

15. Note that the per-capita output data here are for OECD countries, which are considerably higher than world averages. However, since these are the countries that have ignited the wealth creation processes discussed herein, their data will be used for this common chart used throughout the book.

Chapter 2

1. I would like to thank Professor Brett Wallace of the University of Oklahoma for providing this quote from a 1968 U.S. Department of the Interior report believed to be titled, "Man—An Endangered Species?"

2. Maddison, Angus. *Monitoring the World Economy: 1820–1992* (Paris: OECD, 1995).

3. United Nations data online at: *www.un.org*

4. Luttwak, Edward. *Turbo-Capitalism: Winners and Losers in the Global Economy* (New York: Harper, 2000).

5. Livi-Bacci, M.J. *A Concise History of World Population*, trans. Carl Ipsen (Oxford: Blackwell, 1997), 31.

6. DeLong, Bradford. "Cornucopia: The Pace of Economic Growth in the Twentieth Century," *History of the 20th Century Economy: Slouching Towards Utopia*, unpublished, 2.

7. Cox, W. Michael and Alm, Richard. *Annual Report of the Federal Reserve Bank of Dallas 1997: Time Well Spent: The Declining Real Cost of Living in America* (Dallas: Federal Reserve, 1997), 4.

8. My own anecdotal observation on bicycles is that the deflation factor, or productivity multiple, is even greater than what DeLong suggests. While he notes a one-speed bike today costs $130, I've recently purchased a pre-assembled 18-speeder for my daughter for approximately $65 at Toys R Us. While I've never seen a bike from 1895, one would have to believe the one I purchased is infinitely better in quality, including more advanced alloy composition (lightweight and rust-proofed), technologically better gear and brake components, and a wicked metallic fuchsia paint job! Since my purchase price was half of DeLong's example, this makes the productivity multiplier for bicycles closer to 72 versus 36.

9. Based on average U.S. industrial wages of approximately $15 per hour in 2000.

10. DeLong, 6.

11. I use the 1991 325P desktop model to compare to the 2003 4500 Dimension desktop. To get the same "quality of computer," you need between 125–250 of the 1991 computers to match the memory and hard drive, respectively. This equates to $459K–$896K in today's dollars, or between 766–1,496 times what it cost in 1991. Interestingly, Moore's law predicts a 2^{10} increase in processing speed, or a 1,024 times improvement over those 10 years—roughly what has happened.

12. Critics may argue that 100–250 PCs in 1991 might have more "value" than 1 PC from 2003, even though the more recent model has 100–250 x the computing capacity of the older model. True, more productivity may be derived out of 100–250 older computers than only 1 new model. But, we could also buy an old computer like this on eBay today for $40–60 (versus $2,699) if we could find one,

which translates into more than a 95% drop in price. Moreover, using the simple idea of what a $1 buys in terms of computing capability, the above example is fairly sound. And by the time this book is published, Dell will be offering even more features for less money. Suffice it to say, a dollar clearly goes considerably further in what it buys in computing today versus 12 years ago.

13. Perhaps the most balanced study I've read on this subject is *Globalisation and Inequality: World Income and Living Standards, 1960–1998*, authored by Arne Mechoir, Kjetil Telle, and Henrik Wiig at the Norwegian Ministry of Foreign Affairs (Report 6B:2000, October 2000), available online at: *http://odin.dep.no/archive/udved-legg/01/01/rev__016.pdf*

14. Ibid, 14.

15. With this said, one should look at Xavier Salai-I-Martin's May 2002 study, "*The World of Income (Estimated from Country Distributions)*," available online on his Columbia University Web site. The professor notes that from 1970–1998, $1 per day income dropped by 234 million. From 1976–1998, the number of people living on $2 per day dropped by 450 million people (p. 30).

16. Kuznets first described his "U" curve in the 1950s, but also see Robert E. Lucas's "Some Macroeconomics for the 21st Century," *Journal of Economic Perspectives* (Winter 2000, vol. 14, no. 1), 159–168.

17. See David Dollar and Aart Kraay's World Bank study of 40 years of income statistics of 80 countries, "Growth is Good for the Poor" (March 2000), available online at: *www.worldbank.org*

18. *The Economist, Pocket World in Figures 2001* (London: Profile Books, 2001), 82, 120.

19. World Bank, *World Development Report 2000/2001: Attacking Poverty* (London: Oxford, 2000), online at: *www.worldbank.org/poverty/wdrpoverty;* Hungary, Japan, and U.S. car statistics are from *The Economist, Pocket World in Figures 2001.* China's car figures come from *www.bbc.co.uk;* India's car figures come from *www.indiainfoline.com;* Brazil's car figures come from *www.it.bton.ac.uk* China's newspaper figures come from *Statistical Abstract of the United States–1991,* U.S. Department of Commerce, Economics, and Statistics Administration, Bureau of the Census. Coca-Cola figures are from area per-capita averages from Coca-Cola, *Enduring Value: The Coca-Cola Company Annual Report 2001* (Atlanta: Coca-Cola, 2002), online at: *www2.coca-cola.com/investors/annualreport/2001/*

20. DeLong, 27.

21. According to National Council of Applied Economic Research's report on the growing Indian middle class as cited online at: *www.aliciapatterson.org/APF2001/Wells/Wells.html.* The survey said the very rich consisted of approximately 6 million (or 67/100 of 1%). Below

them were three sub-classes: the consuming class, about 150 million people (17%); the climbers, about 275 million people (30%); and the aspirants, about 275 million (30%). Beneath these were the destitute, estimated to be 210 million (23%).

CHAPTER 3

1. This quote came from McLuhan's 1960 "Report on Project in Understanding New Media" presentation to the National Association of Educational Broadcasters in Washington, D.C.

2. I think Karl Marx might have been the first to attempt explaining it in the mid-19th Century, but I've found that many writers have contributed to my understanding, including Ester Boserup, Brad DeLong, William Easterlin, Robert Fogel, Ron Inglehart, John Kenneth Galbraith, Lawrence Harrison, Samuel Huntington, Keynes, Nikolai Kondratieff, Simon Kuznets, David Landes, Robert Lucas, ML Schumpeter, Amarya Sen, Julian Simon, Robert Solow, and Alvin Toffler, among others.

3. Maddison, Angus. *Monitoring the World Economy: 1820–1992* (Paris: OECD, 1995), 37.

4. See David S. Landes' *The Unbound Prometheus: Technological Change and Industrial Development in Western Europe from 1750 to the Present* (Cambridge: Cambridge University Press, 1969).

5. Ibid, 5.

6. "The view from afar: immigration also affects those left behind," *The Economist* (November 2–8, 2002), 11.

7. If pressed for one *single* invention, I might suggest liquid ammonia, created by Fritz Haber in the first decade of the 20th Century. Haber was the one who figured out how to use the earth's vast reservoir of nitrogen gas and convert it into liquid ammonia, the basis for nitrogen fertilizer. With fertilizer, the world was able to grow more per acre and feed growing populations—one of the great feats of humanity. See Vaclav Smil's *Enriching the Earth: Fritz Haber, Carl Bosch and the Transformation of World Food Production* (Cambridge: MIT Press, 2000). Unfortunately, nitrogen is also one of the great pollutants of our time.

8. Ricardo's key work is *On the Principles of Political Economy and Taxation* (1817).

9. I'd like to thank the firm Systemics for supplying me with this specific example of Ricardo's theory.

10. Systemics notes that the simple theory of comparative advantage outlined above makes a number of important assumptions, including: (1) there are no transport costs; (2) costs are constant and there are no economies of scale; (3) there are only two economies producing two goods; (4) the theory assumes that traded goods are homogeneous

(i.e., identical); (5) factors of production are assumed to be perfectly mobile; (6) there are no tariffs or other trade barriers; and (7) there is perfect knowledge, so that all buyers and sellers know where the cheapest goods can be found internationally.

11. See Richard Rosecrance's excellent *The Rise of the Virtual State: Wealth and Power in the Coming Century* (New York: Basic Books, 2000).

12. The best source of global trade information and research is available through the World Bank's Trade research online at: *www1.worldbank.org/wbiep/trade/Pubs/tradepubs.htm*

13. Frankel, Jeffrey A. and Romer, David. "Does Trade Growth Cause Growth?" *American Economic Review* (Volume 89, Issue 3, June 1999), 379–399.

14. See Paul Zane Pilzer's *The Wellness Revolution: How to Make a Fortune in The Next Trillion Dollar Industry* (New York: John Wiley).

15. Insurance companies and pension funds are also miraculous inventions. Insurance helps facilitate an endless variety of risk-taking activities that stimulates wealth creation. Long-term savings through pensions also helps fuel long-term economic well-being, while also providing financial security for savers.

16. Beyond securitized residential and commercial mortgages, remember there are thousands of banks and other lenders that support real estate development.

17. According to DeSoto as reported in *Businessweek Online's* "Global Poverty" (October 14, 2002), 6.

18. According to chief economist David Hale of the Zurich Group. See online at: *www.davidhaleonline.com/pdf/1199_smm.pdf*

19. Sources of stock data include IDD Information Services (1992–93), Securities Data Company (1994–97), and CommScan EquiDesk (1998–current).

20. Levine, Ross and Zervos, Sara. "Stock Markets, Banks and Economic Growth," *The World Bank*, unpublished (October 1996).

21. According to the National Venture Capital Association. See online at: *www.nvca.org*

22. Not all forms of financing are created equal. In general, a more diversified flow of capital for developing countries is desirable because it is less vulnerable to shocks in any one given market segment. In addition, some forms of capital are more volatile than others and do not confer spillover benefits into the economy. Portfolio investments in stocks and bonds, for example, can increase or decrease quite quickly compared to strategic investments such as foreign direct investment (FDI), or property, plant, and equipment. FDI is considered "better" because it provides not only capital, but also often know-how and technological knowledge that can be applied to other areas of a developing economy.

23. Found online at: *www.cardweb.com*

24. As my good friend and scholar Michael Lewitt notes: "In the late 1980s, black limousines used to pull up each afternoon in front of Madame Onoe Nui's house in Osaka, Japan. Men wearing business suits and carrying briefcases would enter her house. While neighbors believed these gentlemen were visiting Madame Nui's popular restaurant (or perhaps that the restaurant had begun serving more than just food), they were in fact coming to pay homage to a figure who was later revealed to be the single most important participant in Japan's stock market bubble: Madame Nui's pet ceramic toad. Toads are considered mysterious and powerful creatures in Japanese and other Eastern cultures. Senior executives from Industrial Bank of Japan (IBJ) would travel from as far as Tokyo to mingle with senior stockbrokers from Yamaichi Securities and other major trading houses at a weekly midnight vigil to honor the toad. Homage to the toad included first patting its head, then reciting prayers in front of a set of Buddhist statues in Madame Nui's garden. The climax of the ceremony would come when Madame Nui seated herself in front of the toad, went into a trance, and delivered her stock market predictions, which were considered oracular and moved the Tokyo markets. Madame Nui parlayed her toad and a small set of loans into an enormous financial empire. At its peak, Madame Nui's borrowings reached $22 billion. But, alas, Madame Nui soon came to a now all-too-familiar end. She was arrested for financial fraud in 1991. It turned out that her borrowings were based on fraudulent deposit vouchers forged by friendly bankers. Madame Nui's bankruptcy resulted in losses of more than $2 billion, the resignation of the chairman of IBJ, and the collapse of two banks." Lewitt's account is based on Alex Kerr's *Dogs and Demons Tales from the Dark Side of Japan* (New York: Hill & Wang, 2001), 77–79.

25. While the discussion probably began with Max Weber, it has been more recently explored by Francis Fukuyama, Samuel Huntington, David Landes, and Hernando DeSoto, among others.

26. Harrison, Lawrence. *Who Prospers? How Cultural Values Shape Economic and Political Success* (New York: Basic Books, 1993), 16–17.

27. Ibid, 18. Note that I have reordered, numbered, and edited down Harrison's translation of Grondona's typology (which was originally unpublished and available only in Spanish).

28. See Daniel Etounga-Manguelle's "Does Africa Need a Cultural Adjustment Program?" in Lawrence Harrison and Samuel Huntington's *Culture Matters: How Values Shape Human Progress* (New York: Basic Books, 2000), 68.

29. Ibid, 69.

30. Harrison cites Potter, Diaz, and Foster, eds. *Peasant Society: A Reader* (Boston: Little Brown, 1967), 304 (and further in 305–18).

31. Brooks, David. "Why the U.S. Will Always Be Rich," *The New York Times Magazine* (June 9, 2002), 90.

32. Ibid, 91.

33. I'd like to thank some of my Columbia University students for reminding me of this development, as well as Amity Schlaes in her *Financial Times* article, "Unbalanced by a Wealth of Oil and Diamonds: Radical Islam Is Often Blamed for Middle Eastern Instability but There Is Another Reason for the Problem: Commodities" (November, 20, 2001).

34. Ibid, Schlaes.

35. Ibid.

CHAPTER 4

1. The *Index of Economic Freedom* is published annually by the Heritage Foundation and the *Wall Street Journal*. The *Index* includes the broadest array of institutional factors determining economic freedom, including corruption; non-tariff barriers to trade; fiscal burden; rule of law; regulatory burdens; restrictions on banks; labor market regulation; and black market activity. Countries are ranked from 1 (most free) to 5 (least free). It is available online at: *www.heritage.org*

2. Freedom House, *Freedom of the World Report, 2002: The Democracy Gap*, available online at: *www.freedomhouse.org*

3. See press releases on TI's Web site: *www.transparency.org*

4. Ibid.

5. Keep in mind that democracy is often defined as "universal suffrage," meaning all citizens having the right to vote. Even in the U.S., women, for example, didn't have such rights in the 19th Century.

6. Fukuyama, 179. It is also interesting to note that in 1990, the then-Communist countries under the former Soviet umbrella recorded the lowest levels of subjective well-being ever recorded by the World Value Surveys. It is no surprise that the system didn't last that much longer.

7. Freedom House, *Democracy's Century: A survey of global political change in the 20th Century* (New York: Freedom House, 1999), online at: *www.freedomhouse.org*

8. Ibid.

9. Seymour Martin Lipset was probably the first to highlight the correlation between democracy and high levels of economic development in the late 1950s. See "Some Social Requisites of Democracy: Economic Development and Political Legitimacy," *American Political Science Review* (53, 1959), 75. However, many subsequent refinements, additions, critiques, and developments of his thesis have since been put

forward. Barro in "Determinants of Democracy," *Journal of Political Economy*, December 1999, S158–183, supports the Lipset hypothesis that a higher standard of living promotes democracy.

10. Mueller, John. *Capitalism, Democracy and Ralph's Pretty Good Grocery* (Princeton: Princeton University Press, 1999), 17.

11. Inglehart, Ronald, "Culture and Democracy" in Lawrence Harrison and Samuel Huntington's *Culture Matters: How Values Shape Human Progress* (New York: Basic Books, 2000), 95.

12. According to the Institute for Democratic and Electoral Assistance (*www.idea.int*). For complete voter election rates for most countries, see the Web site.

13. Statistics are from the Inter-Parliamentary Union, available online at: *www.ipu.org/iss-e/women.htm*

14. Inter-Parliamentary Union. See "Culture and Democracy," by Ronald Inglehart, in Lawrence Harrison and Samuel Huntington's *Culture Matters: How Values Shape Human Progress* (New York: Basic Books, 2000), 95.

15. See International Institute for Democracy and Electoral Assistance, online at: *www.idea.int/gender/*

16. Inglehart. *Modernization and Postmodernization*, 77.

17. I would suggest beginning with Richard Rosecrance's *The Rise of The Trading State: Commerce and Conquest in the Modern World* (New York: Basic Books, 1986).

18. See John Mueller's *Capitalism, Democracy, and Ralph's Pretty Good Grocery* (Princeton: Princeton University Press, 1999).

19. United Nations Development Program, *Human Development Report 1996* (New York: Oxford, 1996), 58.

20. Ibid, 72.

21. Data is cited in Inglehart's *Modernization and Postmodernization*, 30.

22. The Soviet Union was not alone in failure. Many statist regimes and policies in Latin America, Southeast Asia, and Africa also proved of little value in wealth creation.

23. Fukuyama suggests that the Soviet Union ultimately failed because of a pent-up demand for recognition and status: People seek self-esteem and in certain structures, they are not allowed to build it. "Men seek not just material comfort," writes Fukuyama, borrowing from Plato and Hegel, "but respect or recognition, and they believe that they are worthy of respect because they possess a certain value or dignity." Fukuyama. *The End of History and the Last Man*, 152.

24. "For 80 Cents More," *The Economist* (August 17, 2002), 20–21.

25. Ibid.

26. Tyson, Laura D'Andrea. "For Developing Countries, Health Is Wealth," *BusinessWeek Online* (January 14, 2002).

27. Many developing countries—particularly in Latin American but also in the former Soviet Union, India, and China—were following strict Import Substitution (IS) strategies while the East Asian economies were experimenting with more outward-looking policies. IS is the deliberate government policy to increase the share of domestic production in the home market. IS policies often involve buying up the products no longer being exported and promoting the development of local industries capable of producing the goods that were once imported. In the 1950s through 1970s, IS was a popular attempt in many developing countries to generate domestic growth and capacity. Governments in many developing countries, after wild market gyrations during the Great Depression, decided to create their own economies and markets. Many governments actively protected their import-competing industries through fixed, over-valued exchange rates and high tariffs. In addition, governments tried to guide economic development through interest rate, credit, and price controls. Capital flows to these countries were primarily in the form of official loans and aid that were used to finance deficits and balance payment imbalances. IS was in complete defiance of free-market principles, yet, at the same time, the policies were seen as important stepping stones to building a more sustainable domestic economy. State-led economic policies supported the notion that the state could accelerate the process of industrialization. However, the state controlled production and prices, virtually erasing free markets. Unfortunately, the distortion of capital allocation led to weak financial markets and highly leveraged national economies—the policies ultimately proved unsustainable as they were built on weak domestic institutions. The developing world was particularly hard-hit by the oil and debt crises of the 1970s and 1980s. Their highly leveraged and mismanaged economies were extremely vulnerable to external shocks. In the 1980s, many developing countries—particularly in Latin America—found themselves trapped in a cycle of bad debt, high inflation, and a loss of confidence that led to massive capital outflows as investors sought shelter in safer places. When the IS system was exposed for its weaknesses, a global shift toward privatization, deregulation, and freer markets took root and began the dismantling of IS.

28. Megginson, William L. and Netter, Jeffrey M. "From State to Market: A Survey of Empirical Studies on Privatization," *Journal of Economic Literature* (June 2001).

29. Refer to the Frankel and Romer study cited in Chapter 1.

30. "Great–if they really happen," *The Economist* (August 10, 2002), 45–46.

31. Shen, Raphael. *China's Economic Reform* (Westport: Praegner, 2000), 3.

32. Naughton, Barry. "The Third Front: Defense Industrialization in the Chinese Interior," *China Quarterly* (115, 1988), 351–386.

33. As sited in address by Michael Camdessus, managing director of the IMF, October 15, 1998, in Paris. "Worldwide Crisis in the Welfare State: What's Next in the Context of Globalization?" available online at: *www.imf.org*

34. Mandatory spending includes funding for government entitlement programs such as Medicare, Medicaid, and Social Security, as well as interest held on the public debt.

35. See U.S. Federal budget figures from the Office of Management and Budget, available online at: *http://w3.access.gpo.gov/usbudget/*

36. The tension between the desire for a less intrusive government and one that still protects the populace has been highlighted through the Enron collapse of 2001–2002. Enron, a huge advocate of deregulating the energy sector, ultimately collapsed under the weight of its own fraudulent and opaque accounting policies and partnerships. It is a case when the American population has reconsidered the commitment to free markets and has asked, once again, that the government step in and investigate the promise of energy deregulation. Such intrusions are often called for after stock market or other financial collapses. I am reminded of a 1980s capitalist scapegoat, Michael Milken, who was demonized for his formidable invention of junk bonds and jailed on insider trading violations.

37. The Conference Board *"Changing Values Challenge the Canadian Way"* December 2000.

38. For the historical context as to how Argentina's problems developed, see the short but well documented book *The Sorrows of Carmencita* by Mauricio Rojas (Timbro, Sweden) 2002.

39. According to the Internal Revenue Service for 1997.

40. Ibid.

41. See U.S. Census Bureau data, available online at: *www.census.gov*

42. According to the Institute for Democratic and Electoral Assistance (*www.idea.int*). For complete voter election rates for most countries, see the Web site.

43. Ibid.

44. Ibid.

45. Ibid.

46. *www.historylearningsite.co.uk/political_action_committees.htm*

47. National Public Radio, *Kaiser/Kennedy School poll.* All results are available online at: *www.npr.org*

48. *New York Times/CBS News* poll, "Mixed Views on Civil Liberties," *New York Times* (December 12, 2001), B9.

49. Inglehart. *Modernization and Postmoderization*, 38.

50. Another interesting development of wealth creation may actually be a slightly reshuffled UN Security Council. For example, some suggest that the EU might ultimately replace the UK and France as permanent members (along with China, Russia, and the U.S.), and some new players—Japan, Brazil, India, and South Africa—may be invited to expand the permanent council in the coming decades.

51. Sales figures are from *Fortune* (July 31, 2000); GDP figures from World Bank, online at: *www.worldbank.org*

CHAPTER 5

1. "Major Religions of the World," *Factmonster.com* (July 30, 2002), available at: *www.factmonster.com/ipka/A0772923.html*

2. Princeton Survey Research Associates for *Newsweek* (Gallup Organization, December 1996).

3. Inglehart, Ronald. *Modernization and Postmodernization: Culture, Economic, and Political Change in 43 Societies* (Princeton: Princeton University Press, 1997), 32.

4. Ibid, 40.

5. Toffler, Alvin. *The Third Wave* (New York: Bantam, 1991), 21. While Toffler was talking mostly about Europe, one can also look to parts of Asia, such as Hindu India, where similar caste systems were in place.

6. Riesman, David. *The Lonely Crowd: A Study of the Changing American Character* (New York: Doubleday, 1953), 11.

7. Putnam, Robert. *Bowling Alone: The Collapse and Revival of American Community* (New York: Touchstone, 2001), 13.

8. Islam and secularization: *www.secularislam.org/separation/seculariza-tion.htm*

9. Refer to the Muslim Women's League at *www.mwlusa.org* for a detailed discussion of the rights given to women through the Qur'an and authentic Hadith versus the rights that are granted to women in modern Islamic societies. The site does a nice job of tracing these changes and identifying the ways in which women are trying to recapture their own voice within Islam rather than deciding they must leave Islam to express feminism.

10. Wolf, Martin. "The Economic Failure of Islam: Muslim animosity towards the west has its roots in an inability to respond effectively to centuries of financial progress," *Financial Times* (September 25, 2001).

11. Lester, Toby. "Oh Gods," *The Atlantic* (February 2002). Available online at: *www.theatlantic.com/issues/2002/02/lester.htm*

12. See Katie Bacon's interview with Philip Jenkins in "Christianity's New Center," *The Atlantic* (September 12, 2002). Online at: *www.theat-lantic.com/unbound/interviews/int2002-09-12.htm*

13. Ibid.

14. Weber notes this in sharp contrast to "traditional" authority based on adherence to inherited customs or "charismatic" authority where allegiance is pledge to leaders professing some extraordinary virtue (possibly military or religious strength, among others).

15. Gary, Jay. "Ten Global Trends in Religion," at: *www.wnrf.org/arti-cles/gtrends.html*

16. Ibid.

17. Woodward, Kenneth. "The Changing Face of the Church," *Newsweek* (April, 16, 2001), available online at: *www.newsweek.msnbc.com*

18. Bacon.

19. Woodward, 81.

20. Ramirez, Margaret. "Less Focus on Church, but More on God," *The Los Angeles Times* (January 15, 2000), 2.

21. Putnam, 70–71.

22. Putnam, 70.

23. Ramirez, 2.

24. Bates, Stephen. "Decline in Churchgoing hits CoE hardest," *The Guardian,* Manchester, UK, (April 14, 2001), 1.

25. Haight, Frank, Jr. "Christianity changing for the new millennium," online at: *www. celebrate2000.cjonline.com/stories/03099/fai_chris-tian2.shtml*

26. Inglehart. *Modernization and Postmodernization,* 58.

27. Inglehart. *Modernization and Postmodernization,* 284.

28. Higgins, Richard. "Sold on Spirituality," *Boston Globe* (December 3, 2000), 6.

29. Hart and Teeter Research Companies for *NBC News/Wall Street Journal* (June 1996).

30. Ramirez, 2.

31. Ibid.

32. Higgins, 3.

33. Ibid, 2.

34. "Stretch Your Mind," *Times-Picayune*, New Orleans, LA (August 30, 2001), 30.

35. Higgins, 5.

36. Lester.

37. For centuries, Jews were on the move, and in many countries were forbid the legal rights to own land, particularly in Western Europe. The relative early detachment from land and economic necessity to focus on general commerce—trading, shopkeeping, and money-lending, for example—may have made the economic and modern cultural shifts easier to deal with.

38. Inglehart. *Modernization and Postmodernization,* 72.

39. Huntington, Samuel. *The Clash of Civilizations and the Remaking of World Order* (New York: Touchstone, 1998).

40. See his speech "New Dimensions: Foreign Policy and Human Rights," available online at: *www.cceia.org/pdf/brzezinski.pdf.* Brzezinski also discusses such extremism within the American context of abortion, euthanasia, and other ethical issues that are intertwined with religion.

41. Bacon.

42. Inglehart. *Modernization and Postmodernization*, 58.

43. Lester.

44. Ibid.

CHAPTER 6

1. This often used quote came from Sir Claus Moser, chairman of the Basic Skills Agency in his report on the state of British education to his government in 1990.

2. *The Economist, Pocket World in Figures 2001*, 69.

3. Achieving universal primary school enrollment by 2015 is just one of the Millennium Development Goals (MDGs) that 180 countries signed in September 2000. The other goals are: eradicate poverty and hunger; promote gender equality and empower women; reduce child mortality; improve maternal health; combat HIV/AIDs, malaria, and other pressing health concerns; ensure environmental sustainability; and build a global partnership for development. More detail on these goals is available at the World BankWeb site: *http://www.world-bank.org*

4. Psacharopoulos, George and Patrinos, Harry Anthony. "Returns to Investment in Education Up to the New Millennium" (2001), unpublished.

5. United Nations Development Program, *Human Development Report 2001* (New York: Oxford University Press, 2001), 86.

6. World Bank. *World Development Report 1998/1999* (New York: Oxford University Press, 1999), 44.

7. Maddison, 37.

8. Ibid.

9. Sperling, Gene. "Toward Universal Education," *Foreign Affairs* (80.5 September/October 2001), 7–13.

10. "High Tech China," *Business Week Online* (October 28, 2002).

11. China Education and Resource Network (*www.edu.cn/20010101/22286.shtml*).

12. "High Tech China," Business Week Online, (October 28, 2002).

13. See "Fertility, Income, Distribution and Growth," by Matthias Doepke, an unpublished paper written at the University of Chicago (May 1999). Available online at: *http://home.uchicago.edu/~mdoepke/research/proposal.pdf*

14. In a World Bank roundtable discussion, Professor Mumtaz Ahmad noted that in the 1980s, many Madrassas shifted toward a more militant stance. Some Madrassas may be grooming Muslim terrorists, but often terrorist camps have used Madrassas as a veneer to cover their

activities. In the wake of September 11, Pakistani authorities have actually enacted legislation to control the influx of foreign students and funding to these schools to safeguard against terrorist breeding grounds. Listen online at: *www.worldbank.org/wbi/B-SPAN/sub_muslim_education.htm*

15. Cook, Bradley James. "Egypt's National Education Debate," *Comparative Education* (Oxford: November 2000).

16. World Bank *Development Report 1998/1999*, Chapter 2.

17. World Bank, Education Advisory Service, "Education and Development," available online at: *http://www1.worldbank.org/education/pdf/EducationBrochure.pdf*

18. World Bank, *Development Report 1998/1999*, Chapter 2.

19. See their Web site *www.dec31.org* for more details on this organization.

20. The World Bank's Education Department and Web site (*worldbank.org/education*) is an excellent source of information on education around the world, including country breakdowns based on spending, enrollment, and gender disparities, and working papers on a range of educational topics around the world.

21. It is important to note that enrollment rates do not necessarily take into consideration retention and completion rates. So while 100% of children attend primary school in any given country, that does not mean they all finish. A major push is now underway to examine retention rates instead of enrollment to get a clearer picture of the quality and length of schooling.

22. World Bank Human Development Network, Africa Region and Education Department, "Achieving Education for All by 2015" (April 24, 2002).

23. World Bank, *World Development Report 1998/99*, 41.

24. Maddison, 77.

25. World Bank, *World Development Report 1998/99*, 43.

26. Card, D., and Lemieux, T. "Can Falling Supply Explain the Rising Return to College for Younger Men? A Cohort Based Analysis" (NBER Working Paper #7655, Cambridge, MA, 2000). As seen in World Bank, *Constructing Knowledge Societies*, 16.

27. World Bank Education Group, *Constructing Knowledge Societies: New Challenges for Tertiary Education* (Draft April, 2002), online at: *www.worldbank.org*

28. Gerald, Debra E., and Husser, William J. *Projections of Education Statistics to 2011* (Washington, D.C.: U.S. Department of Education, National Center for Education Statistics, NCES 2001–083, August 2001), 25 and 29.

29. Source: Eurostat and UOE.

30. According to Japan Ministry of Education, Culture, Sports, Science, and Technology (*www.mext.go.jp/english/statist/index01.htm*).

31. See *www.afs.org*

32. For up-to-date enrollment statistics, see *www.ed.gov*

33. Jones, Carolyn. "Foreign Students Turn to US Colleges in Droves," *San Francisco Chronicle* (November, 13, 2000), available online at: *www.sfchron.com*

34. Christian Science Monitor (*www.csmonitor.com/2002/0709/p13s01-lecl.html*).

35. The Head Start program began in 1965 with only $96.4 million in funding for 561,000 students. By 2001, Head Start programs served over 905,000 Americans with over $6 billion in federal funding—or more than $6,600 per recipient. Minority groups—in particular have been helped by Head Start, with 29.7% of 2001 funding going to Hispanics families and 33.8% going to African-Americans. 13 percent of the Head Start enrollment consisted of children with disabilities (mental retardation, health impairments, visual handicaps, hearing impairments, emotional disturbance, speech and language impairments, orthopedic handicaps, and learning disabilities).

36. According to W. Steven Barnett, Director of the NIEER, in a presentation delivered on September 13, 2002 at a congressional Science and Public Policy briefing on the impact of Head Start.

37. OECD figures cited on *www.korpios.org/resurgent/8Comparison.htm*

38. See *www.elderhostel.org*

39. Harmon, Amy. "Cyberclasses in Session," *New York Times* (November 11, 2001), available online at: *www.nyt.com*

40. World Bank, *Constructing Knowledge Societies*, 20.

41. According to the *Center for Education Reform 2002 Survey.*

42. Ibid. The average per-pupil cost of survey respondents is $4,507, significantly less than the $7,000 average in traditional schools.

43. A key issue in the decision was the fact that many vouchers were being used at religious-affiliated schools—mostly Catholic—which was seen as a questionable violation of church and state laws.

44. "A Supreme opportunity," *The Economist* (February 23, 2002), 35.

45. Meehan, M. Samuel, and Abrahmson, V. *The Future Ain't What It Used to Be: The 40 Cultural Trends Transforming Your Job, Your Life, Your World* (Riverside, 1998), 6. Also, it is interesting to note in Germany, the D21 initiative promises to put a computer in every primary and secondary German classroom by 2003. This was done in partnership with IBM, Hewlett-Packard, Cisco, Oracle, and 280 corporate sponsors.

46. According to the U.S. Departments of Education's National Center for Educational Statistics.

47. Ibid.

48. Surprisingly, 79% of all private schools have religious affiliation, with Catholic schools comprising nearly half. In addition, there are 850,000 U.S. students who are home-schooled, or 1.7% of the population, a majority of which are religious-based programs.

CHAPTER 7

1. Inglehart. *Modernization and Postmodernization*, 30.
2. Zinn, Howard. *A People's History of the United States* (New York: Harper Perennial, 1995). In Chapter 6, "The Intimately Oppressed," Zinn provides an enlightening view of women in colonial America, including the rise of a women's movement.
3. Pillsbury, B., Maynard-Tucker, G., and Nguyen, F. "Women's Empowerment and Reproductive Health: Links throughout the Lifecycle" (New York: UNFPA, March 2000), available online at the UN's online interactive population center: *www.unfpa.org/modules/intercenter/cycle/marriage.htm*
4. I am reminded that even in 2003, there are places where children are asked to perform horrific duties as soldiers as they are kidnapped into armies and paramilitary groups. Reports from human rights groups note that boys as young as 9 are coerced or lured into becoming soldiers, even though international protocols forbid the use of children under 15 in the military.
5. Kane, Hal. *Triumph of the Mundane: The Unseen Trends that Shape Our Lives and Environment* (Washington, D.C.: Island Press, 2000), 100.
6. U.S. Census Bureau.
7. United Nations Population Fund. "Population Trends: The Numbers and Beyond" (New York: UN, 1999), online at: *www.unfpa.org/modules/6billion/populationissues/trends.htm*
8. United Nations. *The World's Women 2000: Trends and Statistics* (New York: UN, 2000), 8.
9. United Nations Development Program. *UN Human Development Report 1995* (New York: Oxford, 1995), Chapter 2.
10. *The Economist, Pocket World in Figures 2001* (London: Profile Books, 2001).
11. United Nations Population Fund. *The State of World Population 2001* (New York: UN, 2001), Chapter 3.
12. United Nations *State of the World Population 2001*, and from the Population Institute, "The Urbanization of the World," available online at: *www.populationinstitute.org/*
13. United Nations. "Population Trends."
14. The Population Institute, online at: *www.populationinstitute.org/teampublish/71_234_1058.cfm*

15. Ibid, Population Institute.

16. United Nations. *Human Development Report 1996*, 176.

17. Klosko, G., and Klosko, M. *The Struggle for Women's Rights: Theoretical and Historical Sources* (Upper Saddle River, NJ: Prentice Hall, 1998), 2.

18. Ibid.

19. United Nations. *World's Women 2000*, xvii.

20. United Nations. *Human Development Report 1995*.

21. O'Connell, Martin. "New Census Bureau Analysis Indicates Women Making Longer-Term Commitments to Workplace" (U.S. Census Bureau, December 5, 2001), online at: *www.uscensus.gov*

22. Ibid.

23. Ibid.

24. U.S. Bureau of Labor Statistics. "Changes in Women's Labor Force Participation in the 20th Century," Editor's Desk, *Monthly Labor Review* (February 2000), online at: *www.bls.gov/opub/ted/2000/feb/wk3/art03.htm*

25. "The real situation...." *Business Week* (January 9, 1943).

26. *Catholic World* (April 3, 1943). As quoted in Dorris Kearns Goodwin. *No Ordinary Time: Franklin and Eleanor Roosevelt: The Home Front in World War II* (New York: Touchstone, 1994), 414.

27. U.S. Bureau of Labor Statistics.

28. United Nations. *World's Women 2000*, xvii.

29. MicroCredit Summit Campaign, online at: *www.microcreditsummit.org*

30. MicroCredit Summit Campaign. "What is Microcredit?" online at: *www.microcreditsummit.org/involve/page1.htm#microcredit*

31. United Nations. *World's Women 2000*, 113.

32. International Gallup Poll Report. "Gender and Society: Status and Stereotypes" (Princeton, NJ: The Gallup Poll Organization, March 1996).

33. Ibid.

34. Campbell, Kim. "Beyond 'Bridget,' a fuller view of single women," *Christian Science Monitor* (April 11, 2001), online at: *www.csmonitor.com/atcsmonitor/specials/women/mirror/mirror041201.html*

35. United Nations. *World's Women 2000*, 41.

36. Ibid., 25.

37. Ibid., 29.

38. Ibid., 24.

39. Ibid., 27.

40. Heredia, Christopher. "Raising a Tulip to Marriage," *San Francisco Chronicle* (April 2, 2001), A–16.

41. Reuters. "Same-Sex Partners Win Legal Status in Germany," *New York Times* (August 2, 2001), Section A, Page 3.

42. In 1993, a Hawaiian court touched off the furor when it ruled that denying marriage licenses to same-sex couples amounted to gender discrimination and violated the state's constitution. States went into a panic, fearing that under federal law they could be required to recognize a gay or lesbian marriage performed in Hawaii, if Hawaii were to legalize same-sex marriages. More than two dozen states subsequently moved to ban same-sex unions. By 1997, however, the Supreme Court in Hawaii rejected the earlier decision. The state legislature proposed a companion "reciprocal beneficiaries" bill, which would guarantee gay and lesbian couples four specific rights: hospital visitation, joint property ownership, inheritance rights, and the right to sue for wrongful death. This would give about 200 rights and benefits to gay and lesbian couples. They include state worker's health and death benefits accruing to a "life partner," the ability to file joint state tax returns, workers' compensation benefits and criminal victims' rights, family leave, and other rights.

43. Abraham, Yvonne. "Swift to Extend Same-sex Benefits," *Boston Globe* (August 16, 2001).

44. Inglehart. *Modernization and Postmodernization*, 45.

45. Ibid, 278.

46. Ibid.

47. According to the Research Action and Information Network for the Bodily Integrity of Women (RAINBO), "Female Circumcision or Female Genital Mutilation (FC/FGM) is the collective name given to several different traditional practices that involve the cutting of female genitals. It does not refer to minor forms of genital rituals, which may involve washing the tip of the clitoris, pricking it with a pin, or separating and cleaning the foreskin (prepuce). The term FC/FGM is reserved to describe ritualistic practices where actual cutting and removal of sexual organs takes place." RAINBO estimates that approximately 2 million girls are at risk of genital mutilation every year, and that an estimated 130 million women and girls have been afflicted by such practices mostly in African countries, but also occasionally in Asia and parts of Latin America. According to some estimates, a purported 90% of the girls in Djibouti, Ethiopia and Eritrea, Sierra Leone, Somalia, and Sudan (North) have been mutilated. In addition, perhaps 50% of the girls in Benin, Burkina Faso, Central African Republic, Chad, Côte d'Ivoire, Egypt, Gambia, Guinea, Guinea Bissau, Kenya, Liberia, Mali, Nigeria, and Togo have been operated on. In the past two decades, there have been a variety of international resolutions and local laws enacted to ban this practice, although there is evidence that it still persists in many agrarian societies.

48. United Nations. *World's Women 2000*, 32.

49. Graphs from the Population Resource Centre, available online at: *www.prcdc.org/summaries/intlyouth.html*

50. It is interesting to note that while children are becoming more protected, particularly in wealthier societies, poorer children still suffer atrocities like slave labor, child prostitution, army kidnappings, neglect, and general poverty that should be addressed and acted on to be eliminated globally.

51. This demographic development could set the stage for wealthy country policy battles based on age in the future. Education, healthcare, retirement, and social security programs may all be affected by such demographic trends. It may also set the stage for labor imbalances that may also generate immigration policy.

52. One can see this in China, as its "one-child" population program produced a remarkable 107 boys versus 100 girls in recorded births. Normally, the ratio is much closer, and there were charges of infanticide and abandonment of baby girls during the 1980s and 1990s, not just in China, but in other countries with large Biological populations, such as India.

53. Niefield, M., O'Brien, E., and Feder J. "Long Term Care: Medicaid's Role and Challenges"(Washington, D.C.: The Henry J. Kaiser Family Foundation, 1999).

54. Arno, P.S., Levine, C., and Memmott, M.M. "The Economic Value of Informal Caregiving," *Health Affairs* (Vol. 18, No. 2, 1999).

55. The term "Club Sandwich" was coined by eldercare entrepreneur Carol Abaya, who has launched the Web site: *www.sandwichgeneration.com*

56. Federal Interagency Forum on Aging Related Statistics. "Older American 2000: Key Indicators of Well Being" (2000), online at: *www.agingstats.gov/chartbook2000/default.htm*

57. U.S. Census Bureau. *Statistical Abstract of the United States: 1999* (Washington, D.C.: U.S. Census Bureau, 1999).

CHAPTER 8

1. Cox, W. Michael, and Alm, Richard. Federal Reserve Bank of Dallas, *1993 Annual Report: These are the Good Old Days: A Report on US Living Standards* (Dallas: Federal Reserve, 1994), 7.

2. Fogel, 185.

3. There are even some wealthy countries such as France and Germany, for example, that have experimented with short work weeks, in some cases, only 4 days versus 5, and in other cases, 6-hour workdays versus 7-hour days.

4. Cox and Alm, 8.

5. Fogel, 184–190.

6. Cross, Gary. *A Social History of Leisure* (State College, PA: Venture Publishing, 1990), Chapter 5.

7. Cox, W. Michael, and Alm, Richard. Federal Reserve Bank of Dallas, *1997 Annual Report: Time Well Spent: The Declining Real Cost of Living in America* (Dallas: Federal Reserve, 1998), 15.

8. Ibid, 10.

9. Taken from the 1977 *Annual Report* of Warner Communications, a predecessor of AOL Time Warner, one of the world's largest media concerns. A special thanks to author Greil Marcus who introduced me to this time-capsule gem in his great cultural survey *Lipstick Traces: A Secret History of the 20th Century.*

10. Weiss, Michael. *The Clustered World* (New York: Little Brown, 2000), 176.

11. Matathia, Ira. *Next, Trends for the Future* (Woodstock, NY: Overlook Press, 2000), 52.

12. Fukuyama, Francis. *The End of History and the Last Man* (New York: Avon Books, 1992), xiv-xv.

13. Bureau of Transportation Statistics. *National Transportation Statistics 2000*, Chapter 1, online at: *www.bts.gov/btsprod/nts/Ch1_web/1-36.htm*

14. UNESCO. Study on International Flow of Cultural Goods, 2001.

15. Ibid.

16. Veblen, Thorstein. "Conspicuous Consumption," *The Consumer Society Reader* (1899), 187–204.

17. Perkin, Harold. *Origins of Modern English Society 1780-1880* (Toronto: University of Toronto, 1969), 96–97.

18. Diane Rehm Show, "Sustainable Development," National Public Radio, Aug. 21, 2002.

19. I recommend MacDonald's *Against the American Grain*, which is an out-of-print collection of entertaining essays and reviews written mostly in the 1950s.

20. Menzel, Peter. *Material World: A Global Family Portrait* (San Francisco: Sierra Book Clubs, 1994), 16.

21. See: *www.un.org/esa/population/publications/wup1999/urbanization.pdf*

22. *The Economist, Pocket World in Figures 2001*, 82, 99.

23. Matathia, 122.

24. Twitchell, James. *Living It Up: Our Love Affair with Luxury* (Columbia University; New York) 2002. Twitchell's line tickled me as I remembered the first time I visited the Great Wall of China and saw more Nike and Michael Jordan t-shirts being sold by locals than Great Wall souvenirs.

25. CNN Presents: "Beneath the Veil: Life in Afghanistan under the Taliban," journalist Saira Shah (August 26, 2001).

26. Putnam, Robert. *Bowling Alone: The Collapse and Revival of American Community* (New York: Touchstone, 2001).

27. United Nations, online at: *www.un.org/esa/population/publications/wup1999/urbanization.pdf*

28. Blakely, Edward J., and Snyder, Mary Gail. *Fortress America: Gated Communities in the United States* (Washington, D.C.: Brookings, 1997).

29. One of the most noted anti-consumerists is Naomi Klein. See her book *No Logo: Taking Aim at the Brand Bullies* (London: Palgrave MacMillan, 2002).

30. Cross, Gary. *An All-Consuming Century: Why Commercialism Won in Modern America* (New York: Columbia University Press, 2000), viii.

31. Bourdieu has written many books that discuss consumption, but most would suggest *Distinction; A Social Critique of the Judgement of Taste* (Cambridge: Harvard, 1987) as his definitive work.

32. A Dahn, Jo. "Mrs Delany and Ceramics in the Objectscape," *Interpreting Ceramics* (Issue 1), online at: *www.uwic.ac.uk/ICRC/issue001*

33. For the complete lowdown on SUVs, check out Keith Bradsher's *High and Mighty: SUVs—The World's Most Dangerous Vehicles and How They Got That Way* (New York: Public Affairs, 2002).

34. Duane Elgin. "Voluntary Simplicity and the New Global Challenge," *The Consumer Society Reader* (1993), 407.

35. Ibid.

36. Fukuyama, 319. Note that I have substituted my term "Experiential" twice in this paragraph, which echoes similar points. The first replaces Fukuyama's phrase "post-historical," and the second "thymotic."

37. Inglehart. *Modernizations and Postmodernization*, 35.

38. TIAA–CREF Web Center. "TIAA–CREF Announces Five New Mutual Funds and Four New Variable Annuity Accounts" (April 3, 2000), online at: *www.prnewswire.com/cgi-bin/micro_stories.pl?ACCT=840938&TICK=TIAA&STORY=/www/story/04-03-2000/0001180358&EDATE=Apr+3,+2000*

39. SocialFunds.com Newsroom. "Five Top Social Investing Stories of 2000" (December 29, 2000), online at *http://socialfunds.com/news/article.cgi/article460.html*

40. Walsh, Mary Williams. "Calpers Wears a Party, or Union, Label," *New York Times* (October 14, 2002), online at: *www.nytimes.com/2002/10/13/business/yourmoney/13CALP.html*

41. SocialFunds.com Newsroom. "Five Top Social Investing Stories of 2001" (January 8, 2002), online at: *http://socialfunds.com/news/article.cgi/article750.html*

42. See *www.SocialFunds.com*

43. Ibid.

44. Matathia, 123.

45. "MTV's World," *Business Week*, European Edition, February 18, 2002. Available online at: *www.businessweekeurope.com*

46. Ibid.

47. Bennett, B. "101 Pixels of Fun," *Time Magazine* (June 2001, Vol. 157, No. 22).

48. Database Marketing Institute, online at: *www.dbmarketing.com/articles/Art112.htm*

49. Cross, viii.

CHAPTER 9

1. World Bank, Environment Department. "Protecting Our Planet—Securing Our Future: Linkages among global environment issues and human needs" (1999), 4, online at: *www-eds.worldbank.org/planet/toc.html*

2. Ibid.

3. Adapted from World Bank, "Protecting our Planet Appendix 2: A Synopsis of Eight Major Global Environmental Issues."

4. This is because the final shape of the environmental 'Kuznet curve' is an inverted-U that resembles the income inequality relationship that Kuznet developed. See Theodore Panaytou. "Economic Growth and the Environment," Center for International Development at Harvard University (Working Paper No. 56, July 2000), 6.

5. Ibid.

6. Johnson, Todd M., Liu, Feng, and Newfarmer, Richard. "Clear Water, Blue Skies: China's Environment in the 21st Century" (New York: World Bank, September 1997).

7. *The Economist.* "Survey: Development and the Environment" (March 19, 1998).

8. International Research Institute 1996 Survey. See: *www.response-analysis.com/whatsnew/environ.html*

9. United Nations. *Human Development Report 1998.*

10. U.S. Information Agency, May 1998.

11. FAO (1998); McDonald's Corporation (1997); UN (1999).

12. World Bank. "Assessing Globalization: Is Globalization Causing a 'Race to the Bottom' in Environmental Standards?" (April 2000).

13. Wheeler D., Hugs, M., and Martin, P. "Process Change, Economic Policy and Industrial Pollution: Cross County Evidence from the Wood, Pulp and Steel Industries," as discussed by World Bank report (April 2000).

14. The matrix of the modern American environmental movement was located, not surprisingly, in the West. The dying days of the American frontier and broad-based public concern over widespread land misuse prompted an early *conservation* movement. In 1897, the federal government enacted the Forest Reserve Act and ushered in an era of greater government participation in natural resource allocation and management. Other legislation aimed at managing the national commons included the Forest Management Act (1897), the River and Harbor Act (1899), the Reclamation Act (1902), and the Antiquities Act (1906). Out of the Progressive era emerged a natural resource strategy based on conservation, or rationing. At the root of this program were principles of economic utility and ongoing use of the land and resources of the nation. President Theodore Roosevelt spelled out the nation's conservation efforts in a 1901 speech: "The fundamental idea of forestry, is the perpetuation of forests by use. Forest protection is not an end to itself; it is a means to increase and sustain the resources of our country and the industries that depend upon them. The preservation of our forests is an imperative business necessity." Rather than a policy of outright *preservation*, the purpose was to use resources sparingly to ensure their continued use for both recreation and enterprise. Roosevelt's speech was cited in Gifford Pinchot's *Breaking New Ground* (New York: Harcourt, Brace, 1947), 190. Not all Progressives agreed with this approach. John Muir continued to argue for preservation. The Sierra Club, founded by him in 1892, was one of the earliest organizations devoted to this issue. Despite this opposition, the federal government's role as chief manager of the nation's resources remained throughout the early part of the 20th Century. This role was seen as an important means to allocate and protect resources to best serve economic development and the gradual accumulation of wealth. Other organizations still in existence that were founded at this time were the Society of American Foresters (1900) and the National Audubon Society (1905).

15. Cable, S., and Cable, C. *Environmental Problems, Grassroots Solutions* (New York: St. Martins, 1995), 68.

16. See Lee, Martha F. *Earth First! Environmental Apocalypse* (New York: Syracuse University Press, 1990), 8.

17. *Warriors of the Rainbow: A Chronicle of the Greenpeace Movement* (New York: Holt, Reinhart, and Winston, 1979), 252.

18. Inglehart. *Modernization and Postmodernization*, 242.

19. Ibid, 243.

20. CBS News/*New York Times* poll (New York: CBS News, April 16, 1990).

21. *The Economist.* "Europe: Green with Envy" (November 14, 1998, Vol 3, Issue 8094), 55–56.

22. Eurobarometer. (Brussels: European Commision, Spring 1999).

23. "PricewaterhouseCoopers Endowment Report Finds Market-Based Regulatory Programs Not a Panacea for Curbing Air Pollution," *Business Wire* (October 21, 1999).

24. *New York Times*/CBS News poll (June 21, 2001), A1. Responses to the following "How is the president handling…" "…the environment" 39% approve, 46% disapprove; "…the energy situation" 33% approve, 55% disapprove. And 55% of respondents said that "protecting the environment" was more important than "producing energy" versus 12% who thought that George W. Bush thinks "protecting the environment" is more important that "producing energy".

25. Brown. "Foreword" *Human Development Report 1998*.

26. Results from a Gallup/Waste Management poll in "Industry Watershed, Year End View of Recycling" (December 1995).

27. The Hartman Group. "Food and the Environment: A Consumer's Perspective," (Bellevue, WA: The Hartman Group, 1996).

28. Holusha, John. "Packaging and Public Image: McDonald's Fills a Big Order" (*New York Times*, November 2, 1991), A1.

29. Victor, David G., and Ausubel, Jesse H. "Restoring the Forests," *Foreign Affairs* (79:6, 2000), 143.

30. Hammond, Allen. L. "Digitally Empowered Development," *Foreign Affairs* (80:2, 2001) 104.

31. IIE Solutions. "Reducing raw materials use to increase profits" (April 1999).

32. See Coors Brewing Company's Web site at *www.coors.com* and Jay Forrest (1996).

33. Arensman, Russ. "The Greening of Technology," *Electronic Business* (27:5, May 2001), 96–104.

34. Ball, Jeffrey. "Warming Trend: Auto Maker Juggle Substance and Style in Green Policies," *Wall Street Journal* (May 15, 2001), A1.

35. Bradsher, Keith and Revkin, Andrw C. "A Pre-Emptive Strike On Global Warming," *New York Times* (May 15, 2001), C1, C14.

36. It is interesting to note that in his 2003 State of the Union Address, U.S. President George Bush actually promoted the notion of hydrogen-powered automobiles. While the technology viability of hydrogen-powered automobiles in the near future is questionable, Bush's proposal underscored the U.S. public's demand for environmental action.

37. World Resource Institute's Global Trends. "Are Businesses and industry taking sustainability seriously?" online at: *www.wri.org/trends/business.html*

38. Ibid.

39. KPMG Environmental Consulting. "KPMG International Survey of Environmental Reporting 1999" (The Netherlands: KPMG, September 1999), 13.

40. Ibid, 16.

41. United Nations. *Human Development Report 1998.*

42. *The Economist.* "Beyond the Bubble" (April 21, 2001), 57.

43. United Nations. *Human Development Report 1998.*

44. IEA, *The Evolving Renewable Energy Market* (June 1999), online at: *www.iea.org*

45. The World Wildlife Fund has this program set up in a number of countries, including Namibia, Zimbabwe, Russia, Thailand, and Cameroon. For more information on all of these programs, refer to their Web site at: *www.panda.org/resources/publications/sustainability/indigenous/*

46. Lovejoy, Thomas. "Aid Debtor Nations' Ecology," *New York Times* (October 4, 1984), A31, online at: *http://web.lexis-nexis.com/universe*

47. Jakobeit, Cord. "Nonstate Actors Leading the Way: Debt-for-Nature Swaps," *Institutions for Environmental Aid.* Keohane, Robert O., and Levy, Marc A., eds. (Cambridge, MA: MIT, 1996), 155.

48. *Futures* (September 1992), 662.

49. Jakobeit, 150.

CHAPTER 10

1. UNICEF. *State of the World's Children 2001*, online at: *www.unicef.org/pubsgen/sow01/.* Also, one cannot forget HIV/AIDs a problem that has spread to virtually all corners of the earth.

2. Mugabe's purported "Africanization" of the country is particularly noteworthy. His recent policies and rhetoric seem like extreme isolationism, with even formerly close allies such as South Africa being publicly rebuffed.

3. Wolfensohn, James. "How rich countries keep the rest of the world in poverty," *Irish Independent* (September 30, 2002).

4. See *www.cafod.or.uk* for more on CAFOD.

5. Estimated by Penny Fowler of Oxfam International, as cited in *The Economist* article "A few green shots" (August 31, 2002), 60.

6. See *www.cafod.or.uk*

7. Ibid.

8. Ashdown, Keith. "Farm Subsidies top $28 billion," Taxpayers for Common Sense (Volume VI, No. 1, January 9, 2001), online at: *http://www.taxpayer.net/TCS/wastebasket/environment/1-09-01.htm*

9. Brooke, James. "An Orange Grove Illustrates Japan's Economic Woe," *New York Times* (Late Edition, Final, Section 1, Page 6, Column 3, January 27, 2002).

10. Lingard, John. "Agricultural Subsidies and Environmental Change,"

University of Newcastle upon Tyne, *http://www.wiley.co.uk/wiley-chi/egec/pdf/GB403-W.PDF*

11. Padilla, Chris. "Market Access: What's at Stake," Co-Chair WTO Working Group (PowerPoint Presentation April 2002), online at: *http://www.wto.org/english/tratop_e/dda_e/1*, citing the Progressive Policy Institute.

12. "America's Hidden Tax on the Poor," *Progressive Policy Institute*, cited again in the Padilla presentation.

13. Ibid.

14. IMF staff. "Global Trade Liberalization and the Developing Countries" (November 2001), online at: *http://www.imf.org/external/np/exr/ib/2001/110801.htm*

15. UNCTAD. "Country Notes" (2000), online at: *http://www.unctad.org/trains/*

16. Padilla.

17. Ibid.

18. International Institute for Strategic Studies (IISS). "The Military Balance 2002/2003," introduction online at: *http://www.iiss.org/*

19. Elbadawi, Ibrahim and Sambinis, Nicolas. "How Much War Will We See?" (*World Bank*, Working Paper 2533), online at: *www.worldbank.org*

20. The three interstate conflicts in this period were Iraq versus Kuwait, India versus Pakistan, and Eritrea versus Ethiopia.

21. Stockholm International Peace Research Institute (SIPRI). "SIPRI Yearbook 2002" (2002), Chapter 1 and Appendix, online at: *http://news.bbc.co.uk/2/hi/business/the_economy/323751.stm*

22. World Bank. "Bosnia and Herzegovina, Lessons and Accomplishments" (May 1999), online at: *http://www.worldbank.org.ba/ECA/Bosnia&Herzegovina.nsf/*

23. Ed Crooks. "The cost of conflict," BBC News (April 21, 1999), online at: *http://news.bbc.co.uk/2/hi/business/the_economy/323751.stm*

24. According to John Sfakianakis, research fellow at Harvard University's Center for Middle Eastern Studies: "War Costs," *AL-AHRAM Weekly* (Issue No. 588, May 30–June 5, 2002).

25. Myers, Laura. "Annual U.S. Gulf Costs Said at $50B" (November 17, 1998).

26. Military expenditures figures from the *Center for Defense Information*, available online at: *www.cdi.org*

27. Looney, Robert. "Economic Costs to the United States Stemming From the 9/11 Attacks," Center for Contemporary Conflict, or CCC (August 5, 2002), online at: *www.ccc.nps.navy.mil/rsepResources/si/aug02/homeland.asp*

28. Gongloff, Mar. "Cost of Fighting Terror Mounting" (September 9, 2002), online at: *www.cnn.com/2002/BUSINESS/09/09/nine11cost/index.html*

29. Ibid.

30. Looney.

31. Bradsher, Keith and Banerjee, Neela. "Indonesia Stocks Fall 10%; Others in Asia Off Modestly; Severe Tourism Losses Seen," *New York Times* (October 15, 2002), online at: *www.nytimes.com/2002/10/15/international/asia/15BALI.html*

32. Department of Defense. "Proliferation: Threat and Response" (January 2001), online at: *www.fas.org/irp/threat/prolif00.pdf*

33. Federation of American Scientists. "States Possessing, Pursuing or Capable of Acquiring Weapons of Mass Destruction" (July 29, 2000), online at: *www.fas.org/irp/threat/wmd_state.htm*

34. See this online at the International Water management Institute's Web site: *www.cgiar.org/iwmi/home/wsmap.htm#a2* There are critics who argue that water "shortages" (and many other resource shortages) may be an overstatement. Fred Smith, President of the Competitive Enterprise Institute, believes that global demand may be adequately met if water was privatized and incentives were made for greater exploration and curbed usage. Smith noted that if water production and distribution—like food or petroleum—were in private hands versus public, supply/demand equilibriums would develop to avoid shortages. Anytime a resource is given away for free, he argues, supply and demand projections become distorted. Poor public policy and little regard for private incentives exacerbate such problems. He aired some of these views in a discussion called "Sustainable Development" on *The Diane Rehm Show*, WAMU radio, August 21, 2002.

35. "The Convention and Kyoto Protocol," online at: *http://unfccc.int/resource/convkp.html*

36. Smith, J.M. "Is Global Warming a Legitimate Concern?" *National Liberty Journal* (July 2002), online at: *www.nljonline.com/july02/global_warming.htm*

37. Oakley, Robin. Citing Bush's public address in "Bush Facing Clash Over Climate," *CNN.com* (March 29, 2001), online at: *www.cnn.com/2001/WORLD/europe/03/29/environment.analysis/index.html*

38. Office of International Information Programs, U.S. Department of State. "U.S. Takes Pro-Growth Approach to Climate Change" (October 23, 2002), online at: *http://usinfo.state.gov*

39. See the speech "Are North/South Population Growth Differentials a Prelude to Conflict" by demographer Michael Teitelbaum of The Sloan Foundation, online at: *http://www.csis.org/gai/Graying/speeches/teitelbaum.html* Teitelbaum notes that unregulated immigration from Bangladesh, for example,

into the 25-million-person Indian state of Assam has created problems, including Hindu-Muslim clashes and a separatist movement. The current political situation in Assam is considered unstable with United Liberation of Assam (ULFA) fighting a low-intensity but widespread guerrilla war for independence from India for more than 10 years.

40. See Pete Peterson's speech, "Global Aging and the Graying of the World Order" (Fall 1998), available online at: *www.his.com/~council/peterson.htm*

41. Hewitt has many articles and speeches online at: *www.csis.org* These works cover Japan's demographic ills.

42. Peterson.

43. Actual World Bank figures for 2000 are closer to $32 trillion, but many suggest the informal, or unreported, economy may total another 25–30%, which brought me to $40 billion. Over time, it is assumed that much of that underground activity will be captured in statistics. My output expansion rate is projected at a conservative 2.70% per annum (10% lower than the 1950–2000 period), adjusted for inflation, and a projected 2050 population of 10 billion.

44. See Edmunds' book *Wealthy World: The Growth and Implications of Global Prosperity* (New York: John Wiley, 2001). This book provides an insightful look into financial marketization and growth. While his projections may seem optimistic based on aggressive growth rates, his methodology is compelling. It is an outgrowth of ideas that Paul Samuelson stimulated with historical studies of markets that typically grew to 2–5x the size of an economy.

45. For this example, I use a conservative 4.05% annualized growth rate representing 1.5x my projected global output's 2.70% expansion. Edmunds suggests that this number could grow even faster. For example, between 1950 and 2000, Edmunds notes that global output climbed approximately 3% while financial assets grew at 6.5%.

Index

8 reasons why you should read the Financial Times for 4 weeks RISK-FREE!

To help you stay current with significant
developments in the world economy ...
and to assist you to make informed business
decisions — the Financial Times brings you:

❶ Fast, meaningful overviews of international affairs ... plus daily
briefings on major world news.

❷ Perceptive coverage of economic, business, financial and political
developments with special focus on emerging markets.

❸ More international business news than any other publication.

❹ Sophisticated financial analysis and commentary on world market
activity plus stock quotes from over 30 countries.

❺ Reports on international companies and a section on global investing.

❻ Specialized pages on management, marketing, advertising and
technological innovations from all parts of the world.

❼ Highly valued single-topic special reports (over 200 annually)
on countries, industries, investment opportunities, technology and more.

❽ The Saturday Weekend FT section — a globetrotter's guide to
leisure-time activities around the world: the arts, fine dining, travel,
sports and more.

FT FINANCIAL TIMES
World business newspaper

The *Financial Times* delivers
a world of business news.

Use the Risk-Free Trial Voucher below!

To stay ahead in today's business world you need to be well-informed on a daily basis. And not just on the national level. You need a news source that closely monitors the entire world of business, and then delivers it in a concise, quick-read format.

With the *Financial Times* you get the major stories from every region of the world. Reports found nowhere else. You get business, management, politics, economics, technology and more.

Now you can try the *Financial Times* for 4 weeks, absolutely risk free. And better yet, if you wish to continue receiving the *Financial Times* you'll get great savings off the regular subscription rate. Just use the voucher below.

---

4 Week Risk-Free Trial Voucher

Yes! Please send me the *Financial Times* for 4 weeks (Monday through Saturday) Risk-Free, and details of special subscription rates in my country.

Name _____

Company _____

Address _____ ❏ Business or ❏ Home Address

Apt./Suite/Floor _____ City _____ State/Province _____

Zip/Postal Code_____ Country _____

Phone (optional) _____ E-mail (optional)_____

Limited time offer good for new subscribers in FT delivery areas only.
To order contact Financial Times Customer Service in your area (mention offer SAB01A).

The Americas: Tel 800-628-8088 Fax 845-566-8220 E-mail: uscirculation@ft.com

Europe: Tel 44 20 7873 4200 Fax 44 20 7873 3428 E-mail: fte.subs@ft.com

Japan: Tel 0120 341-468 Fax 0120 593-146 E-mail: circulation.fttokyo@ft.com

Korea: E-mail: sungho.yang@ft.com

S.E. Asia: Tel 852 2905 5555 Fax 852 2905 5590 E-mail: subseasia@ft.com

www.ft.com

FT FINANCIAL TIMES
World business newspaper

Where to find tomorrow's best business and technology ideas. TODAY.

- Ideas for defining tomorrow's competitive strategies — and executing them.

- Ideas that reflect a profound understanding of today's global business realities.

- Ideas that will help you achieve unprecedented customer and enterprise value.

- Ideas that illuminate the powerful new connections between business and technology.

ONE PUBLISHER.
Financial Times Prentice Hall.

 Prentice Hall
FINANCIAL TIMES

WORLD BUSINESS PUBLISHER

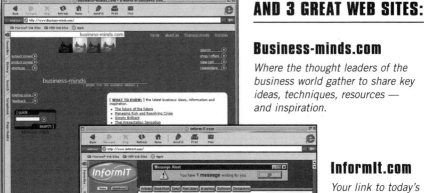

AND 3 GREAT WEB SITES:

Business-minds.com

Where the thought leaders of the business world gather to share key ideas, techniques, resources — and inspiration.

InformIt.com

Your link to today's top business and technology experts: new content, practical solutions, and the world's best online training.

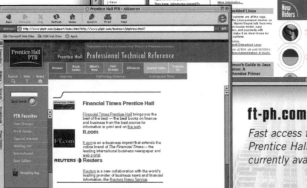

ft-ph.com

Fast access to all Financial Times Prentice Hall business books currently available.